Bus and Coach Operation

Bus and Coach Operation

Fifth Edition

R.W.Faulks FCIT
Bus Consultant

Butterworths
London Boston Durban Singapore Sydney Toronto Wellington

First published 1987

© R.W. Faulks, 1987

British Library Cataloguing in Publication Data

Faulks, R.W.
   Bus and coach operation.—5th ed.
   1. Bus lines—Great Britain—Management
   I. Title   II. Lambden, William
   338.3'22'068   HE5663.A6
   ISBN 0–408–02810–6

Library of Congress Cataloging-in-Publication Data

Faulks, Rex William.
   Bus and coach operation.

   Rev. ed. of: Bus and coach operation / William Lambden.
4th ed. 1969.
   Bibliography: p.
   Includes index.
   1. Bus lines.   2. Bus lines—Management.   3. Bus lines
—Great Britain.   4. Bus lines—Great Britain—Management.
I. Lambden, William. Bus and coach operation. II. Title.
HE5613.F38 1987   388.3'22'068   87–10966
ISBN 0–408–02810–6

Phototypeset by Scribe Design, Gillingham, Kent
Printed and bound in England by
Butler and Tanner Ltd, Frome and London

Preface

Much has been written about buses and trams; most is for the enthusiast and gives little guidance on how to run a bus business. With a trend towards privatization and an increasing number of smaller companies, more and more owner/managers are entering the industry or are attaining local managerial status with direct responsibilities for the satisfactory conduct of their undertakings. It is to this group of people together with the middle managers of the larger combines, wherever they may be, that this book is dedicated.

Although over the years very few authors have directed their efforts to the practising busman, there are some well-known names, all experts in their day, who have made their mark in this particular field although their work has long since dated. One of the first was R. Stuart Pilcher in the late 1930s. In 1947 came L.D. Kitchin's *Bus Operation*, which ran to three editions. In 1969 the successor author, W. Lambden, through the successor (and present) publisher, produced the fourth edition which had by then become *Bus and Coach Operation*. Sadly, Bill Lambden did not live to write a fifth edition, and in 1981 I attempted to fill the gap with *Urban and Rural Transport*, which dealt with all passenger services within the classification as described, including trams and rapid transit. Butterworths has now decided to continue the Kitchin/Lambden productions, hence this fifth edition of *Bus and Coach Operation*—an established work and one with which I have the privilege of becoming associated. The task is formidable because high standards have been set. Bill's untimely death was to me the loss of a personal friend, but strangely the production of this book was discussed with him not long before he died. I feel very strongly that he would be pleased if he knew that his work was being perpetuated, and I hope equally strongly that he would be satisfied with what has emerged.

To potential readers who already possess copies of any of the above-mentioned books, let it be said that this edition is substantially an update of the bus part of *Urban and Rural Transport*, some 55% of the text being brought forward and amended as necessary. The remaining 45% is completely new. References to rapid transit have been omitted for possible inclusion in a subsequent book on railway operation, and references to express coaches have been introduced.

Although aimed primarily at the industry, the book will be valuable for transport students and particularly those studying the Road Passenger Transport subject of the Chartered Institute of Transport, the Transport Operation (Road Passenger) subject of the Institute of Transport Administration, and the Road Passenger Transport Operation subject of the Royal Society of Arts.

It will quickly become apparent that a transport service is the product of the combined efforts of a multiplicity of separate disciplines, the majority of which are independent sciences in their own right. The contents of the pages that follow are, however, confined to pure transport matters. In other words, they cover operating and commercial practices. References to mechanical engineering, accountancy, legal, staff and planning aspects are made only to the extent to which it is necessary for the operating and commercial managers to be familiar with these ancillary subjects. Although entire chapters are devoted to finance, planning and statutory controls, in no way must they be construed as adequate coverage for readers in these particular studies. In any case useful material is already available for aspirants in these fields. Particularly as far as the legal profession is concerned, the information given here is descriptive only and does not represent adequate coverage of law.

The fundamentals of general transport topics are covered in my book *Principles of Transport*. The information contained in that particular work is not duplicated here but the relevant parts are developed to cover in greater detail the operational and commercial techniques within this one facet of transport. The reader should note particularly that statutory control, trade organizations, the structure of the bus industry, administration, staff matters and finance have all been considered in some depth in *Principles of Transport*. The coverage is adequate for bus operating purposes and the information has not been repeated. *Bus and Coach Operation* is complementary to but not an alternative to *Principles of Transport*. By the nature of its purpose, *Principles of Transport* presents facts and I have made no attempt to superimpose opinions on the resultant issues. In proceeding now beyond the principles and into the application of different techniques, I have examined actual working methods in some detail, and it becomes more appropriate for personal views and preferences to be expressed. To this extent, therefore, *Bus and Coach Operation* could become a little more controversial than *Principles of Transport*. Nevertheless, far from wishing to impose upon the reader a set of opinions, I hope that a presentation in this way will stimulate thought and mental argument. Facts and theory must be known and understood but application reflects the attitude of the individual who will develop his own thoughts and inclinations, all with the benefit of knowledge and experience. Where opinions have been expressed, care has been taken to identify them as such. A textbook must contain accurate information but a discussion on resultant practices is also helpful. At this stage subjective thought is appropriate and a subsequent dialogue stimulating (with plenty of scope for the critics!). Fact is one thing and opinion is another, and there must be no confusion between the two.

Finally, even with a single author, a work such as this can seldom be accomplished without some help from other people. *Bus and Coach Operation* has been no exception and acknowledgement of the provision of information is duly recorded where appropriate.

I said earlier that a textbook must contain accurate information, and I sincerely hope that no misrepresentation has arisen. Although every effort has been made to verify certain of the detail with those who are directly concerned, if an error has crept in responsibility must remain with me. Unfortunately the necessary lead time between preparation and publication tends to be such that what is written, whilst correct at the time, is liable to be overtaken by subsequent events. Given an industry that is always in the public eye and hence sensitive to popular opinion together with a dynamic government, all within a changing world, such circumstances cannot always be avoided but again I hope that the effects will be minimal.

In presenting this work I hope that readers will derive some benefit from its pages. Perhaps also it will be of some interest to that strong body of loyal enthusiasts and to anyone else who, although not directly connected with the industry, see a fascination in riding on buses.

RWF
1987

Contents

He who knows not but knows not that he knows not is a fool —
    avoid him.
He who knows not but knows that he knows not has promise —
    teach him.
He who knows but knows not that he knows is asleep —
    ignore him.
He who knows and knows that he knows has wisdom —
    follow him.

Introduction

Transport is an all-embracing subject. Its science covers the movement of passengers, whether travelling a short distance on a local bus or across the face of the earth by a jet airliner; the movement of merchandise—and there are many different ways of doing that—and physical distribution which, as well as actual transport, involves also materials handling, packaging, warehouse location and management and inventory control. Transport management consists of a collection of people drawn from many different disciplines. Engineers, accountants, lawyers, administrators, sociologists and town and country planners all have an important input, but their learning is not confined to transport. The people concerned are specialists within their own particular calling but they are not necessarily also experts in the art of moving people or goods and most could work equally well within an industry other than public transport. The transport specialist as such, and the one who must learn the art of movement and who could not easily exercise his skills in any other field, is the operator and he generally confines his expertise to one particular mode. Road passenger transport which is being considered here is therefore a subject within a subject—only one particular branch of the collective science.

Alternatives to buses may become important if energy supplies become depleted, which they are predicted to do. Although the battery vehicle may have been developed between now and the turn of the century so that it will be able to undertake all of the functions at present being performed by the diesel engine, it has not, as yet, been proved. Even today there are situations where line-dependent systems are more appropriate than the conventional bus and a dearth of oil could easily accelerate a swing in this direction in order to maximize the use of electricity for propulsion. Hence although the bus is the predominant feature of this subject, trams and trolleybuses are also a part of the overall urban transport scene and must be recognized as such.

Although public transport facilities are more profuse in some areas than in others, there are few parts of the inhabited world that have no bus service at all. It follows that many different operating organizations are managed by many different types of people with as many different methods of conducting their businesses with varying statutory rights and obligations. All, however, have the common purpose of carrying passengers to the places where they want to go as expeditiously and as economically as possible. Passenger requirements and accepted standards vary not only between countries but in different areas within the same country. Local customs and practices have grown up within managements and amongst the staff and passengers. What might be regarded as an impossible inhibition in one town could be seen as an indispensable aid to operation in another perhaps less than 100 miles (160 km) away. This parochial outlook is gradually being broken down within the senior and middle management fields with much of the in-breeding which at one time existed being eliminated. Similar circumstances do not apply within the trade unions whose platform staff members are less likely to move around. Hence local habits die hard, and in the treatment of a subject of this kind it is neither practicable nor particularly necessary to discuss the infinite variety of local practices. Readers with some local experience may, therefore, see statements within these pages that are strange to them and with which they might not readily agree. This does not, however, make anybody wrong. Even at managerial level there are differences of opinion regarding such fundamental issues as the practicalities of one-man operation, methods of fare collection and vehicle design, not to mention different staff agreements and working practices. What this really shows is the inadvisability of being too dogmatic on a particular topic as it is unlikely that any one line of thinking will be completely in error or completely right.

It was said in the Preface that this book is dedicated to bus managers wherever they might be. In so doing, however, the usual problem presents itself in that when discussing statutory controls it is not possible to treat this aspect of the subject on a world-wide basis. Even if different countries have legislation that is similar in principle, the detail will be different. Remembering what was said earlier, the law is a profession in its own right. Lawyers do not have to be busmen and busmen do not have to be lawyers. Nevertheless, because the operation of public transport is so closely bound with the statutes busmen cannot be ignorant of these legal requirements and the subject must form an important part of any work on transport operation. But this notwithstanding, it is clearly impracticable to give comprehensive coverage of the statutory background as it applies to each individual country. Hence although the text deals with the science of running buses and trams as is applicable to the world at large, references to legal matters relate only to British law.

Transport is movement and where there is movement there is a potential hazard. It is right, therefore, that there should be strict controls backed by the force of law in the interests of public safety. But the provision of transport facilities is also very much a political animal. Certainly as far as local public passenger transport is concerned it is something that is always in the public eye and in this more than in any other science the average layman seems to consider his knowledge and wisdom to be infinitely superior to that of the professional manager. Therefore, although some regulation is essential, there is also political whim and when the pendulum swings periodically between left and right it is not surprising that successive governments have seen fit to introduce new arrangements. Thus in Great Britain over the past three decades there have been transport-related acts in the years 1947, 1953, 1962, 1968, 1969, 1977, 1978, 1980, 1981, 1982, 1983, 1984 and 1985, all of which have had an impact on some aspect of bus management although some of this legislation makes little contribution to the science of running buses and trams.

In 1969 Mr W. Lambden wrote in the introduction to his fourth edition of this work that:

'the all-round efficiency of bus and coach operations is bedevilled by persistent staff shortages, falling passenger demand, intense competition from cars and television, punitive taxation and an apparent growing love by national and local governments alike for excessive planning. Hardly a post-war year has not brought heavy increases in basic costs, principally because of upward trends in wages, whilst improvements in working conditions for platform workers have also raised annual expenditures considerably. The effects of this has more than outweighed the economies of the big-capacity single-decker bus or coach and likewise those of the 78-seater double decker. Consequently there has been next to no stability in the level of fares.'

He was, of course, referring to British circumstances. It will be seen from the text that Government some 3 years later did something about the financial predicament but at the expense of yet more bureaucracy and even higher costs. 18 years after Lambden there is still a familiar ring to some of the things that he said. Now it is the 1985 Act that has contrived to do something about it and it has tackled the problem in a completely different way. At the time of writing the detail can be documented but the effects cannot. When these words appear in print maybe everybody will be a little wiser.

   In introducing this subject it is important to remember that it is the science of running buses and trams that is the basic consideration and this must not be subordinated to any political policies or preferences.

1 Historical background

Introduction

This is not a historical treatise. The development of buses and trams has been well documented and a host of excellent literature on the subject is readily available. But if there is to be an appreciation of the present and an understanding of why certain things are happening now and are likely to happen in the future, there must also be a knowledge of how things have developed in the past. Nevertheless, references to what has gone before will be no more than is necessary to acquaint the reader with the events that have led to the situation as it is now in the late 1980s. Therefore, although a little bit of history is essential, this chapter will not be a long one.

The growth of a network

In 1829 George Shillibeer introduced the first horse bus in London from the 'Yorkshire Stingo' on the Marylebone Road to the Bank and the subsequent nearly 160 years has seen a process of evolution and development, both in the UK and overseas, leading to the network of services which is now provided. From that time onwards, enterprising bands of people set themselves up to provide transport services as a means of earning their livelihood and in so doing, destined the shape of the things to come. Certainly it was done for private gain (with financial risk) and some perished in the process but the services provided fulfilled a community need. Small privately owned undertakings mushroomed and, with a view to maximizing revenue, concentrated on what were regarded as the more lucrative routes. But bus proprietors knew, perhaps better than the passengers, which areas were likely to have the greatest potential. They decided what the people would most probably use and provided the services accordingly. The technique of what is now known in popular parlance as 'marketing' is not, therefore, really so very new. More is to be said about marketing in Chapter 7. This early development of lines of communication helped to determine subsequent geographical patterns of our towns.

So far, reference has been confined to the conventional bus, a simple vehicle with its wheels running along the surface of the road and hauled by a horse. But it was realized that a horse could pull a greater load if the vehicle had smooth steel wheels which ran on smooth steel rails than it could if running on the uneven surface of a road on account of the lower resistance. It was the same principle as

4

applied to water transport and which had already justified the construction of canals. Steel lines were therefore laid in the roadway on the more important traffic routes and so the street tramway was born. The first horse trams came to Great Britain in the early 1860s and electric traction followed with Magnus Volk opening his short electric railway along the seafront at Brighton in 1883. The first successful electric street tramway in Great Britain became operational at Blackpool in 1885, i.e. before the introduction of the petrol engine. Trams, therefore, became electrically powered (made practicable by their fixed track) when buses were still being drawn by horses.

However, it was not only private enterprise that helped to lay the foundations of the local transport systems. For the best part of a century municipalities owned and operated first tramways and then local bus services in many of the larger towns in the United Kingdom. The reason why they are not the operators now is subject matter for Chapter 4 but there are nevertheless still many examples of this form of ownership and control overseas. As far as Great Britain is concerned, the reason for the entry of local government into public transport can be traced to parliamentary action in the nineteenth century when, as already noted, trams were becoming very much a part of the urban scene. To encroach a little on Chapter 5 and referring now to British law, parliamentary authority is necessary for the construction of a railway, light railway or tramway (which includes trolleybuses). This was a complication at a time when tramways were developing and the Tramways Act 1870 was passed with a view to simplifying the procedure. This it did, which is a matter for Chapter 5. What, however, is important in this context and what will lead into Chapter 4 is that this Act of 1870 was also instrumental in bringing local government into the urban transport arena. With tramways being developed by private enterprise, the Tramways Act, 1870, among other things, gave to local authorities the power to acquire compulsorily if they so decided (but not necessarily to operate) local tramway systems. These powers could be exercised at 21 years from their inception and thereafter at seven yearly intervals and the purchase price for such acquisitions needed to contain no recognition of goodwill. In other words, the price was based virtually on scrap value of the assets to be acquired. This, of course, gave very little incentive to tramway promoters even though, in the event, some systems were never acquired in this way. What it did do was to introduce local authorities to local passenger transport. Many such authorities did exercise their powers if only to resuscitate tramways that had become run-down for the very reason that owners would not risk sinking capital into an enterprise that could be taken from them on unfavourable terms. Other tramway systems came into being under local authority control at the outset and in due course their tramway interests led to bus interests as well and hence the patterns of ownership as will be considered in Chapter 4 were evolved.

So much for the political background. To return to the development of the 'system' regardless of the form of ownership and control, the electric tramway came into being in the 1880s and from that time onwards local networks spread out from urban centres into what, in some cases, could almost be termed the nearby countryside. This process was often followed by the construction of rows of terraced houses adjacent to the routes and so the neighbourhoods began to develop. It was in this way that local transport (in the form of tramways) moulded the pattern and the layout of many of our older established towns, particularly within the first few miles of the centre, and the development process can be traced in this way. The important point to note here is that in this example transport came first and development followed. The ability to travel made the area attractive for living and increased land values, and readers will doubtless be able to identify districts within their own home towns that owe their origins to the tram.

The development and demise of the tram

No study of road passenger transport would be complete without reference to the tram, even though, in the United Kingdom, there is now only one undertaking— Blackpool Transport Services Ltd.—which continues to operate this form of transport. In many other parts of the world, including Europe and North America, some excellent tramway systems are still functional and they make a valuable contribution to the transport requirements of the communities they serve. There could, if circumstances happen to be appropriate, even be a repetition of history with a universal tramway revival in the future but that is a matter for Chapter 12. The present situation is that trams had their heyday in the 1920s and the mode has since suffered a decline and has now become extinct in some places and severely truncated in others. Only by a historical review can it be seen why this has come to pass.

Remember two important factors to which attention has already been drawn. The first is that a horse can pull a greater weight on rails than on roads. The second is that electricity as a form of motive power came before the general acceptance of the petrol engine. Trams generally had the advantage in terms of capacity right up to the time of the introduction of the large front-entrance, rear-engined buses such as the Leyland Atlantean which first appeared in 1958, by which time trams were disappearing anyway. Whilst, however, capacity was a major reason for the introduction of the tram, it was not also a reason for the final supremacy of the bus as the tram still has a capacity potential. Popularity focuses on comfort and in this respect the tram has been at a disadvantage in the United Kingdom, not because of any inherent characteristic but because no attempt was made to modernize antiquated hardware. Whilst a rail-borne vehicle is able to give a very comfortable ride it is hardly surprising that a bus new in the 1950s compared favourably with trams built up to some 40 years earlier but which were, nevertheless, still running. As far as comfort is concerned, a high standard can be expected from the modern tramway. The explanation why tramway systems were allowed to run down in favour of the bus would therefore seem to lie elsewhere. This is in fact the case and the reasons are economic as a result of the high cost of the way, the vehicles and the power together with the inflexibility of a fixed track. However, as far as the cost of fuel is concerned, although the price of electricity became less favourable in comparison with petrol and diesel oil, there are indications that such a situation may not remain.

To summarize, therefore, it can be said that originally the tram progressed in advance of the bus. But new technology (which in the case of buses included pneumatic tyres, improved suspension, better performance, greater comfort and more economical operation) in due course put the bus ahead of the tram in terms of public appeal. Add to this the growing diseconomies of the tram and the operating disadvantages of being tied to a track, particularly when the road is heavily congested with other vehicles, and there were reasons for not applying the benefits of similarly advanced technology to the trams, with the results as have been shown. Not all trams, however, were directly replaced by buses. Some undertakings, although not prepared to spend money on updating their tramways, were also not ready to dispense with electric traction.

Trolleybuses

The trolleybus, or trackless tram as it was known in some places, was a vehicle designed to combine the electric propulsion of the tram with the manoeuvrability of the bus. Whilst it certainly achieved the former it did not go more than part way towards the achievement of the latter as although it could to some extent weave amongst other traffic, this was possible only to the limits of its trolley booms and the vehicles could not be diverted at short notice along other thoroughfares. Nevertheless, as far as flexibility was concerned, this represented something better than the tram and for all intents and purposes the trolleybus took over where the tram left off. The point has already been made in the previous sub-section that

Figure 1.1 For much of road passenger transport, steel wheel on steel rail gave way to rubber tyres but in many cases electric traction was preserved, at least for the time being. This was certainly the case in the UK. The tram and the trolleybus pictured here, both at one time a part of the London fleet, are seen preserved and operational at the East Anglia Transport Museum near Lowestoft, UK. Although this particular tram was one of a later delivery, it is really only a continuation of the basic body design (less the windscreen) which was adopted as standard by London County Council Tramways (the operator at the time) in 1907. Compared with the bus, the tram in the early 1900s was superior indeed but subsequent generations of buses first reached and then surpassed them in terms of comfort.

whereas each generation of new buses became more impressive than the last, the trams, after a flying start, were not similarly progressive and by the 1930s they had lost most of their attractiveness with the general public. This is not to say that they could not have been made equally if not more acceptable than buses had managements and national policy been so motivated. In the event, however, the electric vehicles' answer to the bus, at least in Great Britain, was not better trams but trolleybuses, the comfort of which and hence passenger acceptance was equal to that of the bus. Although isolated examples of trolleybus systems had been around since 1911 the heyday was not until the 1930s when local networks were developed on a large scale throughout the UK and elsewhere. When, however, the vehicles and equipment became time expired, decisions were taken not to renew but instead to close the systems and run buses in their place. By that time, as has been stated in the case of the tram, electricity as a form of motive power together with the need for capital equipment had made it uneconomic relative to the diesel bus. By so converting to form one common system, complete integration could be achieved and the disadvantages of running two separate systems were eliminated.

As was the case with trams, as the number of different systems diminished, so also did the demand for vehicles and equipment. Manufacturers gradually dropped out of the business and the systems that were left found it increasingly difficult to survive. The result was that in the UK, the last trolleybus ran (in Bradford) in 1972. Like the tram, examples of the mode remain overseas, including Europe and North America.

But history has a habit of repeating itself, and even as this book is being written, South Yorkshire Transport Ltd. has a test track at Doncaster in the UK where a prototype trolleybus—a standard bus converted for electric power—is being evaluated. More about the viability of trams and trolleybuses is contained in Chapter 11.

Buses

Although the animal-powered vehicle required two horses it had a seating capacity of only 26. The early motor bus had a body similar in style to that of the horse bus which it replaced. *Figure 1.2* shows the London 'B' type, which is typical of the period and shows the original body style perched high above the rear axle on a motorized chassis. Like its predecessor the driver was seated behind the power unit. Then came a forward control arrangement whereby the driving position was brought nearer to the front of the vehicle beside the engine. This gave a better range of vision and enabled the provision of greater body space. The London 'NS' type (*nulli secundus*—second to none) was one of the first to be designed with a lower centre of gravity which subsequently allowed the covering of the upper deck. This type also had fitted within its lifetime an enclosed driving cab and pneumatic tyres. Subsequent generations of vehicles embodied inside staircases and the ultimate development in body design during the petrol-engined era came with the extension of the upper deck right to the front of the vehicle over the driver's cab (*Figure 1.3*). This further increased accommodation which by now had risen to about 56 seats.

Over the years new technology has produced at every stage bigger and better vehicles. Such features included the replacement of the petrol engine by diesel, hydraulic servo-assisted brakes, fluid flywheel transmission, air suspension,

Figure 1.2 The first landmark in standardized bus design came in 1910 when the erstwhile London General Omnibus Company introduced its B type, one of which is shown here preserved in the London Transport Museum at Covent Garden, London. The body is very similar to that of the horse bus which it replaced, in fact it is little more than a horse-bus body on a motorized chassis. A preserved horse-bus can just be seen behind and to the left of the picture and the similarity can be detected. The source of power (a 30 hp petrol engine) was, like the horse, forward of the driver and the bus had 34 seats. As a matter of interest, the destination boards and route number, accurate at the time, represent a service which is still in operation today. Route planning and traffic investigation there must be but passengers resent disturbance of their regular routine. Change is sometimes necessary but there must never be change for change's sake.

automatic gear boxes, power-assisted steering, etc. Within the last three decades the outer appearance and technical design has changed considerably as a result of the engine being re-positioned from the front to either under-floor or the rear. At last the wasted space at the front because of the half-cab was utilized. This new arrangement allowed the driver to be placed ahead of the front axle and an entrance/exit immediately adjacent on the near side. This design brought the driver within the main body of the vehicle into real contact with passengers and in a good position to control boarding and alighting. It also made it physically possible for him to collect fares and thereby dispense with the conductor.

Along with new technology have come relaxations in permitted vehicle dimensions and the original 34 seats of the 'B' type with a two-man crew has now become 80 seats with a one-man crew with even larger capacities available with longer maybe three-axled vehicles.

Figure 1.3 A design of vehicle which was never popular with upper-deck passengers but which served a useful purpose in its day was the lowbridge type double-deck bus of which this vehicle of the then London Transport Executive is an example. By sinking a gangway along the length of the offside of the top deck (low over the heads of passengers seated on the offside downstairs) passengers were able to walk along and step up into rows of four seats (again with little headroom). By this means the overall height could be reduced thereby permitting it to be used on routes which passed under low bridges and on which single-decks would otherwise have been necessary. The design is not found today as with the increase in permitted lengths single-deck buses are now able to carry the same number of passengers as did this bus assuming always that there are that number wishing to be carried.

In this context, in the British bus industry, working without a conductor has by popular acceptance become known as 'one-man operation' or 'OMO' for short. Some will say that in the UK this violates the terms of the Sex Discrimination Act, 1975. However, the Interpretation Act, 1889 stipulates that in statutory documents, the term 'he' will be deemed to embrace 'he' or 'she' where appropriate. It is, therefore, regarded as unnecessarily pedantic to elucidate further on nouns or pronouns of an agreed common gender. As parliament is prepared to accept this, the writer also proposes to use the masculine which, by inference, includes the feminine, and no violation of the Sex Discrimination Act is intended.

Private cars

Although private transport could be said to have no legitimate place in a textbook on public transport, it does, nevertheless, have some very important repercussions. The private car shares the use of a common highway, causes congestion and hence delays buses. It also abstracts traffic from buses. On the other hand, if all of the car drivers and their passengers who travel in the peak periods demanded instead a seat on a bus, it would produce at best a heavier peak commitment which would probably be uneconomic and at worst an extra demand at a busy time for which it would be difficult or impossible to cater and hence would be an embarrassment. However, regardless of the effects on buses, people want cars and it cannot be denied that for those who are prepared, able and qualified to drive, nothing can match the private vehicle in terms of convenience and comfort.

Private feeling in this respect is amply demonstrated by *Table 1.1* which shows the number of private cars licensed in the UK at five yearly intervals from 1930. The trend is clear. In the 1930s, to run a car was a prestige symbol and the exception rather than the rule. True, many people did so but there were plenty who did not and were pleased to utilize the services of public transport, not only for the journey to work but for pleasure purposes as well. Then came World War II which completely distorted everybody's way of life and traffic patterns along with it. More congenial conditions did not return until the late 1940s. In the aftermath of war, although there was money, there was little to spend it on. Food and, more importantly for this topic, petrol, was rationed, and new cars were virtually unobtainable. Only then, however, after years of restriction and gloom could pent up feelings be released and people wanted to get out and about. Private transport was not available and public transport was in great demand. This was the heyday of the bus but it was not to last. As cars and petrol became more easily available and society became more affluent, so the private vehicle appeared on the roads in ever-increasing numbers and bus patronage dwindled, particularly outside the peaks when travel was optional and mostly for pleasure purposes. On many of the rural services double-deck vehicles were replaced by single deckers; hourly services were reduced to two-hourly and then to odd journeys prior to being withdrawn altogether. In the towns the trend was less apparent but it was still there. What was very noticeable was the persistently increasing volume of vehicular traffic and the resultant congestion and delay.

This, therefore, is the background that has led to the changing fortunes of buses largely as a result of the greater use of cars and which may be summarized as follows:

1. The combined effects of the erosion of traffics and heavy increases in costs have necessitated hefty fares increases.
2. With a large part of the traffic already gone, high fares discouraged much of what was left.
3. Bus loadings, particularly in rural areas, fell to negligible proportions.
4. Bus services were no longer economic, even after allowing for cross-subsidization, and were reduced and withdrawn.
5. There remains a hard core of people, mainly the young and the elderly, without access to cars and who suffer hardship without buses.

Subsidies

The conclusion that can be drawn from the previous paragraphs is that when private car ownership reaches a certain level bus networks are no longer viable but they remain a necessary social service. In Great Britain the fortunes of the bus industry began to dwindle in the late 1950s. At that time Britain had a population of around 51 million which suggests that when car ownership exceeds about 80 vehicles for every 1000 people (see the figure for 1957 in *Table 1.1*), commercial operation of local bus services becomes difficult. From around that threshold viability begins to disappear but the need does not and therein lies the question regarding the extent to which subsidies should be provided which governments of those countries with a high car ownership factor have had to face. Operators in the developing countries might like to reflect on the extent of their car ownership. It might not be very great in which case there should still be good business for the buses, and this sub-section should not have any great relevance for them. Further reference to this issue is contained in Chapter 11. But in those countries where there is such a problem this is a contentious issue. On the one hand some people will suffer hardship without an adequate bus service coupled with the fact that the bus can make one of the most positive contributions to the relief of traffic congestion; whilst on the other any losses incurred must be made good and that can only come from rates and taxes.

Table 1.1 Number of private cars licensed in the UK at approximately five yearly intervals from 1930 and number of cars per thousand people

Year	Number of cars (000)	Cars per 1000 people
1930	1056	23
1939	2034	43
1946	1770	36
1950	2344	46
1955	3673	72
1957	4308	84
1960	5648	108
1965	8794	162
1970	11 192	201
1975	13 423	239
1980	14 772	262
1985	16 453	291

Source: *Transport Statistics—Great Britain*. London, HMSO and Central Statistical Office (UK).

Experience in Great Britain was that the rural areas first felt the harsh repercussions of this trend. In the towns, high-frequency services could be reduced and still give an acceptable albeit more expensive facility for a smaller number of people. These passengers were, within limits, able to afford, perhaps unwillingly, higher fares, at least for travelling to and from work where their salary justified a certain level of expenditure for travel purposes. To what extent they were prepared to go is a matter for consideration in Chapter 7.

In 1959 the British Government set up a Committee under the chairmanship of Professor D.T. Jack to study rural services. This Committee, which reported in 1961, concluded that the decline in rural bus services was causing hardship to a few people and inconvenience to more. Among the possible solutions considered by the Committee were the carriage of fare-paying passengers on school buses, extended use of mini-buses, combination of the carriage of goods and passengers and carriage of passengers in 'postal buses'. The major recommendation, however, was a measure of financial aid to support rural bus services. This report was followed by a series of local enquiries, the findings of which were published in 1965. A white paper of the British government entitled *Transport Policy* published in 1966 drew attention, among other things, to the problems arising as a result of the proliferation of the private car. But by this time it was not only rural transport which was finding it either difficult or impossible to survive. The finances of all bus undertakings were in a parlous state and the white paper contained some of the first indications of Government thinking towards subsidies for public transport.

In 1967, *Transport Policy* was followed by another white paper—*Public Transport and Traffic*—which was, in effect, a prelude to the Transport Act, 1968 which duly came and with it a reorganisation of much of Britain's transport together with subsidies for local passenger services, be they road or rail.

These arrangements stood for the best part of 20 years and survived a reorganization of local government under the Local Government Act, 1972. The injection of both capital and revenue support into what had become an ailing industry was instrumental in bringing forth a properly planned and co-ordinated system of local passenger transport throughout Great Britain with facilities and fare levels set in accordance with the policies of the different county councils. But—as will be seen from subsequent references to this subject—with a policy of subsidization, costs to the taxpayers and ratepayers began to reach astronomical proportions, particularly in the conurbations, and the government of the day decided that once again something would have to be done. Accordingly another white paper, *Buses*, was published in 1985 which drew attention to this situation. One of the main issues was that it identified London and the former metropolitan counties as the big spenders in this respect, noting that in England those areas with 40% of the population accounted for over 80% of the revenue support, the amount of which was still rising. To put the situation into perspective, the figures quoted were that a £117m bill in 1978/79 had become nearly £400m in 1984/85, only 6 years later. One of the conclusions was that the way in which the bus industry was organized, the protection it worked within and the way in which subsidies were being paid had together conspired to keep costs higher than they need have been.

The result was the Transport Act, 1985 which, as far as Great Britain is concerned, brings things through to the present day. In the following chapters numerous references will be made to this enactment whenever British law is discussed.

Conclusions

The purpose of this brief historical review is to see how and why the present situation has been reached. The background to the changes is, of course, finance. All the time that operators could give an acceptable service without recourse to public funds the managements went their way subject only to licensing and other statutory controls, as will be described in Chapter 5. Once taxpayers' and ratepayers' money is used for revenue support or capital grants, however, politics must inevitably become involved. In a country such as the UK which is somewhat finely balanced between opposing shades of political opinion it is likely that government policy towards transport (and everything else for that matter) will change occasionally. This does not facilitate management's task. Neither does it facilitate writing a book because what is government policy at the time of preparation might have changed by the time the work is published but this is only repeating the remarks made in the Introduction. However, the result of the 1987 general election does now suggest that there will be a degree of political stability in the UK, at least for the next few years, and the 1985 Act should therefore remain valid into the foreseeable future.

2 The infrastructure

Interpretation

The term 'infrastructure' is relatively new and will not be found in all dictionaries. Having said this, it is not the intention of the author to do anything that might perpetuate the use of words that have now become popular albeit inaccurate common jargon, however widely accepted they might be. Neither is it intended to repeat for the British reader fashionable phrases imported from across the Atlantic unless there are good reasons so to do. There are occasions, however, when it is not easy to find in a single word something that adequately embraces a broad subject which has many parts. There is just such a case with the mass of different items on which capital must be spent to run buses such as highways and bus stations. The term 'infrastructure' has been aptly described by the European Commission as 'a system of communication and services as backing for operation' which is precisely what this chapter is about. Now to be considered are the highways, the bus stations, the garages and all the physical assets and facilities that are necessary for operation or, in a word, the infrastructure.

Roads

The highway network

A general review of the different forms of way applicable to the various modes of transport is contained in the contemporary work *Principles of Transport*. Very briefly, the way may be natural or artificial and it may be available either for the sole use of one particular transport service or it may be shared by many different users. Buses, of course, use the national highway network (which consists of artificially constructed roads) along with all other types of road user, be they for the conveyance of passengers or goods either as part of a public transport service or in the form of private and personalized vehicles, together being collectively referred to as vehicular traffic. The use of the highway is, therefore, very much on a shared basis. Although this inhibits free movement, some amelioration of what is becoming an increasingly unsatisfactory situation lies in the fact that the cost of using that way is also shared.

   National or local government is responsible for the construction of roads and they are paid for out of public funds derived from taxation and local rates. Road users, however, which includes bus operators, are taxed for the privilege of so doing. As a general principle this can take the form of a vehicle tax and/or a fuel tax. A third method is the application of tolls. Different countries apply different methods to varying degrees. In Great Britain there is a tax on both vehicles and fuel with only a few isolated examples of tolls which are payable for the use of certain bridges and tunnels. There is also a tax on the purchase price of private vehicles when they are bought. Elsewhere there are examples where the entire revenue is derived from the sale of fuel which, unlike the vehicle tax, relates expenditure directly to the extent of use. Although in Great Britain there is now no direct link between revenue (from fuel and vehicle taxation) and expenditure (on construction and maintenance of roads), the writer does not accept a popular contention that road users have the free use of a permanent way. It is true that a road fund, created by the Development and Road Improvement Funds Act, 1909, was finally abolished by the Miscellaneous Financial Provisions Act, 1955 after being raided for other purposes since 1926. Nevertheless, the fact must remain that road users are taxed and this can be construed as payment for the use of the way for if they did not use the way they would not pay tax. Whether or not there is a specific fund for this purpose is a technicality. In the event, British road users not only pay for their roads but for a lot of other things as well. In Great Britain in the year 1985/86 according to *Basic Road Statistics* (British Road Federation, London), less than a quarter of the total revenue from motor taxation was actually spent on highway

Figure 2.1 The ubiquitous bus—a vehicle of South Yorkshire Transport Ltd. negotiates a narrow road in the village of Bradwell in Derbyshire, UK.

Figure 2.2 Gravel roads mean more wear and tear on the vehicle but in rural Africa this is what they must contend with, hence the need for a bus able to withstand these pressures. Here two Leyland vehicles with locally built bodies are about to pass on the inter-urban service between Musome on Lake Victoria and Tarime for the Kenya border in Tanzania. Note the baggage on the roof.

construction and maintenance. However, even if it is acknowledged that it is those who use the roads that have to pay for them, they do share the costs. This means that expenditure by bus operators, for example in respect of vehicle taxation is small compared with the tramway which has to lay and maintain its own tracks even if in a public street; a matter which is further discussed in Chapter 11.

In Great Britain roads are classified according to their traffic value and those that provide a national network for through traffic are known as trunk roads or special roads such as motorways. Traffic and highway functions are the responsibility of county and metropolitan district councils who are, therefore, the highway authorities except that central government deals with trunk roads and motorways. District councils maintain minor roads and possibly other roads as well for county councils on an agency basis. Both county and district councils may provide car parks.

But this information is of only partial concern to bus operators. The piece of real interest is who is in overall control of the highway, being not only its construction but also its use, which means responsibility for traffic movements. The tramway, particularly a segregated tramway, has its own private way, is an authority only unto itself (subject to any government regulations). The bus operator is one of many users of somebody else's way and he must, therefore, know and have satisfactory working arrangements with that third party. It has been said that it is the appropriate county or metropolitan district council which is the highway authority and it is Section 1 of the Highways Act, 1980 as amended which so decrees.

Traffic control

It has been said that the road is a public and common way shared by many different types of user of which the bus is but one. It is for this very reason that there must be an independent highway authority. The users may be classified into various broad groups as is shown in *Table 2.1* which refers to road traffic, i.e. vehicle mileage, in Great Britain in 1985.

Table 2.1 Classification of road traffic in Great Britain in 1985

Basic classification	Types of vehicles included	Percentage of whole in terms of road traffic in 1985
Passenger		
Private personalized vehicles	Private transport in the form of private cars	
Taxis	A hybrid. A public facility whilst plying for hire but private once the vehicle is engaged	81.1
Motor cycles etc.	Private transport in the form of motor cycles, mopeds and three wheelers	2.0
Buses and coaches	Public transport providing public passenger transport services and excursions and tours. Also private hire which is in effect private transport once on the road under contract	1.1
Goods		
All vehicles adapted for the carriage of merchandise	A very wide variety of vehicles and traffic carried. Vehicles range from small vans to very large tankers, pantechnicons and the like with some exceptional loads. Many are specialized and may be rigid or articulated. Some are providing a public haulage service whilst others are 'own account' being used as part of a trade or business other than transport	15.8

Source: *Transport Statistics in Great Britain*. HMSO, London.

This information puts into sharp relief the ratio of buses and coaches to other traffic. In the western world, public passenger transport is only a very small part. The figures shown are correct to only one decimal place but put in another way, on average only about one vehicle in every 92 which actually appeared on the British roads in 1985 was a bus or coach. This gives a measure of the situation although in reality traffic is not, of course, as evenly spread as this. On certain thoroughfares buses could on occasions be the only vehicles in sight. Nevertheless it is clear that the bus has a lot of competition when seeking not only passengers but road space as well. This aspect will be further considered in connection with bus priorities. In the absence of any such priorities (and overall there are few) the bus must take its place with every other vehicle and conform to general traffic regulations. Certain rules of the road are laid down by the minister which drivers have a statutory duty to observe. Further advice on road behaviour is contained in a Highway Code, an official document which is not in itself mandatory although any violation would not help the driver in proceedings resulting from a subsequent accident. Traffic discipline is regulated by signs and light signals and is subject to the overall supervision and control of the police.

A glance again at *Table 1.1* will remind the reader (if he is not already only too well aware) that the number of private cars on the road is multiplying rapidly. As

Figure 2.3 Urban transport vehicles in southern Africa have to cope with a good deal of none-too-smooth terrain and rather longer distances than their UK counterparts. This is one of United Transport International's Highveld United buses negotiating a ford on the outskirts of Witbank in the Transvaal, South Africa. (Reproduced by kind permission of United Transport International.)

Figure 2.4 In Taipai, Taiwan, although most of the female population seem to ride on buses, the males favour motor-bikes which proliferate throughout the capital. Although individually they are not extravagant in road space, in the numbers that there are they do contribute to traffic congestion which would be reduced if their riders used buses instead.

the numbers grow, so traffic congestion increases; road construction programmes have failed to keep pace with the ever-increasing demands and various palliatives have been and still are being introduced. The British government has tended to veer away from building new urban motorways because of the cost and the impact on the environment. Instead, the general policy is to maximize the use of existing resources aided by less ambitious projects designed to speed traffic flow, and traffic management schemes are constantly being introduced by highway authorities to ease pressure. These provide for better use of available roadspace by such measures as uni-directional traffic flows, the reduction or elimination of conflicting traffic movements which means particularly the banning of turns across the path of facing traffic and the prohibition or control of kerbside parking or even loading and unloading merchandise. On occasions these measures require some relatively minor road reconstruction work before they are introduced but even what is thereby becoming traffic engineering is far less costly than the provision of new highways.

These traffic management and traffic engineering schemes do, however, often result in somewhat devious routes, and important traffic objectives within the central cores of towns are sometimes no longer directly accessible as a result. Vehicles are, therefore, on occasions forced to travel, for example, beyond a commercial centre via a newly created one-way system on the periphery to approach the required destination from the opposite direction. For a through bus route this is at worst impracticable and at best inconvenient and unsatisfactory. Either a setting down/picking up point somewhat distant from the popular traffic point is necessary or else a circuitous time-consuming and hence costly working is necessary. It is the duty of the bus operator to protect the interests of his passengers as far as he is able and to take them where they want to go. To the highway authority, which is responsible for the free flow of all traffic, the bus is just one of many in terms of vehicle numbers and as was shown in *Table 2.1* a relatively small part. Note, however, that this is in terms of vehicle numbers and not the number of people which would present a very different picture and will be the subject of further discussion. Not only is there an obvious need to avoid the use of additional vehicles and staff which longer routes could easily require, it is the purpose of buses to take passengers where they want to go and as expeditiously as possible. It is understandable, therefore, that operators like to be very closely involved in any traffic management and traffic engineering considerations and to get if possible some preferential treatment. More is to be said about bus priorities and their justification but before so doing, there is one further aspect of traffic management that deserves special attention. It is urban traffic control.

One method of traffic management not so far mentioned is the co-ordinated control of traffic light signals over a wide area. This produces benefits when the density of such signals is relatively high which, according to Department of Transport guidelines, means more than 30 sets in total and not less than 10 per square mile. Traffic management of this kind is known as urban traffic control and its effect is to reduce vehicle journey times by co-ordinating the operation of traffic signals and by giving priority to the heavier traffic flows. There is also a built-in system to monitor faults in traffic lights which otherwise can pass without official detection for indeterminate periods and cause much havoc in the process. The system requires a control room in which a computer governs traffic signals in accordance with various time plans which may be selected automatically and which cater for most of the predictable traffic patterns. The controller may, however, override the system manually to cater for any exceptional circumstances either by substituting an alternative fixed plan or by controlling the signals at a particular junction. To enable this to be done, the controller is assisted by closed circuit television. Strategically placed rotatable cameras are able to scan the area and by display on a series of screens in the control room the controller has a visual indication of the actual traffic situation. Also, a wall map of the area is necessary on which is portrayed the main road network with illuminated indications of the operational modes of control of each set of traffic lights in force at the time.

There is, of course, scope for further types of traffic control and traffic restraint by adaptions of this type of arrangement. For example, by computer calculation, access on to particular highways could be controlled to ensure that the volume of traffic at any one time does not exceed road capacity with the resultant congestion which is now becoming almost a way of life. This would, of course, involve queueing at the entry points but even then the subsequent improved traffic flow could compensate for time spent in this way.

Although the highway authority (in Great Britain the county and metropolitan district councils) is responsible for traffic control, with the availability of the

Figure 2.5 To reduce the use by cars of residential roads in housing estates a possibility is a bus gate. This allows buses a direct run through to maximize the convenience of the service with, in pursuance of the Radburn principle, the creation of residential pockets free from through traffic. But the idea is only good if it can be enforced and it would be impracticable to have somebody standing guard throughout the day. This example on the outskirts of Sheffield in South Yorkshire, UK, confirms that principles are one thing and practices another.

equipment as described there is clearly a case for a link-up with the police (who are responsible for enforcement) and bus managements. The system offers considerable scope in this respect. Alternatively, these bodies could institute their own closed circuit television systems but if there is to be any control over general traffic arrangements, consultation and agreement with the highway authority is necessary.

Bus priorities

With traffic congestion becoming increasingly acute there can be little dispute on the need for measures designed to relieve some of its worst effects. Even so, it is debatable whether any resultant restraints should be applied as much to the bus as to the private car. Although the bus operator will probably make a case for preferential treatment for buses, motorists, supported by motoring organizations will take a different view and make representations accordingly. To this background it must be remembered that the resultant arrangements rest with the highway authority branch of the county or metropolitan district council, which means that local policy is in the hands of locally elected politicians subject only to the broad framework as laid down by central government. Some councils are more bus minded than are others but there are very few places where an anti-bus lobby is without at least some support. This exemplifies just one need for effective public

Figure 2.6 A contra-flow bus lane in Piccadilly, London.

relations to make sure that the public gets the message, but this is something for Chapter 7.

When considering the ratio of buses to other vehicles as depicted in *Table 2.1*, the case for bus priorities might not appear to be very strong. However, in terms of potential capacity a different situation emerges. Buses are able to carry anything up to about 80 passengers and those running on local services within large towns frequently do, particularly in the peaks. This is in stark contrast to the private car whose average occupancy is about 1.6 people. Certainly the bus is a larger vehicle, but in about four times the road space compared with the car it can carry some 50 times as many people. When road space is at a premium, therefore, the case for moving people by public rather than private transport is very strong. Looked at in this light it is surprising that some politicians and some local authority staff as well still remain unenlightened in this respect. It must, nevertheless, be accepted that it is right and proper for the highway authority to do everything in its power to facilitate the free flow of traffic generally. It is also true that people want cars and it is understandable that no politician would be prepared to antagonize public opinion by imposing restraints on private transport without very good reason and that reason will have to be something better than just making life easier for the buses. But it has been shown how traffic management schemes can react unfavourably on buses and a plea for special recognition should in no way be interpreted as a bid to muzzle a competitor.

Bus priority measures may take the following forms:

1. Facilities for stopping on freeways and other roads where parking, loading or unloading is prohibited.
2. Authority to make right turns (or left turns where the rule of the road is to keep to the right) barred to other traffic for the purpose of reducing conflicting vehicular movements.
3. Activation of traffic lights in their favour by buses by means of special equipment placed on the vehicle.
4. Special bus lanes (usually the near side lane) which allows buses (in single file) to proceed ahead of other road users held in traffic blocks. (The practicability of a bus lane is dependent of course on there being an adequate width of road to allow at least a second lane for general traffic.)
5. Contra-flow operation along what have otherwise become one-way streets. This is, in effect an extension of the bus-only lane principle but against the normal traffic flow. The use of through routes denied to other traffic by the provision of special 'bus gates' being, in effect, no entry signs which buses only are permitted to pass.
6. The use of roads denied to all other traffic; in other words, bus-only roads.
7. Special provision for buses built into a system of urban traffic control. This could take the form of special computer programming for selected bus routes, separate and unrestricted access for buses on to a highway for which other traffic might have to queue and participation by bus operators in the control of such schemes.

Examples of all of these different types of bus priority can be found both in Great Britain and overseas but there is still much scope for extensions to the principle. In Great Britain, once a proposal has been accepted a statutory order will be prepared. The necessary signs can then be erected and observance will be enforced by the police. In the case of bus priorities, although the sign will refer just to 'buses' the

Figure 2.7 A bus priority enables buses to negotiate a particular movement which is denied to other traffic. Here, a bus is permitted to cross an intersection into a special contra-flow bus lane in Victoria, London. Other traffic is required to turn left and use a permanent diversion.

Figure 2.8 Entry to a bus priority zone in Singapore. Adjacent to the gantry there is a notice which prohibits the entry of cars into this particular part of the central area in the peaks on weekdays. Singapore has a traffic problem and it has been tackled by putting restraints on the private car which is extravagant in road space.

Figure 2.9 The town and traffic planners have done their work at Uxbridge on the outskirts of Greater London. The one-time busy High Street can now no longer be used by buses and the station entrance on the left, instead of containing bus stops has parked cars. A new relief road to the south-west (to the right of the picture) contains all through traffic and buses whilst a bus station lies behind the station on the left.

vehicles which are authorized to take advantage are as specified in the Order and there is not necessarily consistency in this respect, not even within the same town. The word itself is open to interpretation and only the specific order will indicate whether 'buses' means vehicles operating on local services (*see* Chapter 5) or also includes long-distance services, excursions and tours, vehicles working under contract and those running out of service. Even within the PSV category, therefore, there is no automatic definition of vehicles that may legally take advantage of bus priority measures. More than that, however, there are also other classes of traffic which might have bestowed upon them the right to use these special facilities. Examples are taxis, vehicles of the police and emergency services such as fire and ambulance and pedal cyclists. Clearly it would be a nonsense to deny access to the police acting in the interests of defending law and order or to the fire and ambulance services on the occasions of an emergency when there is some urgency in their mission (which is not always the case). Furthermore, it would be hazardous for cyclists not to use a 'with flow' bus lane, for example, where one is provided. When the total number of cyclists is small their presence on a bus lane is not likely to impede buses unduly and only if this mode of conveyance became much more popular (as in Holland, for example) would some better arrangements need to be made. Bearing in mind, however, the justification for bus priorities in the first place, it is, on the face of it, not easy to see a case for their use by taxis. A taxi takes up as much road space as a private car except that it does not need to park indiscriminantly. Similarly, long-distance coaches, excursions and tours and private hire would seem to be outside the spirit of the thing. But a works bus or a school journey might be under contract; it is very difficult to generalize.

Pedestrianization

It is not only buses for which there are priorities. Special facilities for pedestrians are still fashionable. The concept really began to catch the public eye in 1963 when a working group led by Professor Sir Colin Buchanan produced its report *Traffic in Towns*. This report drew attention, among other things, to the undesirable effects of the conflicting and competing demands for limited road space, including vehicular and pedestrian traffic, with the resultant congestion, harmful effects on the environment and sometimes personal injury. The Radburn principle, which is the creation of residential pockets free from through traffic but with a system of

Figure 2.10 Although Bournemouth in Dorset, UK, has a pedestrianization scheme on the western exit of the town, buses are still allowed through, at least in one direction. Once the shoppers have filled their baskets the bus is to hand, and note the queue-type shelters conveniently placed without obstructing the footpath.

Figure 2.11 Although it has been proved that the operation of buses through what are otherwise pedestrianized areas works well, trams lend themselves even better to this arrangement. In any case they are difficult to divert even if the planners do have ideas of that kind. This example at Hannover in West Germany shows that trams and pedestrians are quite good mixers. Note that this tram is drawing a non-powered trailer.

footpaths entirely separate from vehicular routes and linking places generating pedestrian movement, was quoted. This in turn led to thoughts regarding business and shopping areas, concluding with the view that there are advantages in these activities being undertaken in a completely traffic-free atmosphere. The general theme of the report continued on traffic segregation with proposals on how it might be implemented.

Certainly it is pleasant to stroll and shop and perhaps rest awhile in a traffic-free area. That is, free from noise and fumes and narrow pavements and sometimes crossing problems to get to the shops on the other side. Local politicians have their chance to impress the electorate with their interest in people and the environment and planners have an opportunity to exercise their skills with trees and bushes, seats and ornamental lamposts, all in the alleged interests of improving the quality of life. In reality, however, it is seldom possible to start from nothing with controlled planning at the outset. Any such new arrangements have to be superimposed on old-established development. Traffic has to be diverted elsewhere, sometimes conveniently but often inconveniently. Sometimes the surrounding roads can accommodate the extra load but on occasions they cannot. To the bus operator, this in itself is bad enough, particularly if the revised route is longer and twisting, which so often is the case. But not only that. It has already been said that it is the duty of the bus operator to take people where they want to go and what is more, passengers want to be taken where they want to go, being right to their ultimate destination which is usually the shops and the commercial centre. Furthermore, longer routes will entail additional costs, the only return to the bus operator for which is loss of goodwill and a host of public complaints. Proper penetration of shopping centres, therefore, is a must if adequate facilities are to be provided and once again the bus operator has the task of making the case and convincing local councils accordingly. Pedestrianization is ideal when it can be provided without creating other undesirable situations but a tortuous alternative route can, among other things, produce a greater safety hazard than ever the buses would be in the main shopping street. Falls inside vehicles are one of the more common accidents, and a difficult route with sharp bends does much to increase these occurrences. Further reference to pedestrian and vehicle segregation is contained in Chapter 6.

Out-town shopping centres

Another concept, not catching on quite as quickly in Great Britain but popular in North America and spreading across Europe, is the out-town shopping centre or 'hypermarket' as it is sometimes called. This is something that need not take up very much space in a book on bus operation as the bus undertaking is not the party that is principally affected.

Shopping areas of this kind do rather split the resources of the retail trade and if a sufficient amount of patronage is lost by shops in the established commercial centres, these areas could wither and eventually die. There are reasons, therefore, why applications for development of this kind are not always welcome and chambers of trade in particular might see detrimental repercussions. Nevertheless, such centres are highly convenient for those who wish to shop by car and that includes a lot of people. It is not the intention here to pronounce on whether vested interests should be allowed to deny the facility but if the concept did become established it could alter some bus route patterns. Like the shops, this might not always be to advantage as off-peak travel could be disturbed with traffic objectives diversified, assuming always that some people would wish to shop out of town and travel by bus to do so.

So concerned was the main department store in the centre at Fort Worth, Texas in the USA of the attraction of out-town shops with ample parking that a tramway of over a mile in length was constructed to link a suburban 5000 capacity car park with the basement of the shop. Free parking and free rides on the tram are available to those who wish to use them, regardless of whether they shop at the store concerned when they arrive.

Bus stops

Bus stops might seem a somewhat obvious and rather minor part of bus operation to which the operator is required to give his attention. On the contrary, it is more complex than at first might be apparent. Before bus stops are sited, policies must be determined. At one time it was usual for buses to stop almost anywhere on request although trams generally had designated albeit frequent stopping places. Circumstances have now changed, and in built-up areas fixed stops are the rule. Nevertheless, in the more rural districts a fixed stop system is still unnecessary.

The distance between stops is a matter for discretion and there must be a balance between the convenience of frequent stops and maintaining the speed of the service. Historically, as noted above, buses, unlike trams, generally developed without very many fixed stops and even today there is a tendency for stops to be more closely spaced on those routes that were at one time worked by trams or trolleybuses. The Department of Transport recommended guidelines is four or five

Figure 2.12 Typical standard British bus stop sign of the nationally approved design. This illustrates the minimal infrastructure requirements of the bus compared with other modes.

stops to the mile. Stops on opposite sides of a single two-lane carriageway should be staggered, if possible by about 150 feet (46 m), and so arranged that buses pass each other before stopping and move off away from each other. Undertakings that operate local town services usually have both compulsory and request stops. Compulsory stops are at the more heavily used locations where drivers are required to bring their vehicles to a halt regardless of passenger requirements. The remainder are of the request type and need a hand signal to the driver from the intending passenger. Other undertakings, particularly those that run into the more rural areas, use a universal type bus-stop sign without any reference to request but nevertheless, operationally regard them all as request stops and generally observe them only when required.

For the convenience of passengers, stops need to be sited at popular traffic points and elsewhere at places where people will most likely have occasion to use them. This, however, might not be in the best interests of vehicular traffic circulation generally and might even be a safety hazard. As will be seen in Chapter 5, the ultimate authority for approving the physical use of roads, stops, etc. in Great Britain is the traffic commissioner. However, reliance is likely to be placed on the views of the highway authority and the police and bus operators will, therefore, wish to seek agreements with those bodies on matters concerning bus stops. Stopping places are not, for example, placed immediately adjacent to road intersections, on narrow sections of road or on bends, etc. where it would be dangerous for other vehicles to overtake. At the more heavily used stops there should be adequate room on the pavement for people to queue and possibly for the erection of a shelter (*see* below). For queue control and vehicular congestion reasons there is a limit to the number of different services that can use any one stop and it is, therefore, sometimes necessary to group routes geographically on to two or more separate stops at the same point.

Figure 2.13 Bus shelters need not involve expense as contractors will erect them free in exchange for advertising rights. In Great Britain this involves planning permission but in Greece it would seem that the formalities are not quite as rigid. This example at Glifada near Athens shows the shelter well astride the footpath leaving very little room for passers by. Shelters are an asset to intending bus passengers but discretion must be used regarding siting.

Very much a part of the bus stop topic is the provision of lay-bys. Any stationary vehicle is an impediment to free traffic flow and a bus waiting at a stop is no exception, particularly if it is one-man operated and the fare collection procedure is not of the most speedy kind (*see* Chapter 9). Once again, the agreement to and the construction of a lay-by is the responsibility of the highway authority and it is policy to provide this facility where practicable. To the bus operator it does remove a source of objection to one-man operation which thereby facilitates such conversions. Apart from that, however, the lay-by offers no great benefit to bus operation. The fact that other traffic might be delayed whilst buses stop in the nearside lane is not really the concern of the bus manager unless of course the situation became so serious that in the absence of a lay-by the stop would have to be removed. On the other hand, once in a lay-by, difficulty can be experienced by bus drivers in pulling back into the stream of moving traffic. As a rule of the road, priority to the bus when indicating an intention to make this manoeuvre would be helpful. A case where a lay-by is particularly useful to the bus operator is for stand purposes at the end of a journey. It is often a problem to find adequate terminal facilities, particularly in built-up areas, and lay-bys are convenient in this respect.

Having determined the stopping arrangements, the erection of suitable signs is necessary. This, however, is more a part of publicity and will be considered in Chapter 7.

Shelters

Closely allied to bus stops is the bus shelter. There is public clamour for some sort of protection from the weather when waiting at the kerbside and whilst it could be argued that the operator's responsibility for passengers is when they are on the bus, there must, nevertheless, be some sympathy with such requests. In any case it enhances the attractiveness of the service if people can wait (hopefully not too long) in reasonable comfort, and shelters offer a site to display publicity. Overall there is no reason why operators should be opposed to the principle. On the other hand they cost money, they have to be maintained and they are targets for vandalism. It does not, of course, have to be the bus company who provides the shelters and very often it is not. As a public amenity they could be and are provided by local authorities and there are even cases where shelters have been donated by private individuals. An alternative is the free erection and maintenance of shelters by commercial firms in return for advertising rights, expenditure being covered by advertising revenue. Although this would seem an admirable arrangement, in Great Britain at least, the erection of a structure that carries advertisements does require planning permission and the practice does tend to offend the environmentalists even though it is a way of providing a measure of comfort for people waiting for a bus. One possible disadvantage is that sites required for traffic purposes and those most suitable for advertising displays are not necessarily the same. Nevertheless, shelter provision by a third party can only be welcome. To the public, however, it does tend to be identified with the bus organization who will always like to be consulted in connection with design and location. A poorly maintained shelter produces a bad image and the bus operator is criticized even though it might not be his responsibility. But good shelter facilities have the opposite effect and goodwill is engendered.

Shelter design takes many forms and is to some extent dictated by the numbers of people that are likely to be involved and the space available. In Great Britain, old habits die hard and the practice of queueing, born nearly 50 years ago in time of war and scarcity (and, in fact, made obligatory at the time when waiting for a bus by virtue of the Defence Regulations) is still observed today. Nobody would wish to alter this arrangement, particularly after experience in some other countries where the local populace is more precipitant and it is the strongest and the fittest who succeed in boarding. At the same time, the need to queue does have its effect on shelter design and where larger numbers congregate it is not a wooden hut or similar edifice which is required but a queue type shelter under which people can line up in traditional style and still have protection from the weather. One other factor that has some influence in shelter design is the type of vehicles that use the stops in question. The queue-type shelter becomes a little complicated when buses of different designs serve the same queue. It will be seen from Chapter 3 that whilst boarding is now usually at the front, on some vehicles it is still at the rear. On others passengers may alight from a separate centre exit and if one is not careful, directly into a queue or the railings of a queue-type shelter. But this is something that can be solved more easily by bus design than shelter design.

Bus stations

Mention has already been made of the use of lay-bys for stand and terminal purposes. Even these are not necessary if side roads are available where vehicles can park without causing an obstruction. If a lay-by, therefore, is not an essential part of a terminal facility, far less is a purpose-built bus station.

Those responsible for town planning often like to incorporate a bus and coach station in their proposals if only for prestige purposes. But local authority planners are not bus operators and there is always the danger that the needs of passengers and the interests of efficient bus running will be subordinated to the ideology of a separate self-contained and in the event even a somewhat remote area designated for the use of public transport, perhaps with a circuitous approach designed to avoid a pedestrianized area. The upshot is that passengers are not taken where they want to go and route mileage and running times and hence operating costs are increased. Furthermore, the owner of the bus station, which again is likely to be the local authority, will require recompense for the facilities provided which will probably take the form of a departure charge on the operator. All of this extra expense can only reflect in fare levels which could be avoided by direct routes through town centres with kerbside setting-down and picking-up points.

This, then, is the extreme case against bus stations, and it does illustrate the need for operators to maintain close contact with local planning authorities. But throughout the world there are many hundreds of bus stations in daily use. Large bus undertakings, perhaps with route networks protected by a route licensing system, have themselves even built and thus own and operate their own bus stations. The principle cannot, therefore, be entirely wrong. Indeed, it is not; but it is a question of degree and judgement according to local circumstances and the types of services. To encroach on Chapter 6, it will be seen that seven different types of services are listed ranging from local town bus services through to long-distance coaches and it is noted that the local services could be of the cross-town variety. It is to this group in particular that the remarks made at the

Figure 2.14 Example of a 'head-on' type bus station but one which does not derive full benefit of the basic concept. Here, Victoria coach station in London, although large, has a tremendous amount of traffic to handle. It is congested, and so much so that a new site is being sought. The passenger platforms (on the left of the picture) are narrow and coaches pull up short which also enables them to move off in a forward direction and thereby eliminate the need to reverse which would be difficult anyway as there would probably be another vehicle behind. But passengers do tend to mingle with moving coaches. Note how double-decks have come into the coaching scene at a time when many former double-deck bus routes have been converted to single-deck operation.

outset apply. On short-distance journeys such as this passengers do not require the special facilities afforded by a bus station. For shoppers with heavy baskets the top priority is a bus stop immediately adjacent to the shops. Likewise, commuters have no desire for a long walk between a 'central' bus station and their offices.

Progressing through the classifications from rural services, medium-distance limited stop and long-distance express, the scale of benefits tips gradually away from a kerbside pick-up in the centre and becomes more weighted both passengerwise and operationally towards the amenities of a bus station. Furthermore, for the routes described, a series of different terminal points scattered throughout the town is difficult for passenger interchange and, if the services are worked by the same operator, it is inconvenient for control purposes. However, with a trend away from the larger operating units to fragmentation into smaller concerns it is likely that more bus stations will become separate entities with operators paying on a departure basis.

The lesson then is that operators must maintain a close liaison with the planning authorities and resist to the extent that they are able the use of a badly sited bus station. It is important that passengers are taken precisely to where they want to go, particularly on their local daily trips. Remember always that people need very little encouragement to use their own private cars and this they will do if the bus is not sufficiently attractive. In consequence traffic congestion becomes a yet more serious problem. This is something that highway authorities do not (or should not) want although they are often loathe to accept the advantage of the bus in this respect. This, therefore, is a feature that operators must continually stress and it is important that car parks are not placed in more advantageous positions than are bus stops.

To summarize, operators must be circumspect in their willingness to accept the use of a bus station and in their representations make known the contribution which they make to the relief of traffic congestion together with the social character of the services which they are providing, probably on slender profit margins. On any bus station proposal look particularly at:

1. The facilities provided in terms of stands, space including a parking area, offices and passenger and staff amenities, all of which might be either inadequate or excessive.
2. Access and egress in terms of physical suitability and added mileage to the route.
3. Location in terms of passenger convenience and proximity to the main traffic objectives and relationship with public car parks.
4. Costs including departure charges and their effect on the viability of the services, remembering that the ideal location is where space is least likely to be available or if it is where land is most expensive and also most attractive for other commercial development.

Inevitably, therefore, there is a conflict of interests and prices are bound to be high but some of this might be alleviated by developing the airspace of a central site for other commercial purposes. There does sometimes have to be a compromise, particularly for long-distance coach services.

Turning now to the design of a bus station, the number of stands must be determined and this will be governed by traffic demand and the number of services. Total departures is not a good guide as ideally medium frequency services or a series of services geographically grouped need a stand on their own to avoid a conflict of queues and a multi-user is only practicable where journeys are sufficiently widely spaced that neither queues nor vehicles are likely to clash. On the other hand, very frequent services might call for two (or even more) vehicles on the stand at any one time unless there is a separate parking area. If this is the case, space must be earmarked accordingly: Adequate arrangements must be made for vehicles to manoeuvre and stand, for passengers to queue, for all the supporting passenger and staff amenities and for supervisory and control facilities.

There are two basic principles on which bus stations are designed, each with their advantages and disadvantages. The theory is explained by *Figures 2.15* and *2.16*. Briefly, the first alternative comprises a series of island platforms. If passengers are to approach these platforms on the level then they must cross the vehicle runways and if the walkways are grade separated (either above or below) then it becomes necessary to negotiate stairs or escalators. This is a disadvantage but is balanced by the fact that vehicles can be driven progressively through the bus station compound without any manoeuvring or reversing movements. The alternative is a single platform with vehicles nosing on from a large circulating area. This provides maximum convenience for passengers but it does entail substantial manoeuvring with vehicles reversing out and in so doing crossing the paths of

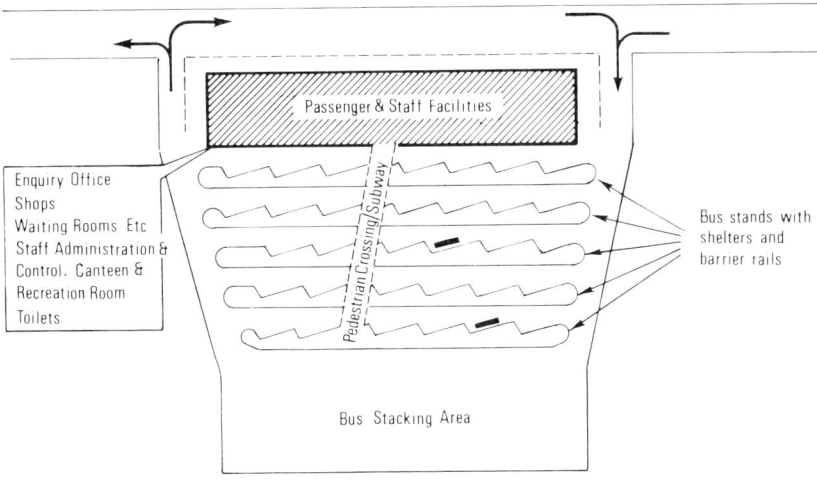

Figure 2.15 The principle of the 'drive-through' type bus station. In this example, the 'sawtooth' pattern for easy bus movement has been adopted. The runways must be sufficiently wide to allow buses to overtake others, which are parked on the stands.

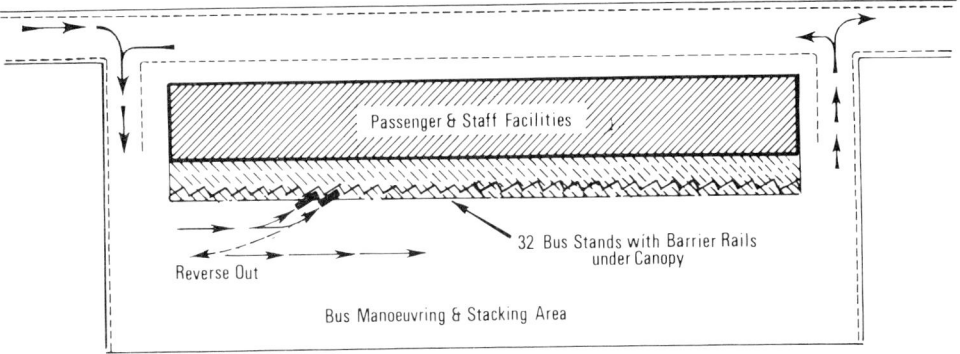

Figure 2.16 The principle of a 'head on' type of bus station. As in *Figure 2.15* the 'sawtooth' pattern has been adopted. Although this design eliminates the need for passengers to cross the runways, the vehicles themselves must undertake reversing and conflicting movements.

others coming in. The latter arrangement is more economical in terms of space but there are many examples of each basic design.

Another principle to be decided is whether a bus station should be combined with a bus garage. The answer can be determined only in relation to local circumstances but generally it is likely that it should not. Bear in mind that for route planning, the siting of a bus garage is less crucial than that of a bus station, and to the passengers the garage is really of no interest at all. If space is a problem, and at the ideal location it usually is, then the garage can be expected to be at some place elsewhere. Exactly where will be considered in the next sub-section. Exceptions, however, do arise, often in the smaller towns where more than one property holding could not be justified and no point is very far from the centre anyway. A possibility here is to use a large forecourt for passenger boarding and alighting purposes. Occasionally the garage itself is similarly used, but for safety reasons any practice that allows passengers on foot to mingle with garage activities is not ideal.

Bus garages

It was acknowledged in the Introduction that people in the bus industry, as in most big businesses, represent many professions. Some are fundamental to the basic function of the industry whilst others assume more of an ancillary role although they are no less important for that. A 'busman' in this context is regarded as the operator and the commercial manager; in other words, the 'traffic man'. The engineer could well regard himself in similar vein and it is true that the design, construction and maintenance of buses is also somewhat fundamental. Without such support the operator would be ineffective. Nevertheless, this book is not being written by an engineer and there is no pretence of teaching engineering skills. A bus garage is primarily a place to service and overhaul vehicles and mechanical engineering is a science in itself. At the same time, managers and others who are not skilled in this respect do need a sound layman's knowledge of the subject as well as a good chief engineer and this side of things cannot therefore be completely disregarded. Furthermore, the operator (as distinct from the engineer) has some interest in bus garages in his own right if part of the premises is used for control, supervision and cash paying-in purposes as described in Chapter 10.

There are numerous policy decisions that must be determined at the garage planning stage as also must the role which the garage is to play within the organization be decided. The main considerations are as follows.

Size

Whilst adequate facilities must be available for the entire fleet this in itself does not necessarily dictate the size of any one garage. What is the optimum size for a superintendent on the engineering side and a chief inspector on the traffic side to handle is largely a matter of opinion and different undertakings have different policies in this respect. It is not easy to generalize but provision for less than 40 vehicles could be regarded as rather small whilst a capacity for more than 200 too unwieldy. Geography also plays some part in determining size. Only a few vehicles might, for example, need to be housed at a small town location—but, being so far distant from a neighbouring centre, allocation elsewhere would be uneconomical or impracticable. To take the argument one stage further, it is at times appropriate to stable odd buses at a village to avoid a long empty run back to town and back again next morning. In circumstances such as this there is sometimes a case to have an 'out-station', being a small shed or even a piece of open ground able to accommodate one or perhaps two vehicles manned by drivers who live locally. Under this arrangement, staff bring back their buses to the out-station in the evening, probably sweep them out and collect them the following day, the vehicles being otherwise serviced at the parent garage.

It is the larger and more heavily trafficked urban areas where it is appropriate to consider alternative policies on garage capacities. Such decisions, however, are likely to have been taken long ago and it is never easy and often costly to reverse garage policies which have been followed over the years. That apart, there is at least a theoretical choice between a lesser number of larger garages or a greater number of smaller garages and it is not only the elusive optimum size which determines this. The function and location must also be taken into account and the fewer the garages are in number the more difficult it will be to satisfy the location requirements. On size alone, that is disregarding these other circumstances, it is suggested that a total capacity for about 120 vehicles is sufficiently large to exploit properly the potential of local garage managers whose traffic work is described in Chapter 10 but which at the same time avoids the organizational and operational complexities which a very large unit can bring.

The actual size of a garage in terms of area occupied is determined not only by vehicle allocation (that is, buses required for service plus an agreed percentage of spares) but also on the size of the vehicles in terms of length and width. It has already been seen from Chapter 1 that over the years buses have become bigger, and the larger the vehicle, the fewer that can be accommodated in any given space. In this sense, however, size does not also mean capacity as subject to adequate headroom a double-deck bus will occupy no more garage space than will a single deck of similar dimensions. In the 1930s the standard measurements of a bus were 27ft 6in × 7ft 6in (8.4 × 2.3 m). As regulations have been relaxed so sizes have been increased even to very long articulated vehicles and the following table showing approximate capacities by a selection of vehicle sizes of a garage which could accommodate 100 buses of the one-time conventional 27ft 6in (8.4 m) dimension is of interest:

Size of bus	Number of buses in garage
27ft 6in × 7ft 6in	100
30ft 6in × 8ft 0in	82
33ft 0in × 8ft 2in	75
39ft 0in × 8ft 2in	63
57ft 0in × 8ft 2in (articulated)	44

These figures are essentially an approximation and much will depend on the design of the garage but they do give an order of magnitude and it is quite clear that length and breadth has a strong bearing on garage capacity and hence cost. On the other hand, as far as economics are concerned larger vehicles would hopefully also mean fewer vehicles and this is the other side of the equation.

Function

On the engineering side, vehicles need to be parked when not in use (which does not have to be under cover—this is an engineering expediency), washed, swept, refuelled and generally made ready for use on the following day, inspected as a routine, serviced (that is, greased, etc.) at the required intervals, repaired as necessary and made good and overhauled periodically which will sometimes be a major overhaul. Not all garages need be equipped to undertake this work. There could be a centralized overhaul centre to take care of all recertification work, major overhauls and serious accident damage or this type of work could be put out to an independent contractor. Even if intermediate dockings and lesser services are to be undertaken at garages, every establishment still does not have to be so fitted. There could be dormitory sheds and parent sheds with the dormitory units used mainly for stacking at night and perhaps engineering work of a minor nature. Beyond that is the out-station to which reference has already been made.

Mention was made above that on occasions it is sensible to combine bus station and garage and allow the garage or the forecourt to be used as a passenger terminal. Although operationally the use of the forecourt for this purpose is quite acceptable if the location is right, special care is necessary if the public is permitted to enter the precincts of the garage itself, particularly when buses are being shunted for parking purposes.

Location

From a physical point of view, a bus garage must have adequate access roads and freedom to use them. For a new construction, however, it is unlikely that the necessary planning permission would be granted if this was not the case. Operationally there are other reasons why the location of a garage is important. It must be strategically sited in relation to the bus route network if a lot of empty running is to be avoided, and more will be said about that in Chapter 8. Bus garages provide work for a large number of people and for this reason it is an advantage if they are sited in an area where labour is most likely to be available. At the same time, a bus garage might not be popular with local residents on account of noise and the continual passing of heavy vehicles. There is also a divergence of views as to whether garages should be as near as possible to the centres or out in the suburbs of the larger towns. In this context there is the question not only of land values and accessibility but also of duty schedules and again this is a matter which will be further considered in Chapter 8.

Design

The design of a bus garage is conditioned by its size and function and whether facilities are required for traffic as well as engineering staff, which is usually the case.

As far as engineering facilities are concerned it must be decided whether some open-air parking is acceptable and then the number of pits and what equipment is necessary. One pit for every 15–20 buses is generally regarded as an acceptable norm. Pit design has altered as different types of engine position have been adopted. Furthermore, the one-time long, straight 'hole in the ground' with steps down at one end has in more recent installations given way to an adequately heated sunken area which includes a workshop with the white-tiled pits properly lit and equipped with air lines, power points, outlet tubes for coupling to vehicle exhausts so that fumes can be led to a high-level expulsion point and oil drainage points with the used oil passed to an outer tank. A popular arrangement is the 'swimming pool' layout where vehicle wheels stand on ramps placed over a large pit with room for maintenance staff to move from one vehicle to another at full or near-full height. A hoist is employed to lift items to and from floor level.

Vehicle flows in garages should, so far as is practicable, be kept on a one-way basis with the minimum of conflicting movements. Refuelling usually takes place at the nearest point to where the vehicle enters the main building with the subsequent route through to the stacking area being via the washer. *Figure 2.17* portrays a modern bus garage with facilities for undertaking any work up to major

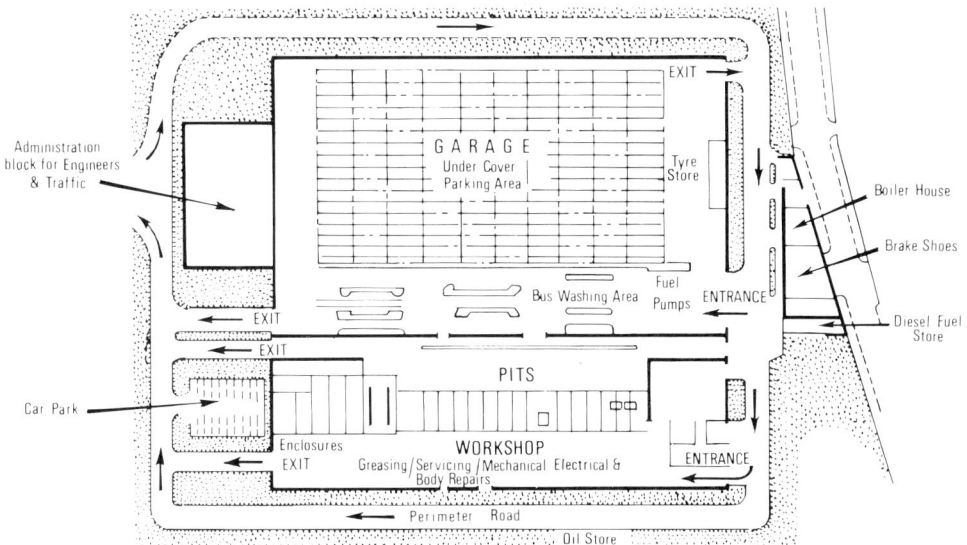

Figure 2.17 The basic requirements of a bus garage. The example shows covered parking accommodation for 180 buses with an adjacent workshop with pits for routine servicing and greasing and mechanical, electrical and body repairs. Separate enclosures are available for chassis cleaning and painting and there is a workshop for brake-shoe relining. Special facilities are necessary for stores, including tyres and fuel, and there must be provision for waste oil. Fuel pumps and bus-washing facilities are required near the entrance. The administration block will include suitable accommodation for traffic supervisory and control staff, including a paying-in room and cash office. Welfare facilities include a canteen and first-aid room and an outside car park.

overhauls. This gives an indication of the range of equipment that is necessary but the design and the facilities provided in this example are nearer to the ideal than to minimum requirements. Only the larger undertakings could justify provision of this kind. At this stage, however, the subject passes from bus operation to mechanical engineering which is not a part of this study.

Remember that as far as the engineering department is concerned the functions of a garage are to:

1. Park vehicles.
2. Refuel.
3. Wash and clean the exterior and interior.
4. Rectify faults reported by drivers, lubricate and undertake routine servicing.
5. Check and change tyres.
6. Re-paint and tend to advertisements.
7. Repair accident damage.
8. Undertake major overhauls.

Whilst functions (5) to (8), although essential, might well be put out to separate contractors, functions (1) to (4) are inescapable and are part of the daily running activities even of the smallest operators.

The responsibility of the garage engineer is to make vehicles of the right type available, properly cleaned and serviced, at the times required by the traffic department. At one time it was customary to do much of this work at night when most, if not all, of the vehicles are available. Penalty rates of pay for night work make this practice less economic and it is a matter for decision according to local circumstances whether to keep plant and equipment fully occupied day and night or to concentrate on daytime work with the vehicles on which work has to be done allocated to low mileage peak hour only runnings, assuming that there are some. Although there is no objection to substituting a vehicle in service for engineering purposes, the practice can become expensive if the route on which it is operating does not pass in close proximity to the garage. Again this calls for the judicious allocation of vehicles to runnings. The number of vehicles allowed for engineering spares will also have a bearing on this. Although a 10% allocation for this purpose could be regarded as very efficient, more than 20% should give cause for concern and hence investigation. This is a case where the larger undertaking has some advantage as there will be more spare vehicles available to meet emergencies. To quote the extreme case, the operator who has only one bus in service has the choice of 100% spares (i.e., a fleet of two and very wasteful) or super-efficient with no spares at all (very optimistic).

To summarize, therefore, as far as size and design is concerned, it is impracticable to describe a typical garage—there just is not one. Regardless of any economies of scale, unless the proprietor is also in the garage business the capacity and facilities must not be in excess of what is actually required by the bus fleet subject to allowing room for possible expansion. Site sizes and terrain also play a large part in garage design. But having considered the engineering requirements, the traffic function also needs facilities which again are generally contained within the garage complex.

The requirements of the traffic people include offices for the control staff (there is a similar requirement by the engineering department), a cash office and a paying-in room suitable also for the display of duty schedules and notices. Coupled with this are the welfare requirements of all staff employed at the garage regardless of the department to which they belong such as canteen or mess-room, recreation or games room, locker accommodation, washing facilities, first aid equipment, car park and other amenities for which the local trade unions will be eager to make representation. The arrangements for the collection, safe custody and disposal of cash, again a traffic function of a bus garage, will be considered in Chapter 10.

Fixed track systems

Tramways

As was shown in Chapter 1, the tram has been very much a part of the urban passenger transport scene. In the world-wide context it still is and no study on the subject can ignore it, particularly as the forthcoming energy situation could result in its numbers multiplying rather than further decreasing. The same could apply to trolleybuses but this is something for Chapter 12. Trams, however, are capital intensive and hence expensive animals. They need a specialized way which may also be a part of the normal public highway. To that extent therefore, discussion is appropriate for this study.

Tram lines may be laid either in a normal road or partially on a private right of way, in which case the system becomes 'grade separated' to use a more recent but appropriate term. The provision of special tracks together with electrical equipment for power purposes is a costly affair, particularly when compared with the diesel bus whose only contribution towards the provision of its way is the annual vehicle licence and for all the extra money, a very inflexible form of transport has been provided. There is nevertheless a capacity advantage which is discussed in Chapter 6. The statutory control of tramways is something for Chapter 5 and it is sufficient to say here that when considering the situation in Great Britain as far as tracks in the street are concerned, attention must again be directed to the Tramways Act, 1870 and the need for parliamentary approval.

A tramway undertaking whose line is on a private right of way is, of course, responsible for the entire cost of the land. At this stage the tram is only one stage removed from a light railway, in fact there is no clear delineation between the two. This in turn leads into what is now known as 'rapid transit'; a system of completely

Figure 2.18 The guideway of West Midlands Passenger Transport Executive on the outskirts of Birmingham, UK. Conventional buses are used on this specialized way along which vehicles can enter and leave at any suitable opening. In this case the space which was at one time a centre reservation for trams has been converted for this purpose. When trams gave way to buses some 30 years earlier this special facility was lost but passengers were able to board buses at the kerbside. Once again it is necessary to cross the stream of traffic to the middle of the carriageway to reach what is now the bus stop but to install a guideway alongside the footpath means restricting access to properties and side roads or to have frequent gaps which reduce the effectiveness of the system. (Reproduced by kind permission of West Midlands PTE.)

grade separated urban transport. A similar title is also suitable for the upgraded tramway as the term 'light railway' is generally associated with a branch of the more conventional type of railway on which certain standards and legal requirements have been relaxed in return for specified operating restrictions. This sort of line is now fast disappearing and a more popular and perfectly apt description of an upgraded urban tramway system is 'light rapid transit'.

Rapid transit

The public passenger transport needs of an urban agglomeration are often met by train as well as by bus, particularly if the area is large and densely populated, although the infrastructure of a railway is considerable and its capital cost formidable. As this is a book about road passenger transport it is reasonable to talk about trams but not about railways. But both can be part of some form of rapid transit. As the former is for discussion and the latter is not, some sort of imaginary demarcation line must be drawn. Just how blurred the distinction really becomes can perhaps be further appreciated by looking at the following modes and their progression from local bus to main-line railway:

1. Diesel bus.
2. Trolleybus.
3. Street tramway.
4. Segregated tramway.
5. Light rapid transit. ⎫ both could have
6. Rapid transit.   ⎬ rubber tyres
7. Suburban railway.   ⎭
8. Fast main-line railway.

Quite clearly the diesel bus is the subject of one study and the fast main-line railway another. Modes (1) to (4), however, are legitimate road passenger transport subjects, particularly if part of an otherwise segregated tramway system has its tracks in a normal road whilst modes (7) and (8) are obviously 'rail transport'. Modes (5) and (6) are arguably either a part of both or a part of neither but light rapid transit certainly cannot be divorced from the subject under review.

Heavy rapid transit is likely to be of the steel wheel on steel rail variety and any discussion on this is appropriate for a book on railway operation even though it caters for the same type of traffic as the bus. But it has been shown that a street tramway is only one stage removed from light rapid transit, and the same system can in fact be part one and part the other. But more than that, there are examples where conventional buses run on segregated rights of way, sometimes, as in the USA, in the centre median of new motorways on a 'pre-metro' basis. To take it one stage further, conventional buses may be used on guided tracks as at Essen in West Germany (where the objective was to interwork them with the tram system, thereby giving fast access to the town centre) and a limited experiment of West Midlands PTE at Birmingham, UK (*Figures 2.18* and *2.19*). Although in this latter instance the track was not only experimental but also quite short (little more than 1/3 mile (0.5 km) in fact), the principle is significant. It means that existing standard double-deck buses (or trolleybuses) only slightly modified to incorporate guide arms can exploit the benefits of a segregated fixed track system where demand cannot justify a more specialist light rapid transit and at the same time retain the flexibility of the bus wherever it leaves the specialized route.

Figure 2.19 The guide arm and roller as fitted to a vehicle of West Midlands Travel Ltd. for use on the special guideway at Birmingham. (Reproduced by kind permission of West Midlands PTE.)

Figure 2.20 Although a street tramway, many of the continental European systems have a considerable amount of segregated track. At this stage the tram becomes very much akin to a light railway (not really light rapid transit because on the in-town sections the tracks are in the centre of the street). This double-articulated tram is one of the Gemeent Vervoer Bedrijf fleet seen in suburban Amsterdam, Holland.

As a matter of interest, as a result of the construction of the Essen and Birmingham guideways, new dimensional world standards of the type that are more familiar in railway parlance have been determined. With the standard width of a bus at 8ft 2½in (2.5 m) the track width between the guide kerbs or rails has been set at 8ft 6in (2.6 m). This is, of course, narrower than would be necessary for a conventional bus lane in the normal highway. Similarly, the height of the guide rail has been set at 7¼ in (185 mm). Again as a matter of interest and this time a British domestic issue, the protruding (not very far) guide arms fitted to the bus caused it to exceed the maximum width as laid down in the Road Vehicles (Construction and Use) Regulations, 1986 and referred to in Chapter 5. A special order for such vehicles to operate was therefore necessary (*vide* Section 42 of the Road Traffic Act, 1972).

3 Vehicle design

Buses and coaches

Definition

A satisfactory distinguishing line has never been drawn between the general use of the term 'bus' and that of the term 'coach'. Broadly speaking, a bus is built for utilitarian traffic while a coach is employed when passengers are riding for pleasure or making a medium- or longer distance journey where a greater element of comfort is required. Whether or not the vehicle is being used on a 'local public passenger transport service' as defined by British law has little relevance and whether it is a single-deck or double-deck has no bearing on the matter. Nevertheless, with the distinction already made, in British parlance the coach is a more luxurious vehicle unsuitable for short trips with their heavy pick-ups and set-downs because of narrow entrances, gangways, etc. Operators sometimes have a few vehicles in their fleet of a general-purpose design with seats rather more comfortable than those of a bus but with entrance/exit and general layout nevertheless suitable for bus work, which can be used for all types of operation.

Types and capacities

The range of types and sizes of buses and coaches in service today is extremely wide with maximum dimensions and weight limited more by the topography of the route and the regulations of the country concerned than by any physical aspects of construction. In very general terms and disregarding now the bus and coach distinction, vehicles may be classified into five broad groups, as follows:

1. *Minibus*—The smallest type of vehicle that can really be classified as a bus, carrying 9–16 passengers. The length is usually between 13 and 20 feet (4–6 m).
2. *Midi-bus*—Something more than a minibus but less than a standard single-deck and will carry up to about 30 passengers. The length is generally in the 20–26 feet (6–8 m) range.
3. *Single-deck*—Medium- to large-capacity bus according to length and seat configuration. The length ranges from about 33 to 39 feet (10–12 m) with a capacity for about 40–60 passengers, but if of the standee variety then many more can be accommodated.
4. *Double-deck*—High-capacity bus with seats for 80 or more depending on length of which the usual range is between 31 and 33 feet (9.5–10 m) but vehicles of 39 feet (12 m) length are available.

Figure 3.1 One of the stalwarts, the rear-entrance open-platform half-cab bus, the backbone of the industry in its day. It still survives in some places as does this Leyland bus of Kerala State Road Transport Corporation working on a local service in Trivandrum in the south of India.

Figure 3.2 Rear-entrance open-platform buses may be obsolete and require a two-man crew but they do offer maximum convenience in towns where vehicles frequently have to stop for traffic reasons at places other than official pick-up/set-down points. Not only is a closed door frustrating to passengers, the fact that some do board and alight in this way reduces the amount of time spent at the official stops and once doors come on the town services, a little additional running time might be difficult to refuse. London Buses still have some vehicles of this type, and one is seen here in Oxford Street in London.

Figure 3.3 The size of the bus must fit where it is intended to go. This Bristol VRLH of London Buses Ltd. seen here travelling along the Finchley Road in north-west London is on a route that traverses residential roads heavy with parked cars. Small buses may not be suitable for moving the masses but they can penetrate those areas where the larger buses cannot go.

5. *Articulated*—Usually single-deck with a length up to about 59 feet (18 m) and a high capacity, able to accommodate 150 passengers including standees.

The above classifications are purely descriptive and have no legal significance. As a matter of interest, in Great Britain, Section 19(1) of the Transport Act, 1985 defines a bus as a vehicle adapted to carry more than eight passengers. A 'small bus' means a vehicle able to carry more than eight but not more than 16, and those that do carry more than 16 are designated 'large buses'.

Basic features

The most appropriate type of vehicle for a given set of circumstances is a matter for consideration in Chapter 6. The development of the bus was dealt with in Chapter 1 and here it is the features of the vehicle that are for consideration. This covers the chassis and mechanical parts which is primarily the responsibility of the Chief Engineer and the body features in which the Traffic Manager has a considerable interest. Again, as this is not a book on engineering technicalities it is not proposed to elaborate on this side of things but those responsible will have their views on such matters as engine makes and design, ease of maintenance, reliability, fuel consumption, ground clearance, ride quality, acceleration, noise levels, heating, ventilation, air suspension, automatic gearboxes, power steering, etc. Whilst the Traffic Manager will call for a different specification for long-distance work, the Chief Engineer will also have a strong interest in this aspect. For example, an automatic gearbox is much more valuable to a one-man driver on a busy town service than it might be to his counterpart on an express coach on a motorway service but the ability of the motorway coach to cruise at 60 or 70 mph (100–110 km/h) is not a feature of the local bus which seldom needs to get above 40 mph (65 km/h). However, the all-important feature which has such a fundamental effect on vehicle design and has strong repercussions on both the engineering and traffic departments is the positioning of the power unit.

Figure 3.4 Buses to fit the route. In Andorra in the Pyrenees roads are narrow and winding and in the town heavily congested. Small buses are therefore standard, the one shown being typical of the Andorra bus fleet.

Figure 3.5 In a country ravaged by war the services provided by the state-owned bus company have fallen to negligible proportions. But their absence has enabled the privately owned midi-buses to flourish, legally or illegally. This midi-bus station in Kampala, Uganda, unlike the neighbouring conventional bus station, has buses in abundance but they keep to the more popular routes and ensure that they have a good load before departing.

   To continue the story from Chapter 1, the one-time conventional position of the engine at the front now has alternatives at the centre under the floor or at the rear. As far as the central position is concerned, this normally necessitates a higher floor, which means that it is suitable for single-deck vehicles and with steps up at the entrance, boarding and alighting becomes more difficult. However, the higher floor makes underfloor luggage accommodation practicable along the centre opposite the engine as well as at the rear. In short, the design lends itself to long-distance coaches where frequent and speedy boarding and alighting is not a feature but where passengers are more likely to have a considerable amount of accompanied baggage. With an engine at the centre or rear, the ability to place the driver and the passenger entrance ahead of the front axle and hence put the driver in an ideal position to collect fares has already been explained. It is true that such an arrangement is also physically possible with the engine at the front, but the inevitable large and bulky cowling on the near side of the driver occupies what would otherwise be an open platform area. The entrance for passengers therefore becomes more narrow and tortuous and space provision for sophisticated fare collection equipment becomes more difficult.

   The advantage of the engine at the rear compared with a central location is that whilst it preserves the driver's position ahead of the front axle, it eliminates the need for a high floor which means that not only does it make for easier boarding and alighting, the arrangement becomes eminently suitable for double-deck designs. Even so, there are disadvantages. With the engine next to the driver he is able to discern the sounds that it emits and hence is in a better position to respond to its needs, whereas with the engine in a remote position at the rear the first indication he might have of any malfunction is when the vehicle has stalled. A front engine is more easily cooled and the transmission is simple in comparison, all of which means that the rear-engined bus has tended to be less reliable and has had the effect of forcing up spare vehicle allocations. However, the advantages in body design are sufficiently overwhelming to justify living with these deficiencies.

Figure 3.6 A typical bus for town work in East Africa. Note entrances/exits both forward and rear but no safety hazard is involved as conductor(s) are carried. This vehicle working on a local service of Kenya Bus Services Ltd. is seen at a central picking-up point in Nairobi.

Nevertheless, the bus with the engine at the front remains the trouble-free workhorse of the industry, and where conditions are rigorous, where roads are rugged and where there is a need for the minimum of maintenance and supply of spare parts, the old original arrangement has much to commend it. This is why the front-engine, front-entrance single-deck bus with a high floor and hence good ground clearance is still ideal for use in some of the developing countries.

In many areas and certainly in the United Kingdom the design features are strictly controlled by regulation. The Road Vehicles (Construction and Use) Regulations, 1986 and the Public Service Vehicles (Conditions of Fitness, Equipment, Use and Certification) Regulations, 1981 as amended stipulate in a depth of detail statutory requirements regarding the construction and use of buses and coaches in Great Britain. The sort of things that are dealt with include:

1. *Body*—General construction requirements with dimensions stipulated for body sides, steps, platforms, stairs, entrances and exits, doors, emergency exits and their access, gangways, seats and driver's cab. As a matter of interest, the maximum box dimensions are:
   Length 39ft 4½in (12 m)
   Width 8ft 2½in (2.5 m)
   Height 15ft (4.57 m)
2. *Stability*—Both double deck and single deck, when loaded to be able to tilt to specified degrees without overturning.
3. *Suspension*—No excessive body sway.
4. *Turning circle*—Vehicles to turn within a swept circle of maximum defined radii according to length (a swept circle is that which is traced by any part of the body of the vehicle and not just the track of the wheels).
5. *Guard rails*—Minimum requirements between front and rear wheels.
6. *Side overhang*—Limitation on the protrusion of the body beyond the wall of the outer rear tyre.
7. *Brakes, steering gear and hubs*—Technical requirements.
8. *Fuel tank and exhaust pipe*—Requirements regarding positioning, filling and fuel to the engine.
9. *Locking of nuts*—Need for lock nuts or split pins.
10. *Lighting*—Minimum requirements and methods of fitment.
11. *Windows including windscreens*—Demisting device and provision against breakage.

These regulations are made in the interests of public safety and general well being as interpreted by Government and it would be both impracticable and unnecessary to reproduce them here, even only as they apply to Great Britain. Manufacturers must design and construct their vehicles in a way that will comply with these regulations and operators must live with them. At best they will make representations (probably through their trade associations to be described in Chapter 4) for relaxations as new technology is developed. This has been an ongoing process over the years—a fact that becomes particularly apparent when it is realized that, for example, in Britain the Road Locomotive Act, 1865 restricted the speed of all mechanically propelled vehicles to 2 mph in towns and required a man to walk in front with a red flag. To quote another British example, The Public Service Vehicle (Conditions of Fitness) Regulations, 1941 restricted one-man buses to small 20-seater vehicles with special dispensation being possible up to 26 seats.

So far, then, it has been established that the Chief Engineer has numerous

49

Figure 3.7 Standard single-deck buses, in this case both on Ashok Leyland chassi of Sri Lanka Transport Board seen in the bus station at Hikkaduwa in the south of Sri Lanka.

matters for consideration and decision when drawing up his vehicle specifications and that he, together with the manufacturer, must work within the limits of the regulations of the country in which the vehicles are destined to operate. But this book is essentially for the traffic side of the business, so the more important of those features of the bodywork within the five broad groups already referred to in which the Traffic Manager has a particular interest will now be reviewed in greater depth. Which of those five groups should be used for any one service is something for Chapter 6.

Figure 3.8 (left) At one time the Ceylon Transport Board had a large number of double-deck buses running in Colombo and in other main towns on the island. When they became time expired what had become the Sri Lanka Transport Board made a conscious decision to replace them with locally built single-decks. Now bus operation in Sri Lanka is again under review which includes further consideration of what are the most appropriate vehicle types. Pictured here in Colombo are three buses of SLTB, one of which is an ex-London double-deck under trial; and coming up in the rear, privately owned midi-buses which abound.
Figure 3.9 (right) A privately owned Tata bus in rural Uganda about to cross the line (0° latitude). It is heavily laden, with much of the accompanied baggage being bananas from the Musaka area destined for the market in Kampala.

Entrances and exits

Fitment of doors

Front-entrance buses are fitted with doors which are under the control of the driver. It has been the trend over many years to fit doors on buses, partly (with the assistance of heaters or air-conditioning equipment and forced ventilation) to give better control over the interior temperature but more importantly to prevent boarding and alighting accidents. Even before one-manning, doors were being fitted to both rear- and forward-entrance buses (a forward entrance is an entrance at the front but behind the front wheels). At first these doors were worked manually by conductors but their use was never really practicable on busy town services. Although subsequent development permitted them to be opened and shut by the driver or conductor at the push of a button, they always had a mixed reception on local routes. Whilst passengers are glad of the extra internal comfort that a door provides they often resent the obstruction to boarding and alighting at places other than approved stops. 'Hop on a bus' was once a well-known catch phrase launched to encourage local riders and one of the characteristics of this mode of transport is its convenience for local trips for which the ability to hop on, take a short ride and then hop off is important. The advantage of this practice is particularly apparent when buses are stationary in heavy traffic. People are able to board vehicles that they would otherwise have missed and tempers quickly become frayed when they have to stand on the platform but are unable to alight

Figure 3.10 A typical British bus. The one pictured here is one of Eastern Counties Omnibus Co. It is a Bristol VR and has 78 seats. With front entrance (i.e., in front of the front wheel) and engine at the rear it is eminently suitable for one-man operation. The vehicle is seen standing on the forecourt of its garage in Great Yarmouth, England, which also doubles as a small bus station.

Figure 3.11 Standard type double-deck Leyland Atlantean of Singapore Bus Service (1978) Ltd. approaching the centre of Singapore.

Figure 3.12 In common with normal continental European practice, urban buses are normally of the single-deck crush loading type which means standing space at the expense of seats. Passengers board at the front and alight at the centre as in the case of this Renault based bus of Régie Autonome des Transports Parisiens seen in Paris, France.

whilst the bus is held in congestion and cannot get to the stop. In the western world, London is a classic example where some rear-entrance vehicles without doors are still in service and where passengers frequently board and alight between stops. Once doors are provided, passengers have no alternative but to use the authorized stops. On some busy town services the additional time taken to complete a journey when buses with doors have been allocated, has been noticeable. Of course, without doors there are boarding and alighting accidents which the industry cannot condone. In any case, the use of buses without doors for one-man operation is not acceptable. For more than one reason, therefore, doors are here and here to stay. Their provision is in the interests of safety and comfort but in towns not of speed and convenience.

Centre exits

The full-front design with front entrance and driver's cab contained within the vehicle as with the now conventional double decks was already in vogue for single decks (which had underfloor engines) when the rear-engined double decks were introduced. The underfloor engine put up the height of the floor and hence the need for steps at the entrance but, be that as it may, vehiclewise, the way was thus paved for single manning. When, therefore, British regulations were relaxed in the mid 1950s and buses larger than the 20- or 26-seaters became eligible for this type of operation (single decks at first), thoughts turned to how boarding times could be minimized. At first it was those existing vehicles with front entrances that were converted, but the next generation was to be designed with one-man operation specifically in mind.

In the United Kingdom it was in the 1960s when consideration was first given to large-capacity buses purpose built for one-man operation. Every possible device was then being explored to reduce time spent in boarding and alighting and it was felt that a separate exit could only speed the process. Accordingly, large numbers

Figure 3.13 Buses in Mahatma Gandhi Road, Ernakulum in Kerala, India. Note the influence of the climate in the construction of the bus. Windows are not glazed but a sun (or rain) blind is provided. Although not clearly visible, hinged doors are provided forward and rear.

of vehicles, first single-deck and then double-deck, were built to this arrangement. But in the light of experience the design has produced operational difficulties and in the case of a double-deck, in the absence of a second staircase, passengers cannot, of course, ascend and descend simultaneously which to some extent negates the advantage of a separate exit. Although most operators are now standardizing on a single entrance/exit, the matter is still of some controversy and the disadvantages of the separate exit are summarized as follows:

1. Lower capacity (usually four seats less which, on a frequent service, could mean the allocation of an additional bus).
2. Unpopular seating arrangements in the forward portion of the lower deck.
3. Higher initial capital cost.
4. Passenger safety hazard.
5. Inability of drivers to check on the number of passengers alighting with consequent difficulty in knowing how many may be permitted to board without overcrowding.
6. Difficulties with shelter and queueing arrangements at stops.
7. Additional maintenance costs.

Note: If a second staircase is provided on double-decks the effects of the disadvantages at 1, 2 and 3 are magnified considerably.

What, in the opinion of the writer, is of overriding importance is the safety hazard which results from the driver no longer being able to observe directly the alighting point. It has already been noted that the unguarded exit of the erstwhile standard rear-entrance bus gave rise to boarding and alighting accidents and was a potential source of danger, even with a conductor. The introduction of the first front-entrance bus with a door under the control of the driver was rightfully acclaimed as a significant move towards greater safety. With a centre-exit that advantage is annulled unless the vehicle is so equipped that its wheels cannot turn until the doors are absolutely closed.

Figure 3.14 A bus of Bangkok Mass Transit Authority in Bangkok, Thailand. Note also the motor rickshaw on the left of the picture. This type of chariot is prevalent in parts of the east including the Indian sub-continent. It is regarded as a cheaper alternative to the conventional taxi but to some people's way of thinking, particularly in those areas, more prestigious than riding in a bus.

Figure 3.15 Single-deck front engined full-fronted forward-entrance bus of Utan Singh at the central bus station in Port Dickson, Malaysia.

Much research has been undertaken by various bodies including the Transport and Road Research Laboratory of the Department of Transport in Great Britain into boarding times with different types of one-man operated buses. In its *Bus Boarding and Alighting Times* there is evidence to show that a separate centre exit on a double-deck bus does not achieve a faster alighting/boarding rate. Furthermore, with any type of bus it is only at those stops where there are passengers both boarding and alighting where there could be any possible saving in time, and according to TRRL data this represents no more than about a third of the total number of stops. The alleged safety hazard is, however, a very real one. There have been numerous cases of fatalities and serious personal injuries resulting from

Figure 3.16 A full-fronted vehicle contrasts with an earlier design where the engine is situated way out front. The vehicle on the left is a bus of EGGED (a large Jewish co-operative society) whilst the one on the right is in the ownership of a smaller Arab company. Both are awaiting departure from Hebron bus station in Israel.

Figure 3.17 Another means of increasing passenger accommodation within a limited headroom is the half-decker. With conventional single-deck style forward, a rearrangement of the floor levels at the rear permits a partial second deck. This vehicle is pictured at Hameln in West Germany.

passengers being trapped in the centre doors. A one-time popular arrangement was to operate the doors through a sixth gear position, but even then there are circumstances when the bus can still move whilst they are open. To overcome this danger it is necessary to fit a transmission interlock which directly links the operation of the doors with the movement of the wheels. This, however, has been shown to increase, sometimes quite substantially, the time spent at stops and more than cancels out any advantage in speed that the separate exit might have provided. For various reasons, therefore, most operators have now veered away from separate centre exits.

Nevertheless, there are still circumstances where a separate exit is desirable. In the subsection that follows, capacity is a consideration and for maximum capacity the option is a standee-type vehicle, either single-deck or the inside (downstairs) of a double-deck. Although the merits of this type of design are for subsequent discussion, in this context note that regardless of any legal limit, on a standee bus the number of passengers carried is usually governed by how many can actually squash in. In conditions such as this a separate exit is a physical necessity as it is often impossible to circulate back through the vehicle to reach a door at the distant end. When the nearest door opens passengers alight (voluntary or otherwise) and more can then board at a separate entrance.

The writer believes strongly that on one-man operated buses passengers should both board and alight at a point adjacent to and in full view of the driver. Only in this way can the interests of safety be properly served. If a separate centre exit needs to be provided, i.e. for standee buses, then it must be accompanied by a transmission interlock regardless of the delay factor. With a two-man crew, the position is, of course, different. If a conductor is available to supervise passengers alighting (or boarding) and is required to give the driver a signal when it is safe to start then there can be no objection to a separate exit (or entrance if the arrangement is to alight at the front).

Figure 3.18 One of the few mass produced designs, the single-deck Leyland National. These two vehicles of London Buses Ltd. are seen standing in the bus station adjacent to the large main-line railway terminus at Victoria in London.

Figure 3.19 A coach design for medium and longer distance work where comfort takes priority over the need for wide entrances and exits and hence ease of boarding and alighting. This vehicle is one of the Green Line fleet, the coaching arm of London Country Bus Services Ltd. pictured at Golders Green, London.

Figure 3.20 Although double-deck coaches have become popular, the height can be a problem. This two-deck coach produced by Kassbohrer Setra of West Germany has a lower upper deck for passengers with a spacious lower deck for luggage and toilet provision. (Reproduced by kind permission of Kassbohrer.)

Figure 3.21 Maximum seating double-deck buses are operated by both the China Bus Co. Ltd. (serving Hong Kong island) and the Kowloon Motor Bus Co. (1933) Ltd. serving the Kowloon mainland. The bus pictured is a vehicle of China Motor Bus alongside a Hong Kong tram. Note that it has three axles. It is 39½ feet (12 m) long and licensed for 108 seats plus 60 standing. All are one-man operated with fare boxes and flat fares and have the same running times as the standard sized buses. The provision of vehicles of this size is indicative of the demand for public transport in Hong Kong but note that the Chinese people are relatively small in stature and the space allotted per seat might not suit the average westerner.

Comfort and capacity

Comfort to the extent of smooth riding qualities, heating, ventilation, etc. has already been touched upon. Seating is considered here and whilst standards of comfort and vehicle capacities are really separate considerations, when it comes to seating, one cannot be divorced from the other as in any one body size, generally speaking the greater the capacity the lower will be the standard of comfort. Standards must be set and the traffic for which the vehicle is to cater determined. Consider, for example, the requirements of a passenger on an internal airport bus travelling from the departure lounge across the apron to the waiting aircraft and the passenger on an extended tour visiting a series of holiday resorts. The requirements of the average passenger will fall somewhere between these extremes depending on the type of journey made on whatever of the seven different types of services listed in Chapter 6. Of course, in practice, if only in the interests of standardization or efficient vehicle utilization there will be times when a bus has to work on more than one type of service, and this factor must be taken into account before too many different specifications are ordered and vehicles become tied to specific traffics.

The options are:

1. Minimal seating but ample standing accommodation.
2. Entire floor area except for a gangway devoted to a maximum number of seats.
3. Entire floor area except for a gangway devoted to a lesser number of seats designed for maximum comfort.

In other words, the basic concepts are standee bus, conventional bus and long-distance coach. The policy of whether to accept the standee arrangement is a separate issue and is discussed in Chapter 7, which leaves the seating arrangements for conventional buses and coaches for consideration here.

It is a question of utilizing the space within the maximum permitted width of the vehicle (in Great Britain the 1986 Regulations stipulate a maximum width of

Figure 3.22 Conventional London-style taxi and British-style double-deck coach of National Express at Victoria Coach Station, London.

8ft 2½in (2.47 m)). Although the 1981 Regulations (in Great Britain) detail minimum widths for gangways and seats, there is a degree of latitude, which means that there are options between wider seats with the narrowest permissible gangway or narrower seats with wider gangways. Clearly, therefore, on buses where the journeys are likely to be fairly short but with passengers constantly boarding and alighting the latter arrangement will be required to give the optimum split between seat comfort and ease of circulation, bearing in mind that the gangway may also be used by standing passengers. On long-distance services, ease of circulation is of less importance and the emphasis will be on the comfort of the seat with perhaps armrests. Contrary to popular belief, it is not always necessary to have high backs to the seats, especially on vehicles used for sightseeing excursions and extended tours where overnight stops at hotels are incorporated in the itinerary. Another point for consideration is the territory where the vehicle is destined to operate where not only are different standards of comfort accepted but where the indigenous population is smaller in stature. Under these circumstances it is sometimes possible to fit more seats into a given space, and there are examples in South-East Asia and the Far East where this is done.

One final point on seating and capacity: if any newcomer to the industry has visions of a 'get rich quick' policy with a high payload on the cheapest and smallest buses (i.e. minibuses), let him remember that small vehicles become unstable when overloaded. In Britain at least the Public Service Vehicles (Carrying Capacity) Regulations 1984 stipulate that standing passengers will not be carried on vehicles with 12 seats or less. The total number allowed to stand on larger buses is also controlled.

Steps and staircases

Closely allied to entrances and exits are steps and their height. Quite clearly, the fewer the steps the better as some passengers find them physically difficult and sometimes impossible to negotiate. The principles to follow are the step up from the kerb on to the front platform to be as low as possible and steps from the front platform through into the lower deck as few as possible. Of course it is difficult to win whatever the design. Interestingly, the old rear-entrance type had a step up from the platform into the lower deck. Then Bristol/Eastern Coachworks brought out the Lodekka in the 1950s with a rearranged transmission and rear axle which permitted a lower floor level on the bottom deck with a consequently lower overall height. This eliminated the step from the platform into the lower saloon which was ideal for the purpose under discussion except that some passengers continued to step up the step which was no longer there and fell just the same.

An interesting development and one worthy of mention in this context is the special split-step arrangement widely adopted by South Yorkshire Transport Ltd. where Sheffield's hilly terrain necessitates a slightly higher floor at the front of the vehicle for ground-clearance purposes. Any height inconvenience is mitigated at the rear half of the boarding platform by the provision of three easy steps instead of the standard two larger ones which has the effect of reducing the maximum step height from 14in (36 cm) to 10in (25 cm) which most people can comfortably manage. As with all bus operation, the depth is of course further reduced when vehicles stop adjacent to a kerb but with indiscriminate car parking this, unfortunately, is not always possible.

Figure 3.23 Bus bodies strongly built on to truck chassi are a minimum cost solution and the vehicles can take a lot of punishment. But the high floor means steep steps, and when working on heavily used town services with frequent boarding and alighting on short journeys they are not ideal in terms of passenger convenience. When boarding with encumbrances in one hand and ticket ready to be clipped in the other, a driver anxious to move off in order to complete his trips and thereby earn his bonus and then the need to negotiate through a narrow gap between the engine cowling and the near side front seat with few supporting rails, it is no place for the elderly or infirm. Indeed there is little evidence of these members of the community using buses in Taipei, Taiwan, where this bus of the Taipei City Bus Administration is pictured.

Figure 3.24 Purpose-built buses have easy arrangements for boarding and alighting and with a low floor base steps are at a minimum. Even so, ease of entry has been yet further improved by the split-step arrangement as developed and adopted as standard by South Yorkshire Transport Ltd. Some people find the three shallow steps much easier to use and it is surprising that more operators have not so far adopted this arrangement. (Reproduced by kind permission of South Yorkshire PTE.)

The position of the staircase and the controversial separate exit (if one is to be provided) have a major effect on the internal layout. Of the few operators that still specify separate exits, some prefer them off centre and nearer to the front entrance served by a staircase at the front. But regardless of whether there is one door or two, which way the staircase should ascend—with or against the direction of travel—needs to be decided. The writer suggests that the internal layout should be so arranged as to permit the former, that is, in the same style as the rear-entrance bus or, in other words, the passenger faces the driver as he ascends. If there is an emergency stop whilst the passenger is on the stairs and he is thrown forward, the results are not likely to be as serious if he is propelled into rather than away from the body structure.

Miscellaneous arrangements and fitments

Although there is not a large number of different vehicle manufacturers and they each produce their own fairly standard types of body shell, unlike the private motorist, operators are still a long way from buying their buses 'off the peg'. Even so, there has been an exception in the case of the well-known single-deck Leyland National. Different managements order basic types in accordance with their preferences and availability but they are careful to prepare their individual internal specifications. Alternatives to be considered are the layout, design and covering of the seats depending on the required ratio of seated to standing passengers, the degree of comfort that is wanted and resistance to vandalism. As has already been explained, greater comfort is achieved by a lesser number of larger and more luxurious type seats which will be at the expense of capacity. Fibre-glass gives the maximum protection against malicious damage but at the expense of comfort, although it is more hygienic than moquette.

What provision should be made for passengers' luggage and other chattels and for unaccompanied parcels? It is convenient for double-deck buses on town routes to have a small area near the front, say over the front nearside wheelarch, where passengers can deposit bulky articles including children's folding pushchairs. In fact it is surprising that some enterprising operator has not provided a facility in this area from which to hang pushchairs—they have crooked handles. Seats will probably be placed as close together as possible and although this provides maximum capacity it does little to help the passenger lumbered with an awkward parcel or, for that matter, the person sitting next to him. It is on the rural routes where such space is also likely to be useful for unaccompanied parcels. For longer journeys, interior overhead luggage racks are desirable. The availability of space for parcels at the front is to some extent conditioned by the fare collection equipment in use. A ticket machine beside the driver takes up no room and a farebox not much more; it is positioned on the floor but right at the front. It is when two-stream boarding is adopted with secondary help-yourself equipment or ticket cancellator that more space is needed. Right at the extreme in terms of space requirement comes the turnstile and when this sophisticated apparatus is in position there is precious little room left for parcels or passengers either.

In developing countries, particularly on the inter-urban and rural services, passengers tend to carry enormous amounts of baggage ranging from personal effects to local produce, live or dead, destined for sale in the markets. For traffic of this nature the high-floor single-deck buses already referred to often require a strengthened roof with a rack fitted end to end accessible by a fixed-step ladder on the side or rear of the vehicle. Even so, the experience of, for example, East African Road Services Ltd. is that passengers are becoming increasingly reluctant to travel on the conventional roof-carrier vehicle and the company has upgraded some of its buses to coach standards incorporating an underfloor baggage compartment. Then there are the purpose-built vehicles which have a combined function of carrying both passengers and goods (or Post Office mail including parcels). This is the principle of the postbus although some of those that are used in Great Britain are really minibuses and do not carry a lot of passengers or mail. The vehicles in mind here have a much larger capacity (with perhaps a preponderance of freight) and are specially constructed for this purpose. Trailers are also sometimes used for the carriage of merchandise.

With the single manning of double decks it is never easy for the driver to know how many vacant seats he has available on the upper deck. With centre exits it is usually quite impossible for him to know as has already been noted. A periscope will be fitted which gives him a view upstairs, except possibly for the front seats, but even then his task is a difficult one. Equipment has been produced which gives a numerical indication visible to the driver in his cab and to the passenger at the foot of the stairs how many seats are vacant. If accurate, this is a most useful accessory but in arduous service conditions, perfection is not always the rule and wrong information is worse than no information at all.

One further point in vehicle design which arises from the fact that passengers now have direct access to drivers is the need for his protection. Assaults on bus crews are becoming prevalent and in certain areas a protective screen is provided between the driver and the outside world. It is the author's view that unfortunately the time will come when it will be inadvisable to drive a bus that is not so fitted.

Another matter of detail on which operators have their different views is the display of destination blinds. Most undertakings adopt a route numbering system and this, together with the ultimate destination, must be exhibited, at least in the front. What else should be shown besides the final destination is a matter of opinion and there can be no undisputed answer. Whilst in one sense there can never be too much information if the stranger is to be catered for, a wealth of detail becomes confusing; expensive in terms of blind display; longer blinds become necessary which can only cover a lesser number of routes and therefore make vehicle allocation more inflexible and there is a greater likelihood of incorrect blind display (and again incorrect information is less helpful than no information). The writer feels that route number and destination only is reasonable providing there is adequate supporting publicity in the form of maps or timetable leaflets supplemented by information exhibited at stops, although it is appreciated that wilful destruction is giving the latter provision a serious problem. Side blinds are helpful, particularly when buses are standing nose to tail, and there are divided views on the provision of information at the rear. Some managements would like rear blinds but have difficulty in persuading one-man drivers to change them and settle for a compromise of a route number only without the need to alter the destination at the end of each journey. Others maintain that a rear display is essential and that people living in towns where buses are not so embellished 'don't know what they're missing'. One final point on blinds is the display of the route number. An old established practice but one which has become more widespread in recent years is separate blinds for each digit with up to four aspects (to make provision for three figure numbers plus a suffix letter). This arrangement is often not as neat as the individual figures are sometimes not displayed in perfect alignment and, according to the permutation, cannot always be in the centre of the box. However, the system makes for economy in blinds and gives maximum flexibility. In an emergency, a correct route number with everything else blank is much better than nothing. Some operators are now turning to automated destination and route number displays with dot matrix electronic blinds. This, of course, adds to the cost of the vehicle and the writer feels that the clarity is inferior to that of conventional blinds but it does have the great advantage of easing the tasks of one-man drivers. Operation can also be linked in with the electronic ticket issuing equipment as is described in Chapter 9.

Figure 3.25 Although not necessarily involved with cash in the driver's cab, Lagos State Transport Corporation considers it prudent to protect its drivers with built-in wire surrounds. This shows a Mercedes vehicle so fitted in one of the Corporation's garages in Lagos, Nigeria.

Figure 3.26 (left) Both East and West Berlin require high-capacity buses but in the west there is a preference for maximum seating. The double-deck bus of Berliner Verkehrs-Betriebe is therefore standard of which this vehicle shown at Zoolog Garten bus station in West Berlin, West Germany, is an example.
Figure 3.27 (right) In East Berlin the single-deck standee principle is preferred. Here an articulated bus of Kombinat Berliner Verkehrs-Betriebe is seen in Unter den Linden, East Berlin, East Germany.

Figure 3.28 Remember from *Figure 1.2* that the original buses were open top. The covered tops came later with great acclaim. However, although the benefits are great the open top does have an appeal to the pleasure rider in fine sunny weather. This vehicle of Cityrama is seen on a round-London tour near Trafalgar Square in London.

Figure 3.29 Although buses provide a vital service for rural communities, those that cater for these areas are seldom remunerative. Various methods have been adopted to reduce costs and one possibility is to combine the carriage of passengers with mail and parcels as is the practice in the north of Scotland. The illustration shows a dual-purpose vehicle of the then Rhodesia Railways at Nuanetsi en route between Fort Victoria and Beitbridge, Zimbabwe. Note that in this case goods and parcels are carried in the rear part of the vehicle itself, on the roof and also behind in an open trailer.

Articulated buses

In road haulage terms an articulated vehicle is one where a separate tractive unit hauls a non-powered semi-trailer. The design is not often used for passenger vehicles although there are limited examples, particularly in India. A more common adaption of the articulated principle for passenger work is the linking of two passenger-carrying units. This principle is widely adopted in Europe and elsewhere where the standard headroom precludes the use of double decks. In Great Britain this is not the case and the same need does not arise. In fact it was not until fairly recently that British legislation allowed this type of bus; it was the Transport Act 1980 which made it legally possible.

The articulated bus is a long one (about 59 feet (18 m) in fact) but for its length, surprisingly manoeuvrable. It also has a very high capacity; up to about 150 if only 40 seats are provided with the remainder standing, and all with only one driver. For this sort of number ideally three sets of doors need to be provided and the fare collection system must then be geared to a pre-paid or help-yourself basis. If this is not acceptable and it is felt that provision must be made for passengers who wish to purchase a ticket conventionally, then they must either board at the front and pay the driver or at the back and pay a seated conductor. The latter, however, would achieve little in terms of manpower compared with conventional double-deck one-man operation. The use of vehicles of this type is really a part of the double-deck/single-deck issue discussed in Chapter 6, and the articulated concept is most useful where there is a height restriction. Its development in the UK, therefore, where a lack of headroom is the exception rather than the rule, is bound to be controversial.

Figure 3.30 Just as vehicles for long-distance services have an emphasis on comfort, those for very short journeys need hardly any seats at all. Shown here is the interior of an articulated vehicle with a separate tractive unit at Athens Airport in Greece. Its function is to ferry passengers between the airport terminal building and the aircraft.

Whilst acknowledging certain benefits, the articulated bus has a number of disadvantages compared with double decks which may be summarized as follows:

1. Unless it is fully loaded, it takes up more road space per passenger carried, and road space is a scarce commodity in urban areas.
2. It takes up more garage space per vehicle; it is not as easily manoeuvrable for shunting inside garages and it cannot use the normal pits for inspection and repair purposes.

3. It does not mix easily with conventional buses at stops as it requires different queuing and shelter arrangements, it makes the design of bus stations more difficult and reduces the number of stands.
4. It does not exploit the air space which (at least in the UK) is usually freely available.
5. Following on what was said in respect of centre exits, if proper safety precautions are to be observed, a transmission interlock must be fitted to prevent the wheels from turning whilst the doors are open. This together with additional time taken to join traffic streams is likely to annul any time saving achieved by the greater number of doors.
6. If the potential capacity is fully utilized, passengers must travel in considerable discomfort.
7. One-man operation should generally be accompanied by a supplementary pre-paid or help-yourself ticket system.
8. The lower cost per passenger carried is valid only when it is heavily loaded. It has more technical complications, and if the capacity is not fully used it is cheaper and more satisfactory to build on an upper deck rather than employ what is a very expensive articulated vehicle.

Figure 3.31 Articulation with a difference and a style more familiar with road hauliers is this separate tractive unit and semi-trailer which is one of the standard designs which operates in the larger towns in India. The vehicle is 40 ft (12.2 m) long and has seating accommodation for 100 passengers. The example shown here is in the ownership of Delhi Transport Corporation and is seen on a bus stand in New Delhi, India.

In short, the big advantage of the articulated bus is capacity and, incidentally, it does not have to be single deck, although there are very few examples to the contrary. The type under consideration here is the single-deck standee variety as is used extensively on the European mainland and elsewhere. Its capacity is approximately twice that of a standard double decker and three times that of a single decker but only at the expense of items (1)–(8) above. All of these factors are important but, in the opinion of the writer, of particular significance is item (6). If the bus industry is really anxious to attract traffic and, in the national interest, encourage people to come out of their cars and on to public transport, then it must do something better than herd them into standing positions on crush-loading vehicles. And do not be swayed by the protagonists who point to the greater popularity of the lower deck. Do not forget that more and more people are finding smoking distasteful and some refrain from travelling on the upper deck where smoking is generally permitted not because they object to the stairs but because they cannot tolerate the polluted atmosphere. If smoking was banned on both decks instead of on just the lower, then the upper deck would become more popular.

The writer sees a potential for the single-deck standee articulated buses only on routes for which:

1. There are for physical reasons restrictions to single deck.
2. The average length of the journey is short.
3. There is heavy traffic necessitating a frequent service.

To elaborate on (3), if traffic is such as to justify a 10-minute headway of conventional single-deck buses, and the articulated bus can carry three times as many people, then a 30-minute service of articulated buses would suffice. Any greater frequency would result in under-utilization and would be uneconomic but only two buses per hour would not be sufficiently attractive for an urban route, hence the need for a heavy demand. A 2-minute headway converting to a 5- or 6-minute frequency, for example, would be more readily acceptable.

Buses for the disabled

In this context a disabled person is interpreted as someone who is confined to a wheelchair and hence unable to ride on normal buses but is otherwise fit.

Over recent years the western world has given much thought to the requirements of the chairbound fraternity, many of whom are in desperate need of ways and means to get around. As a result, various types of buses have been adapted to carry wheelchairs with access via either a lift or a ramp and with spaces in which to anchor the chairs in lieu of the normal seats. Whether the carriage of wheelchairs should be mixed in with normal traffic is considered in Chapter 7. The purpose here is to note that vehicles can be and are adapted to carry wheelchairs, be they small or large single-decks or the lower deck of double-decks.

The construction of such vehicles is likely to be subject to regulation (in Great Britain the Minibus Conditions of Fitness, Equipment and Use Regulations 1977 as amended in 1981 stipulates dimensions, etc. of tail lifts) and provision is necessary for wheelchairs to be secured firmly to the floor and hence rendered immobile whilst vehicles are in motion. Various capacities are possible according to the size of the bus but as far as actual wheelchairs are concerned, the number is likely to range from one to about six. This assumes that some normal seating will still be available for accompanying passengers. Other disabled people could be accommodated if they are able to be moved from a folding chair which can be stowed into a normal seat.

One of the main considerations here is whether the entrance via the lift or ramp should be at the side in a central position or at the rear (not a rear entrance as such but literally in the back of the bus). A rear-engined vehicle will dictate a side entrance; otherwise the option is available and there are features for and against. A back entrance is likely to necessitate negotiating a kerb and thence go into the road before boarding. But having done that, wheelchairs are able to be pushed straight

Figure 3.32 A Leyland National modified for the use of passengers confined to wheelchairs. Some bus undertakings do operate services specifically for this class of traffic including South Yorkshire Transport Ltd., one of whose vehicles is seen pictured here in service in Doncaster, South Yorkshire, UK. (Reproduced by kind permission of South Yorkshire PTE.)

in to their allotted position (they travel facing forward) and on alighting can be pushed out backwards. A side entrance is likely to mean awkward manoeuvres inside the vehicle and if the ramp or the base of the lift spans the footpath (which it will do if it is narrow or if in a bus station if the platform is narrow) difficulties arise for those in charge of the wheelchairs and there is congestion and obstruction for passers-by. The need to go into the road does not really constitute a safety hazard, particularly if the vehicle has a flashing warning light. This is in fact the accepted practice for ambulances, even for those that cater for the ambulant sick. The writer considers that the need to manoeuvre wheelchairs inside the bus and the obstruction of the footpath (together with a possibility of being unable to alight on a road where there is no pavement—only a bank) are strong disadvantages of a side entrance and outweigh the adverse features of the entrance at the back. Nevertheless there are examples of both types in regular service.

Standardization

Standardization has already been touched upon on the manufacturing side. For consideration here is the wisdom of fleet standardization within an undertaking. There are advantages. Apart from routes where for physical reasons a different type of bus is essential, if there is standardization then there is flexibility in allocation, drivers and maintenance staff become more familiar with the vehicles, fewer spares need to be kept, there is interchangeability of parts and perhaps some

Figure 3.33 Although not a part of bus operation as such the cost effective body system of the standard Leyland National single-deck bus has been adapted by British Rail Engineering Ltd. and Leyland Vehicles for use on the railway. The result is this prototype railbus as pictured here at Coleraine Station of Northern Ireland Railways in Northern Ireland, UK. It can carry about 100 people (64 seated) and has driving positions at each end.

savings in bulk purchases. Standardization can, therefore, produce economies and if such a policy is to be followed, what the standard vehicle will be must be decided. Of particular importance is capacity. An average size might result in a little over-provision of seats on some services whilst on others more buses have to be run than would be necessary if larger vehicles were available but if there are compensating advantages in standardization, this is not necessarily a bad thing. Perhaps the biggest drawback with a large number of identical vehicles is when, with new innovations, different designs permit more efficient operation. In these circumstances there is a danger that the entire fleet could become obsolete whilst still having a period of useful life remaining. If part of the fleet was replaced with latest designs year by year advantage could be taken at an earlier stage but it would militate against the realization of the economic advantages of standardization.

Trolleybuses

For urban transport purposes, electricity as a form of motive power has much to commend it. Extensive research undertaken into battery powered buses has shown this to be the case but technology has not as yet produced a battery that is adequate and in all ways suitable for this type of work. However, having accepted electricity as a form of traction, once a vehicle becomes dependent on power from an outside source which must be fed into the system there is a need for a purpose-built way. This not only adds to the capital cost, it also results in a loss of flexibility. It was noted in Chapter 1 that trolleybuses were at one time in widespread use in the UK but disappeared partly for this reason (although many such systems are still flourishing elsewhere).

As far as costs are concerned, the balance between electricity and diesel varies according to circumstances. Much has been said about the future availability of oil and if it becomes scarce it will also become expensive, quite apart from a need to conserve whatever stocks are available. However, just as oil may or may not be an indigenous product, the purchase of which may or may not use foreign exchange, the cost of electricity is governed by such factors as the availability of coal and hydroelectric power and government policy regarding the development of nuclear power. The relative costs of diesel and electricity are therefore variable and are hence difficult to compare but what is known is that with the trolleybus, the latest type of control gear together with regenerative braking is reducing energy consumption. The provision of overhead-line equipment and necessary sub-stations is, of course, an added capital cost of the electric-powered system (although here again, development in overhead-line equipment technology has reduced installation costs and new pick-up systems have reduced wire wear). The vehicle itself is more expensive than a diesel bus but the trolleybus has a longer life, it is cheaper to maintain and its better reliability means fewer spare vehicles (and it has already been noted that the now-conventional rear-engined bus does leave a little to be desired in this respect). Therefore, in the long run the operational savings that trolleybuses could produce might justify the higher initial capital expenditure at the outset, always assuming that the service is of a sufficiently high frequency to justify such costs. More is said about the viability of trolleybuses in

Figure 3.34 From 1982 until 1986 the City of Johannesburg Transport Department ran seven different types of trolleybuses as a demonstration project. The vehicle pictured here, being one of the seven, is a Sigma TCO with BUSAF body seating 84 passengers. (Reproduced by kind permission of City of Johannesburg Transport Department.)

Chapter 11. But it is still a fixed track system and there has been much research into ways and means of mitigating the effects of the resultant inflexibility. Dual-mode vehicles are now emerging which are basically trolleybuses supplemented by an on-board power pack in the form of either a diesel engine to give direct drive or a diesel alternator set to produce its own electric power. With self-placing trolley booms raised and lowered by remote control (another innovation) on a dual-mode vehicle it becomes feasible to run under or clear of the wires at will and hence optimize the potential of the electric trolleybus. But let the busman beware of too much flexibility. Mention was made in Chapter 2 of the environmental enthusiasts and traffic-free areas. Those 'pedestrianization happy' politicians and planners who are ever ready to divert the versatile bus away from the shops to where the passengers do not want to go might think again if it was a fixed-track system that they had to move. Perhaps this is the way to stay in the market-place and the High Street! Perhaps new technology is not always a good thing!

So much for the resurrection of the trolleybus. But just as this is not a book about mechanical engineering, neither is it a treatise for the electrical engineer. It is not therefore proposed to develop further the technicalities of electric traction and the new hybrid vehicles. Of interest here is the body design. This aspect, however, has already been discussed in so far as diesel buses are concerned and the same body can be adapted for either a bus or a trolleybus. Trolleybuses (sometimes known as 'trackless' or 'railless') are available in double-deck, single-deck and articulated form, and the remarks that have been made in respect of buses apply equally to trolleybuses. Although this is essentially a matter for Chapter 12, some conversions to trolleybus operation can perhaps be anticipated; and if the swing to smaller scale enterprise (*see* Chapter 4) continues, then there is really no reason why the owner of the way (i.e. the overhead-line equipment) and the provider of the power should not be independent of the operator who would pay according to use in the same way as payment is already made for the use of bus stations.

Trams

Although the design of a tram is equally as important as the design of a bus, for various reasons this section need not be a long one. Since engineering technicalities are not a part of this study, again this leaves the design of the body as the main topic for consideration as far as vehicles are concerned, and the principles and preferences already expressed for the bus apply also to trams although not necessarily with the same force. The traditional British tram which is now a museum piece was double deck. The current official concept of trams, presumably drawn from European practices, seems to be a single deck and possibly of the articulated variety with plenty of room for standing.

Once again, the writer questions why passengers should be subjected to enforced discomfort on a lower deck when they could be provided with comfortable seats on an upper deck, although the argument is not as strong as it is in the case of a bus. The quality of the ride of steel wheel on steel rail, assuming always that the track is in good repair, is superior to that of a bus using the public highway. Furthermore, if the road is straight then the tram track will be straight whereas the bus will continue to weave around other traffic. Standing in a tram, therefore, is not as tedious or exhausting as standing in a bus but in the opinion of the author it is still not good enough if alternative arrangements (such as seats on an upper deck) are a possibility. The length of an articulated vehicle is of less concern if the tram track forms a segregated private way. Even then there seems to be no good reason why double-deck trams cannot be used, loading gauge permitting, joined if necessary in the peaks to form trains of trams with one driver. Special arrangements for fare collection would be necessary in any case, but with a train of trams (single or double deck) single manning becomes difficult. Unlike the articulated units, there is no physical communication between the two vehicles and each separate trailer, therefore, may need an attendant. On the other hand, trailers can be detached when not required for traffic purposes, which economizes in power.

Figure 3.35 A tram of Calcutta Tramways Co. Ltd. negotiates a congested thoroughfare near Chowrichi Square in Calcutta, India. Unlike the buses, the trams carry first- as well as second-class accommodation. Also unlike the buses they are occasionally subject to delay as wandering cows sometimes see fit to lie down in the road astride the tracks.

Figure 3.36 A tram *en route* between Soller and Soller Port on the Spanish island of Majorca in the Mediterranean. Apart from passenger traffic which is heavily seasonal and hence the addition of two non-powered trailers in this picture, other small trailers are used for the carriage of fish between the port and the town.

Figure 3.37 This 100-seat double-deck tram might even become the prototype for the next generation of British trams. Unlike the single-deck articulated units with which potential operators seem to be so obsessed, passengers are able to travel in comfort which, in the opinion of the author, is preferable to the crush-loading conditions that must otherwise arise if the capacity potential of the tram is to be properly exploited. As can be recognized, it is based on the Atlantean bus design and like the Leyland National railbus pictured at *Figure 3.33* it has 'a front at both ends'. These trams of Blackpool Transport Services Ltd. are seen at Blackpool, UK. (Reproduced by kind permission of Blackpool Borough Council Transport Department.)

A feature of the tram compared with the bus is that it can be 'double ended', i.e. driven from either end. Operationally, this permits a change of direction in the way that can be emulated by no other road vehicle. Subject to there being a crossover in the tracks (or the tram is on a single track) a reversing movement can be accomplished even in the centre of a road without any of the special arrangements as are needed for a bus or trolleybus. This applies equally to an articulated tram but it could not be done if there are non-powered trailers. For reversing purposes it is necessary that a driving cab be provided at each end, which has repercussions on costs and space and there are considerable consequential effects on body design. Entrances and exits must be provided on both sides of the vehicle (which again takes space) and seats must either be so arranged that half face one way and half the other or they are reversible. A seat where just the backrest can be moved across the base might not be as comfortable as a rigid design but otherwise some passengers are likely to have their back to the driver which tends to be unpopular. There are, therefore, advantages in body design of single-ended trams but the route must always have a return loop at each end. This, of course, precludes any short workings to intermediate points where there is no such facility. For emergency use and shunting in depots it is likely, however, that even for single-ended trams minimum driving facilities will also be provided at the 'back'.

In the UK the railway inspectorate as referred to in Chapter 5 is the responsible authority for approving the design of trams.

4 Organization and management

Government and politics in relation to transport

Central government

The provision of a transport facility is a livelihood for those who are in the business. It is also a service to the nation as adequate means of moving people and goods from place to place is an essential ingredient for economic survival. The importance of transport in this respect is dealt with at length in *Principles of Transport*.

However, in the 1980s, at least on the passenger side, it is not every service that can produce an adequate return on the capital invested. In road passenger transport, some bus services are now a financial liability but at the same time they meet a social need. In other words, whilst there are reasons why commercial operators would not wish to sustain them, equally there are political reasons why they should be preserved. To continue what was being said at the end of Chapter 1, because of the tremendous impact which transport has on community life, governments can no longer allow the provision of socially desirable services to be subject only to the law of commercial viability. What is being done about it is material for Chapter 11. The point here is that if there is a case for something more than a transport policy guided only by the economic forces of supply and demand then there must also be a supporting administrative machine to formulate and determine those policies.

In the event governments do have policies (at public expense) for passenger transport although some spend more of the taxpayers' money for this purpose than do others. However, although subsidies are a more recent phenomenon, transport has long since been an industry that, on the operational side, has required a measure of government supervision, if only to ensure adequate safety standards and sometimes to regulate supply.

The outcome of the circumstances described is that governments will have departments within their administrations to which is delegated responsibility for policy and/or control of the various facets of transport. Great Britain is no exception and once again, the structure of the British government and in particular the parts that have transport responsibilities are detailed in *Principles of Transport*. By way of example, this chapter will elucidate those areas of the British administration at national and local level that formulate and control transport policy in so far as it relates to road passenger services.

In England it is basically the Department of Transport that interprets and administers transport policy as laid down by parliament. For the remainder of the

United Kingdom, this, among other things, is the responsibility of the Northern Ireland, Scottish and Welsh Offices within their respective areas. The British government, in common with many countries overseas, does not directly manage transport undertakings, not even those in public (national) ownership. The operating organizations are autonomous bodies with their own managements and responsible to the appropriate government minister on broad policy matters. Policy control is effected through the statutes. The more important of the transport issues involved and the methods of control are outlined in *Table 4.1*. In some cases, direct compliance with acts of parliament and supporting statutory instruments is required whilst in others, government appointed officers have direct responsibilities for quantity (if any) and quality control. For financial matters there is an intermediary between operators and central government in the form of county councils who are able to determine within limits their own local policies. It follows that government departments must be geared on the one hand to issue and enforce regulations in respect of operating practices as decreed by parliament and on the other to oversee and influence, particularly in financial terms, the policies of local councils.

Table 4.1 Control by central and local government in the UK over certain functions and interests of the providers of road passenger transport

Departmental function	Subject matter	Method of administration	Chapter for cross-reference	Government Department (in England) primarily involved
Operating	Bus routes	Traffic Commissioner	5	Transport
	Safety on tramways and trolleybuses	Inspector of Railways	5	Transport
Engineering	Bus vehicle types and standards of fitness	Certifying Officer (through the PSV machinery)	5	Transport
	Safety on tramways and trolleybuses	Inspector of Railways	5	Transport
Finance	Capital grants for local passenger transport and highways	County Councils and Passenger Transport Authorities	11	Transport
	Revenue support for local bus services through tendering	Policy statements by County Councils and 3-year plans by Passenger Transport Executives	11	Transport
Staff	Bus drivers' hours of duty	Traffic Commissioner (through licensing machinery)	5	Transport
	Rights of employees	Industrial Tribunal	4	Employment
	Licensing of bus drivers	Traffic Commissioner	5	Transport
Planning	Public transport Metropolitan areas	Three-year plans of Passenger Transport Executives	11	Transport
	Non-metropolitan counties	Policy Statements of County Councils	6	Transport
	Land use	Unitary Development Plans of County Councils and Metropolitan District Councils	6	Environment
	Highways	Policies and programmes of County Councils and Metropolitan District Councils	6	Transport

Local government

In Great Britain there is a two-tier system of local government with the country divided into large county (or, in Scotland, regional) authorities which are further sub-divided into smaller district authorities. As far as road passenger transport is concerned it is the county councils and metropolitan district councils that are responsible for such matters as strategic planning, passenger transport, highways, traffic regulation and police. In the UK, with minor exceptions, in no case is local government (or national government either for that matter) the operator of any passenger transport undertaking. Although the policy making bodies are parts of central and local government, implementation of the resultant policies and daily management and control are in the hands of separate autonomous organizations. This is not, however, necessarily the case in other countries.

User committees

A user committee is a body that acts in the interests of passengers and makes representations to operators and maybe government if individual approaches do not produce satisfaction. The first reaction here is that surely managements should be acting in the interests of passengers anyway—they are their *'raison d'être'*. This, of course, is true and in a commercial and competitive environment that is likely to be the case. But if national policy is to introduce large publicly owned and subsidized undertakings providing social services under monopoly conditions, then public need becomes more a matter of interpretation. It is under these circumstances that the passengers sometimes need a stronger collective voice when making representations to the operators about the facilities that they do (or do not) provide. This is usually why user organizations have emerged and an example in Great Britain is the Transport Users' Consultative Committee. Although this Committee is concerned primarily with railways it does go further than that in the London area.

   On the bus side there is very little influence from users' committees in Great Britain. County councils and passenger transport authorities have their transport responsibilities and policies, particularly in respect of services to be put out to tender, and these bodies, being locally elected, should represent the interests of local people. Statutory provision for a users' committee in respect of bus services does, however, exist in London. Section 40 of the London Regional Transport Act, 1984 established the London Regional Passengers' Committee for the purpose of considering and at its discretion making recommendations with respect to any matter affecting the services provided by London Regional Transport, any of its subsidiaries (in this context London Buses Ltd.) and those services that run through an agreement with LRT. This Committee (whose members are appointed by the Secretary of State and are representative of the interests of the transport users) is, in fact, an area committee of the TUCC and is the one that has relevance here.

   User bodies are likely to have statutory backing, in which case managements will have a duty to listen to their recommendations and to explain their actions. The machinery might provide for such replies to be sent also to a government minister who could have the power to override any negative decisions.

This, then, is the theory of user committees. Some operators may find themselves answerable to their deliberations. Terms of reference will vary but where they exist they do provide a forum for debate on service provision and they can also give operators a guide on majority requirements that might not otherwise have come to light.

Trade associations

A trade association is an independent body created for the purpose of giving guidance, information, assistance and support to its members. It acts as a 'clearing house' for the dissemination of technical information, seeks to protect the collective interests of its members, makes representations to parliament when relevant legislation is being considered and acts as the spokesman for the industry which it represents. There is a two-way process on the part of members who not only take benefit from the services provided but also contribute their own expertise without which such an association could not function. For purposes of administration it is normal for an organization of this kind to form a series of specialist committees on appropriate matters with the participants drawn from representatives of senior management within the industry, suitably co-ordinated by a small permanent secretariat.

Associations of this kind are appropriate where there are a large number of separate organizations which together constitute 'the industry'. Although in road passenger transport there are some large individual units, there are also many small private operators. This is in contrast to the railway which, with a few exceptions, consists of one single operator for an entire country. A trade association for road passenger transport is, therefore, opportune, and in Great Britain it is the Bus and Coach Council which fulfils this role.

What has been said so far represents the national scene. But the principle can be and is extended to the international field to facilitate, for example, the exchange of information and formulation of agreements and economic policies between organizations of different countries. As far as the subject matter of this book is concerned, there are two international associations that have relevance, namely the International Union of Public Transport (UITP) which is an association of operators and the International Road Transport Union (IRU) which is an international association of national road transport federations. The International Union of Public Transport represents the interests of those responsible for urban, suburban and inter-urban public passenger transport, which includes buses, trams and trolleybuses and most of the major British bus operators are members. The International Road Transport Union embraces the privately owned sector of road transport on both the passenger and goods side. The affiliated British association representing road passenger interests is the Bus and Coach Council.

Forms of ownership

Most of the different types of ownership that are found in the business world generally and that of transport in particular are contained somewhere within the world-wide structure of the bus and coach industry. By way of introduction to the subject, consider the different types of business units, the more important of which are as follows:

1. Sole proprietors.
2. Partnerships.
3. Co-operatives.
4. Private limited companies.
5. Public limited companies.
6. Public corporations.
7. Municipalities.
8. State departments.

In a work of this kind it is not necessary to pursue an in-depth study of forms of ownership. If, for example, members of a partnership wished to turn their business into a limited company, information on company law would be more appropriate for their purpose than a book about bus and coach operation. All that need be done here is to acquaint the reader with the various types of ownership and see how they fit in to the bus and coach industry.

When discussing forms of ownership, one of the fundamental distinctions lies between what is publicly owned and what is privately owned. At one time nearly all public transport was in private hands, but over the years public money was spent to acquire either compulsory or voluntarily different parts of transport, and the time came when the great bulk of local passenger services was 'public property', that is, nationalized or municipalized. Whilst nationally owned undertakings can be operated directly by the government as a department of state, this is not often the case. Some railway systems are managed in this way but the more usual practice is to create separate autonomous bodies with those in charge accountable to the appropriate government minister and parliament on broad principles only.

Public or private ownership is very much government policy as is the creation of monopolies or acceptance of free competition and also the amount of public transport subsidy which is to be afforded. Generally speaking, with generous subsidies comes public ownership and with public ownership comes large-scale organizations under monopoly conditions. A commercially minded government is more likely to encourage smaller competitive units, and there is sometimes a blend of both according to national policies. On occasions public ownership is pure politics—the eastern bloc, for example, has little room for private enterprise— whilst in the western world, both in the developed and in the developing countries, it is more the result of transport policies (or the lack of them).

In considering the various types of undertakings, the starting point is the sole proprietorship where one man owns and runs the entire outfit, with capital derived from savings and borrowings. Small bus and coach businesses are run very satisfactorily in this way but should progress be hindred by a lack of working capital—making it difficult or impracticable to raise a loan on satisfactory terms—then forming a partnership may be considered.

The partnership is the second form of ownership. Here, licences, etc. will be issued in the names of the partners whilst financial arrangements must be settled by agreement. Only one of the partners might be the working or active partner, in which case he would expect to receive remuneration for his services as well as a return on his capital.

Turning to the third group, the co-operative, this also involves individuals who are willing to sink their own capital into the business of which they are a working part. In a co-operative groups of workers band together, hold equal shares in the undertaking, do the job for which they are most suited, undertake the same obligations and enjoy the same rights and remuneration regardless of their particular work, be it driver, mechanic or manager, in keeping with the status of equal partnership in the common venture.

In many parts of the world, even in the large towns, vehicles owned by small entrepreneurs meet a major part of or even all of the passenger transport requirements of the area. Where many different owner–drivers and other small operators provide between them the public transport service for the community the system will probably be administered through their associations and regulated by the appropriate municipal authority through the issue of franchises. South America is one of the best examples where bus services are provided in this way. To put this type of operation into some sort of perspective, Buenos Aires, the capital of Argentina with a population of about three million, is served by some 13000 midi- and minibuses locally known as 'collectivos', independently owned and administered through route associations. There are also instances of co-operatives in South America but it is in Israel where the bus network is provided in this way. World-wide there are examples where provision is in part a sizeable publicly owned undertaking and in part a series of small independents under some sort of co-ordination scheme such as in Taipei (Taiwan), Colombo (Sri Lanka), Kampala (Uganda), Lagos (Nigeria) and Mexico City (Mexico) to quote but a few. In many of the larger towns small privately owned vehicles in the form of shared taxis and 'jitneys' as described in Chapter 6 compete with the conventional bus services.

Next to consider is the fourth form of ownership—the private company. Speaking now of British law, the formation of a limited liability company gives an important protection to the proprietors as in the event of failure of the business they are liable only to the extent of their shareholding whereas the creditors can seek redress from the owner or owners in the case of a one-man or partnership business in such a way that they might find themselves obliged to sell up their homes and all personal possessions. It is for this reason that many small bus and coach companies have been formed. Note, however, that it is still private money that is being invested and it may be desired to bring in more capital than can be raised privately in this manner. In this case shares need to be offered to the public generally and this, therefore, introduces the fifth form of ownership in those which have been listed, namely the public limited company.

In Great Britain the formation and conduct of companies is regulated by the Companies Act, 1985. Briefly, a public company must satisfy three basic conditions. It must:

1. Be limited by shares or guarantee and have a share capital.
2. State in its memorandum of association that it is to be a public limited company.
3. Meet specified minimum capital requirements.

It can then be called a public limited company (plc) and even the very largest organizations may be owned in this way.

Thus the main distinction between a private and a public limited company is that the former is prohibited from offering its shares to the public. It has nothing to do with public or private ownership, it is the availability of shares. But with shares generally available they do not have to be bought by private speculators. Central or local government could hold some or all of the issued capital. This, therefore, is the point where public ownership comes into the picture and the public limited company structure may fall into either camp or may even be part private and part publicly owned with the controlling side dependent on the majority holdings.

In the United Kingdom the larger bus and coach companies outside the conurbations were until recently all owned in this way. The National Bus Company in England and Wales, the Scottish Transport Group in Scotland and the Northern Ireland Transport Holding Company in Northern Ireland are state-owned holding companies whose bus and coach operating subsidiary companies between them embraced the entire area. It was the Transport Act, 1968 (the Transport Act (Northern Ireland), 1967 in Northern Ireland) which established these state-owned companies. But the Transport Act, 1985 required the operations of the National Bus Company to be transferred to the private sector; and at least for the time being, therefore, there is likely to be a 'mixed economy' in the company structure of the provincial buses in England and Wales.

Having now progressed through from private to public enterprise, the sixth type of ownership—the public corporation, sometimes referred to as a board—is for consideration. A public corporation lies somewhere between the loosely defined responsibilities of a publicly-owned limited company and the direct administration and control of a government department. It is a statutory body with its rights and obligations clearly defined. Capital may consist entirely of loan issues with interest paid according to the terms of the enabling legislation. Many such undertakings are owned by the state—i.e., by national, central or federal government—whatever it may be called; but as they are separate autonomous bodies with management divorced from ownership and a degree of independence not found in government departments, the business is able to be run in a more flexible and enterprising manner subject only to overall policy control. However, in Great Britain, although British Railways is an example of this type of organization, there is now no parallel example in road passenger transport but there are many such undertakings elsewhere.

The seventh on the list is the municipality. A municipality is a town or district having self-government for local affairs. Chapter 2 showed that local government has various responsibilities in connection with road transport, but it can be much more than that. Local councils outside the UK can and do own and operate their own bus, trolleybus and tram systems. This is one of the few instances of direct management by a government department, albeit local government. Policy is determined by a transport committee consisting of elected councillors and put into effect by an employed professional manager. Discretion may be used (to the extent permitted under national law) regarding service provision, fare levels and revenue support from local rates and taxes but there is often a pronounced political flavour to this type of direct local government control.

Municipal ownership and control of local transport systems is found throughout the world in all five continents, east and west. Until recently there were many municipal systems in Great Britain with a history dating back to the Tramways Act, 1870. Remember it was this Act that gave local authorities the power to purchase compulsorily privately owned tramway systems at 21 years after inception and thereafter at 7-yearly intervals. This introduced municipal ownership into local passenger transport and over the years local tram, trolleybus and bus services in the majority of the main towns became owned and managed in this way. However, direct management was reduced when the Transport Act, 1968 introduced passenger transport executives in the conurbations and has now disappeared altogether as the Transport Act, 1985 required all undertakings in this type of ownership (PTE and district council) to be transferred to public companies limited by shares registered under the Companies Act, 1985. Any local authority ownership in Great Britain, therefore, is with minor exceptions now separated from daily management and comes within the public limited company structure as has already been described.

The eighth and last in this list of the major forms of ownership is where national government owns and operates its own system through a state department. Within the bus industry not many instances can be quoted where this actually happens. In Great Britain the Post Office (which does own and operate post buses in rural areas) was at one time the classic example where overall responsibility and daily running was vested in a government department headed by a Postmaster General who was a Minister of the Crown and the employees were civil servants. However, this is not now the case as the Post Office Act, 1969 changed the status of the Post Office from a state department to a public corporation. Examples of this type of operation can be found in urban bus systems in Australia.

Management

Having dealt with the ownership of the industry, the organization of individual managements or, in other words, the organization of the units that together make up the industry, will now be considered. Organization in this sense means the arrangement of the administration to ensure the satisfactory conduct of the business and in common with the other parts of this chapter it is a subject that is fully considered in *Principles of Transport*. The policy making bodies are the owners consisting as they do of politicians in the public sector and shareholders in the private sector. At policy level there is a distinction between the two, the former paying more regard to social issues and the latter to economics, and their terms of reference are likely to be different. But both groups will employ professional managers (or corporate bodies) to run their businesses which they will do to the extent that they are permitted with the expertise and 'know how' acquired through years of study and experience. Their responsibilities are to supply the utility of place and to give their passengers a safe arrival, all within pre-determined policies and financial constraints.

Internal organization

Centralized control

The size of the operating unit is all important as it is this that determines to what extent the manager must delegate some of his work to others, thereby creating a chain of command and hence an organizational structure. An owner/manager of a fleet of, say, five buses might be able to write his own schedules, hire and fire his staff and generally control, supervise and administer the running of the business. Subject to any legal limitations his 'office' might be a room of his own private house and he might do his own vehicle servicing whilst his wife 'keeps the books'. The parking lot could be his own back yard. Apart from a few drivers and possibly conductors, he might need a general hand to help keep the vehicles in an acceptable condition with heavier maintenance arranged through an outside contractor. There would be minimal (if any) supervisory and clerical assistance but the services of a solicitor, an accountant, an outside builder and other specialists might be necessary from time to time. The overheads of a small proprietor are therefore low in comparison with larger concerns.

Imagine now that the fleet expands to 20, 30, 40 or more vehicles. The time will come when the volume of work gets beyond the capacity of one man with the minimum of help to undertake the more menial tasks. He will require some senior assistants to take charge of specific functions. The occasional major overhauls have become a regular job as there is now a continuous succession of vehicles that require attention of this kind. The outside contractor is, therefore, no longer economic as he himself is working to profit margins and it is beneficial for the bus company to do the work itself. Apart from capital expenditure on equipment and supporting facilities, therefore, a full-time engineer is required, assisted by a foreman and mechanics according to the magnitude of the work. Route planning, time and duty schedules, registrations, fares, publicity and staff consultation with an emergent and possibly active trade union element is another full-time job for somebody. The financial side will by now have grown to the extent that a permanent professional input is crucial to this side of the business which could also absorb the administrative work necessary when considerable numbers of staff are employed. For this it would seem that three functional heads are indicated, and in diagrammatic form the organization might appear as in the example shown in *Figure 4.1*.

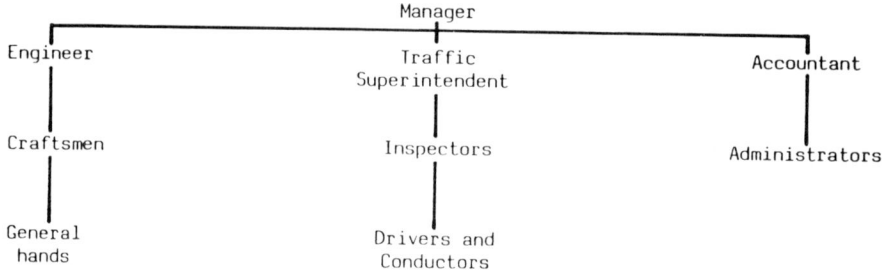

Figure 4.1 The principal department heads and chain of command of a bus company organized functionally.

This is the beginning of the functional or departmental system of the chain of command. Each functional head is responsible to the manager for his department. These officers are the only official links between the departments although in practice there will be daily inter-departmental consultation between staff at lower levels. For example, when fares revisions are considered, traffic staff and accountants are both involved. If a vehicle develops a defect in service both the inspectors and the engineering staff have action to take which must be properly co-ordinated if the service is not to suffer unduly. But the respective staffs are subject to the rulings of their functional chiefs and any clashes of opinion or procedure must, at least in theory, be referred to the top, across the 'functional bridge' and down again before progress can be made. Even the departmental heads might not reach agreement easily and it is only the manager in person who can give a ruling which is binding on all three. Although this is of little consequence in a relatively small unit, there is a stage when the system becomes cumbrous. That stage, however, has not yet been reached. The system represents a natural progression from the single-handed proprietor and it is the most appropriate for the small- and medium-sized undertakings. With yet further growth, so additional staff have to be appointed. If any one department becomes unwieldy, it might be beneficial to divide the responsibilities into new departments. An organization with 800 buses, for example, might perhaps look something like that shown in *Figure 4.2* which lists the possible functions that could be contained within a department. For simplicity the chains of command within each department are not now shown.

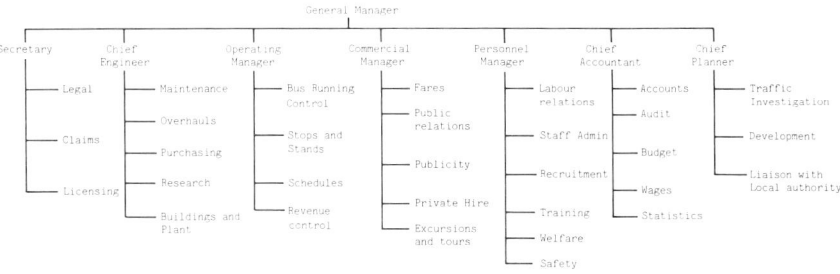

Figure 4.2 The responsibilities of department heads within a bus company organized functionally.

At this stage there has been substantial growth but there is still a clear departmental style. The larger the system the more likely might be the possible administrative difficulties which have been described but at what stage the concept becomes unmanageable is a matter of circumstance and opinion. There are no rules that must be followed when determining an organizational structure except that whatever principle is adopted (and there is an alternative) it must be the one that enables the undertaking to work with the maximum of efficiency and economy and the exercise must not be one of finding jobs for people. The needs of the service must be determined and suitable staff appointed. In other words, the administrative machine will seldom be right if existing personalities are taken as base and the structure built around their capabilities and aptitudes; but this is getting into the recruitment field.

De-centralized control

An alternative concept in this study of organizational methods is the divisional system, the principle of which is the devolution of power.

Consider now *Figure 4.3*. With this system, the operating territory is divided into divisions (or areas or districts; it matters not what they are called), and a manager is appointed for each who reports direct to the general manager. The term 'manager' is significant. It implies that he is responsible for all of the daily work within his division regardless of the function. In other words, he cleans and services the vehicles and ensures that they are available for traffic requirements, he recruits staff, he prepares his schedules, he controls the buses on the road and is responsible for the necessary administrative work within his divisional headquarters. To do this he will need the support of senior assistants whose work could well be organized on a functional basis, such as an engineer, a traffic superintendent and a staff officer. But they will be very small units compared with a centralized headquarters responsible for the entire system.

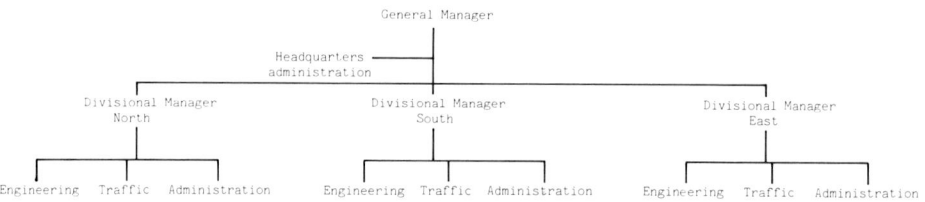

Figure 4.3 The basic organization of a bus company using the divisional system.

Look again at the departmental structure in *Figure 4.2* for a theoretical 800-bus unit. It might now follow the lines shown in *Figure 4.4*, which suggests that there must be rather more to the headquarters organization than might have been apparent from the outline sketch in *Figure 4.3*. One reason for this is that the undertaking as a whole will wish to trade as a single unit with a common policy and not as a series of distinct parts with perhaps different standards. Partly for this and partly in the interests of efficiency there are certain functions that are more appropriate for administration from the centre. If there are to be common standards and the undertaking is to speak with one voice, then the commercial manager will expect his fares officer, his public relations officer and his publicity officer to have responsibility for the entire system. Clearly the secretary would not find it convenient to divide his legal responsibilities and the work of the chief accountant will cover the undertaking as a whole. Similarly, efficiency might be lost if the chief planner lost the advantage of integration between divisions and had to recognize a series of 'independent' units. Major overhaul work, research and the purchase of supplies on the engineering side attracts economies through centralization. It follows that there still must be a sizeable centralized headquarters administration to determine policy and to undertake those functions that do not readily lend themselves to decentralization. On the other hand, divisional managers must have a supporting administrative team if they are to discharge their responsibilities in a satisfactory manner.

Selection of an organizational system

The advantage of the divisional system is that a senior manager with executive power is available 'in the field' as opposed to a 'base headquarters'. Decisions

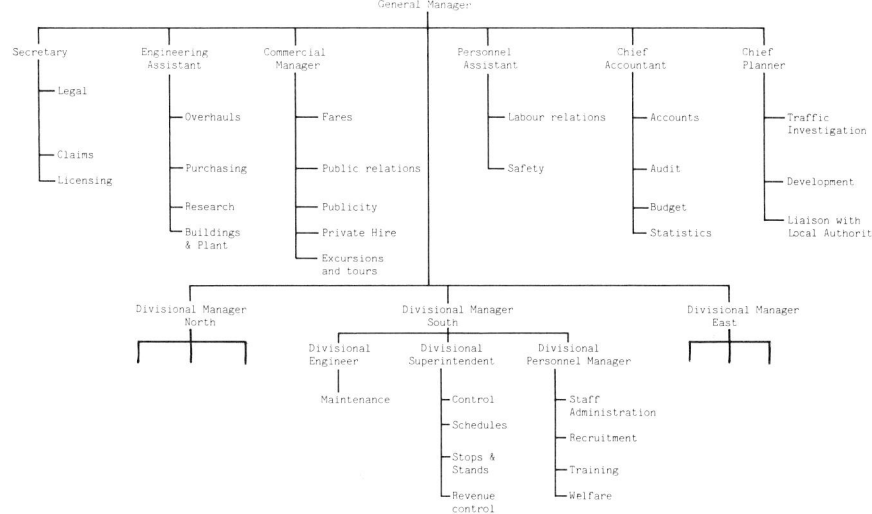

Figure 4.4 The responsibilities of chief officers of a bus company organized divisionally.

within the broad policy framework can be given on the spot and the possible working disadvantages of the functional system as suggested at the outset and which magnify as the system grows larger are avoided. On the other hand, with administration as there must be at central and at local levels, an element of duplication creeps in.

It is at this point where opinions differ and why the determination of an organizational structure is so much subject to discretion at board level. Geography plays a part. If the network is very large, if traffic concentrations are widely scattered with sparsely populated areas in between or if there is a series of physically separate units which do not easily lend themselves to complete operational integration, there is a much stronger case for decentralized control. But bus undertakings do not usually fall into this pattern. Generally their operating territories are smaller and more compact and not of a sufficient size to make the functional system unwieldy. Exceptions can of course readily come to mind such as the organization of London Buses Ltd. which has a fleet of over 5000 vehicles covering Greater London and that of Greyhound Lines Inc. which operates inter-city coach services across the USA and beyond.

Conclusions on types of organizations

The internal structure and organization of an enterprise recognizes, among other things, the amount which it is considered that one man can successfully manage although the size of an undertaking is not necessarily dictated by this restraint as some transport undertakings must of necessity serve a large area. But the internal structures must take size into account and with very large combines there is little doubt that devolution of authority in some form must be considered. At what stage, however, absolute control from the centre ceases to be practicable must depend on personal preferences. It is the opinion of the writer that decentralization is better avoided if at all possible. If that 800-bus unit, a suggested organization for which is depicted in *Figure 4.2*, served a compact operating area it is submitted that the departmental system with centralized control should be practicable. Decentralization not only introduces an element of duplication of administration, it also tends to put the functional heads within each division responsible to two masters: their respective divisional managers and also those in charge of their function at headquarters.

The point was made, however, that there are no rules as such to determine what the chain of command should be. The departmental and divisional systems represent the basic theory. The resultant structure will be geared to one or the other or perhaps to a blend of both. Decentralization within a department is not unknown. A 'divisional superintendent', for example, might carry responsibility for operating matters within his division, being directly responsible to a functional head. Such an arrangement could, however, represent the worst of both worlds as there would be duplication of work without sufficient compensating benefit.

Staff administration

Introduction

The title of this sub-section covers what has become in Great Britain an involved and far-reaching issue. It is a very important part, not only of bus operation but of industry generally but as transport is a large employer of labour, staff matters are now tending to occupy what might be regarded as a disproportionate amount of a manager's time. At one time the chief officers of the various functions as just described were able to handle the staff side of the business. Between the functions, it is the operating department that has the largest payroll but even here the traffic manager, divisional superintendent or whatever his title was generally able, subject to the size of his unit, to handle personnel matters with only the minimum of assistance. Today, the volume and complexity of staff work has grown to the extent that it has become a specialized subject in itself. So much so that in large undertakings a person with particular knowledge of the subject and probably with a sizeable supporting staff is required to deal with the complex day to day isues which arise. Again, this book is about bus operation and personnel management is a separate subject. It will, therefore, remain silent on the teachings of this particular branch of management. It does not mean, however, that the operator can remain ignorant of the subject as it impinges on other work which is more directly related to running buses. This chapter would not, therefore, be complete without at least a reference to the issues.

Industrial relations

Good staff relations are essential if there is to be good service. It is worthwhile, therefore, to look briefly at recent trends and to put into perspective any shortcomings and difficulties that could be a source of discontent both to employers and employed.

Over the years the trade union movement in Great Britain has become progressively stronger, backed by a wealth of social legislation. Several acts of parliament have established a variety of rights for individuals in employment. Most of these rights are now contained in the Employment Protection (Consolidation) Act, 1978 which brought together in one enactment previous legislation which covered redundancy payments, contracts of employment, trade union and labour relations matters and protection of employment although the Employment Acts 1980 and 1982 were introduced subsequently to obtain a better balance between rights and responsibilities in industrial relations. Additionally there are other acts which also bestow rights on employees, the main ones being the Equal Pay Act, 1970, the Sex Discrimination Act, 1975 and the Race Relations Act, 1976. With such extensive rights now conferred on employees, including unfair dismissal, the British government has seen fit to set up a series of industrial tribunals to deliberate and give directions on any complaints that might arise. These tribunals are independent judicial bodies of whom the chairmen are legally qualified and both parties at a hearing (being the employer and employed) may be legally represented if they so wish.

Whilst this may be congenial for employees, it does nothing to help run buses. But the transport industry in general has a history of long hours and relatively low wages. It can also be said that for many years, life for the transport worker (as, no doubt, for many others) was hard and uncompromising with the result that a sense of mistrust and hostility was engendered between employers and employed which is not easily eradicated. The record of management is not without blame in this respect. But even if some harsh decisions were made, it must be remembered that the goodwill of a service is dependent on standards. The service must be reliable if it is to be any good at all. Buses must run in accordance with advertised times, which means that they do not run early, nor must they be subjected to unnecessary delay. The correct destination blinds must be displayed. Uniformed staff need to be courteous and smart in appearance and drivers must not smoke whilst on duty, particularly with the now open cabs which permit the objectionable effects to penetrate the interior of the vehicle (it is illegal anyway). All uniformed staff should be effective public relations officers. It is unfortunate that today, and this applies particularly in Great Britain, too many people regard attention to this kind of detail as petty but such shortcomings (and there are plenty) do more than anything else to accelerate the erosion of traffic. Without proper discipline, service will be lacking and goodwill lost. It is submitted that managements should produce rules and procedures for efficient running which are practical in their implementation, that they should not be impeded by trade unions in so doing and that staff should work to those rules and be disciplined if they do not. It is unfortunate that some members of some trade unions seem to have a different interpretation of 'working to rule'. Managers should therefore impose a strict code of discipline but the British legislation referred to does not assist them in doing it.

Another standard is that charges should not be excessively high but, disregarding subsidies, fare levels depend on working expenses which in turn, to a large extent, depend on wages. The writer accepts absolutely that a fair day's work deserves a fair day's pay, but it is his view that restrictive practices and other measures that enforce inefficient schedules and produce inflated wages for idle time make no contribution to the interests of either the nation, the travelling public or, in the long run, to the staff themselves. Agreements as sought by trade unions, particularly in respect of duty schedules, if restrictive are costly. This is why 'productivity' has become a fashionable term in labour relations but the legislation referred to makes productivity difficult to enforce without agreement and sometimes not easy to negotiate.

The foregoing has but briefly touched upon the complexities of labour relations in Britain today. Because transport is a labour-intensive industry it is something that must enter into the daily lives of all those who have a responsibility for running buses. Part of the staff function involves a knowledge of current legislation (which is always liable to change). Another part—man management and human relationships—calls for a natural gift, the absence of which no amount of technical know-how can compensate. But as this is a book on how to run buses, not how to manage staff the matter will not be developed further. There are other aspects of the staff function which again are not part of operations and these, therefore, will also have only brief mention.

Administration

Having discussed the basic issues of the staff function, there are other more routine matters which usually fall within the scope of this department. Records must be kept of all staff and internal administration must be dealt with. Do make sure that drivers have a valid driving licence and a current PSV licence. The onus of having proper licences might be on the staff but the operator will also be in trouble for employing someone who is not duly authorized by law. Promotions, etc. require advice to the wages section (probably a part of the finance function), entitlement to uniform calls for notification to the supplies section (which might be a part of the engineering department) and management is likely to require statistics in respect of staff utilization. Such examples could continue. Administration is also necessary in respect of certain other activities within the staff officer's domain, references to which follow.

Recruitment and training

Recruitment of staff is something which is normally undertaken by the respective employing officers within the overall policy of the undertaking as applied through the recruitment section. This is another example where two separate functions meet. The staff people ensure that an appointment is appropriate and within an authorized establishment, checking references, etc. whilst the actual employing officer satisfies himself regarding the suitability of the applicant for the job. Having recruited staff, there is a difficulty in some areas of retaining them and the turnover, particularly in the case of platform staff, is sometimes heavy. The most unpopular aspect of this work is the socially inconvenient shifts and weekend working. This, of course, is an essential and unavoidable feature and not something that management can do very much about. But if there is both unemployment and unfilled vacancies for bus drivers and conductors at the same place at the same time then there can perhaps be too much welfare in a welfare state. A bus company cannot match the competing attraction of unemployment pay and supplementary benefits backed with a little unauthorized casual work here and there.

Turning to the training side of the section, most people employed in transport are at least semi-skilled and training is, therefore, an essential feature. Vocational training includes schools for, in particular, drivers, conductors and inspectors. The actual work of training is generally carried out by the undertaking's own staff especially appointed for the purpose and an appointed bus driving instructor may be authorized to examine and certify drivers as competent to hold a driver's licence. Budding engineers normally follow the apprenticeship schemes of their particular trades. Also the responsibility of the training officer are the many different types of courses that are available for general background training and geared to the various levels of management. This category of staff should also be encouraged or required to study for the examinations of the appropriate professional bodies.

Welfare

The welfare input to the transport business is something that has developed over more recent years, particularly amongst the larger undertakings. Not being a sociologist, the writer does not propose even to attempt to consider the many personal and domestic problems encountered by staff and how they could affect their standard of work, let alone to suggest how they might be resolved. The employer of a large workforce, however, might well be advised to have somebody on hand who can deal with such matters.

One of the better-known functions and one that is usually classified as a part of welfare is the provision of canteens. This is a very useful facility, particularly as so many employees are on shift work with the odd hours of work which that entails. It is important that somewhere is available for rest and refreshment at reasonable prices during periods of meal relief and a subsidized canteen service does meet a need in making what can be sometimes rather difficult working conditions more tolerable. If this is beyond the resources of the company then at least a mess room with basic cooking facilities is helpful.

Welfare facilities are really something which are provided by management as a good employer over and above the agreed conditions of service even though probably not now introduced without staff consultation. In this enlightened age, however, some of these arrangements for staff welfare have in Great Britain become legal requirements. An example is safety.

Health and safety

The Health and Safety at Work etc. Act, 1974 is in addition to and only partially replaces hitherto existing health and safety legislation. It also extends its scope as it applies not only to employers but also to those self-employed and to employees. The main aims of the Act are to secure the health, safety and welfare of people at work; to protect other persons against any risks arising out of the activities of those workpeople and to control the storage and use of dangerous substances and their emission into the atmosphere. As the legislation involves the entire workforce, staff as well as management have a legal responsibility to achieve high standards of safety.

The requirements of the 1974 Act are extensive and provision is made for the appointment of safety representatives and establishment of safety committees within the various workforces. The general duties of employers to their employees are contained in Section 2. One of the most pertinent in this context is the requirement to provide and maintain as far as is practicable a working environment which is safe without risks to health and with adequate welfare arrangements. Suitable training must be given as necessary.

Conclusions

This chapter has covered a wide spectrum ranging from government policies to forms of ownership and staff administration. Whilst the attempt has been made to produce a factual survey, it is a subject where there are alternatives and opinions on what is 'best' for the community generally and bus passengers in particular vary.

Where politics are involved things can change rapidly but in 1987 thoughts are turning more to smaller-scale private ownership. Whilst it is really in Great Britain that the pace has been set, the policy is being emulated in the USA, Japan and in other areas scattered world-wide. By no means does public ownership now dominate the bus industry in the way that it did only a few years back.

Although it does not have to be so, large-scale organization with a planned network co-ordinated with other modes, subsidized and working under monopoly conditions is usually associated with public ownership whilst small-scale enterprise, commercially orientated and competitive is generally identified with private ownership. Whilst regulation, planning and finance are subject matters for Chapters 5, 6 and 11 respectively they are concomitants to size and scale. It was seen in Chapter 1 that most bus systems were pioneered by private enterprise. In Great Britain this was followed first by municipalization (the local town services) and then nationalization (the provincial services) although much was the result of voluntary sales. This produced some large units and still larger ones came with the Transport Act, 1968 when passenger transport executives were set up in the conurbations with overall planning powers to produce properly co-ordinated networks. Why, then, has the trend now been reversed?

In this chapter small- and large-scale units have been considered but there has been no suggestion regarding what might constitute an optimum-sized bus undertaking. How much can one man effectively manage? Managerial resources should be fully utilized, for example whilst a manager is controlling ten buses he could equally well be controlling 50, but there comes a point when assistants must be engaged and in due course even a change in the organizational structure must come with a bigger managerial team. True there are some economies through scale but in the bus industry they are not great. What there is is mainly on the engineering side where equipment should be kept fully used, and there is also a limited benefit through the purchase of stores and supplies in greater bulk. But the key issue is administration with the danger that the larger the undertaking the greater this will be. A big house has many servants and more servants are required to serve those servants. In the large undertaking administrative costs are liable to increase without anyone really noticing it or, at least, not admitting that they are noticing it, bearing in mind that a larger workforce is likely to increase the status of the sectional chiefs. Beware of the production of unnecessary information by departments anxious to justify their existence with reports and statistics being produced for other people within the same organization whose only jobs are to file them, store them and then destroy them. This can happen even more easily in a subsidy situation where the need to 'live out of the farebox' in order to survive has been removed. There are real dangers of these sort of things happening in the larger units where there are in any case more opportunities for laxity and loss of efficiency amongst the staff.

Although finance, regulation and planning are not for discussion here, political control is and it has been seen that some types of ownership give local councillors considerable power to pursue their own particular brand of politics which will please some but certainly not all of the potential ridership. This type of control also brings with it an opportunity for policies to be formulated more in the interests of vote catching than of bus passengers. Although this does not necessarily happen everywhere, it is a possibility. And it has been the process of municipalization and amalgamation for co-ordination purposes that has brought the local government controlled category into some of the larger units.

Turning now to industrial relations, the larger the undertaking the easier it is to organize labour and the stronger becomes the bargaining power of the trade unions. The resultant agreements are therefore likely to be more favourable to the staff and more costly to the employer. Where large units have come through amalgamations of smaller concerns with differing pay structures and service conditions there is a history of unions demanding and getting the best features of all of the various systems absorbed.

The theory of a large unified network has much to commend it, but this is for discussion in Chapter 6. Co-ordination is in stark contrast to uncontrolled competition which in theory is wasteful and overall will not produce facilities sufficient to cater for everybodys' requirements. The provision of an adequate, efficient and properly co-ordinated system of passenger transport to meet the needs of the area served in the most economic manner and free from unnecessary and wasteful competitive services, subsidized as appropriate, is the very laudable base on which many of the large undertakings in the public sector have been founded. It was justification in itself for introducing large-scale public ownership. But experience has proved that in terms of costs, the services provided by the large publicly owned units are high in comparison with smaller scale private enterprises to the extent that the degrees of subsidy have become excessive. This does not have to be so but for success the theory has to be made to work and it would seem that this has not always been done. If it is a fact that in some instances politicians, managements and trade unions have put self-interests before service then high costs, inflexibility and passenger dissatisfaction will have resulted and the benefits of co-ordination will have been negated. Maybe this is why thoughts have now turned to smaller privately owned operations. It will be seen in Chapter 5 that in Great Britain opportunities are now being afforded to smaller private operators to exercise their ingenuity in providing bus services at less cost to the nation than those of their larger predecessors. But with all of these extraneous factors, the definition of an optimum size is still as far away as it ever was.

5 Statutory controls

The need for regulation

The provision of a public service of any kind generally implies some sort of control. A special skill may be required which, if undertaken by people not properly proficient, could be damaging or even result in danger to life or property. If it is an essential service, those who provide it might need to be protected from unfair or wasteful competition. If by so doing near-monopolies are created, then in turn the public requires protection with its interests taken into account. There would also have to be safeguards to ensure that essential services are maintained.

Control emanates from the dictates of Parliament. The various edicts which come forth from the legislature either detail in direct terms what will or will not be done, are permissive in that certain provisions may be implemented at the discretion of the appropriate minister or lay down principles and authorize the preparation and issue of regulations, again probably by a government minister. Provision must also be made for the requirements of these enactments or regulations to be properly administered and enforced and a convenient way of doing this is by the institution of a licensing system, which means the establishment of an issuing authority.

There are two basic types of control, exercised through *quality licensing* and *quantity licensing*.

The terms are self-explanatory. Quality licensing ensures that adequate standards are maintained, that vehicles are kept in a safe and roadworthy condition, that the operators are competent and that the business is properly run. Quantity licensing controls the amount of service and where it may be provided.

So much for the generalizations. The controls exercised by any one country (assuming always that they have controls!) will fall somewhere within these broad concepts. It is impracticable in a general work such as this to detail the different arrangements that are adopted world-wide but as far as licensing is concerned this information can be obtained from *Regulation. An International Study of Bus and Coach Licensing* by J. Hibbs.

All of what follows refers to British law and applies to Great Britain where the operator (being the manager), the operative (being the driver), the vehicle and the service are all subject to quality control. The manager and the driver must be proficient, the vehicle must be properly constructed and maintained and the route and stopping points must be physically suitable.

Buses, coaches and trolleybuses

Vehicle definition

The vehicles which are used for public passenger transport and to which the licensing laws to be described apply are known as public service vehicles (PSVs). A public service vehicle is defined in Section 1 of the Public Passenger Vehicles Act, 1981 as a motor vehicle (other than a tram) which is used for carrying passengers for hire or reward and carries more than eight passengers or if it is able to carry only eight passengers or less it is used for hire or reward at separate fares as part of a passenger carrying business (but see under the sub-heading 'car sharing' below). In more familiar terms this generally means buses and coaches. It would also mean trolleybuses if there were any but at the time of writing there are no trolleybuses in Great Britain in normal public service.

Traffic commissioners

The PSV licensing system revolves around traffic commissioners, being semi-judicial authorities appointed by the minister for each of nine traffic areas which between them cover the entire country. Traffic commissioners are the licensing authorities for the PSV industry and are responsible for the issue of operators' licences and drivers' PSV licences. As a matter of interest, they are also responsible for the issue of licences for the road haulage industry but in this capacity they are known as Licensing Authorities.

Traffic commissioners were established by the Road Traffic Act, 1930 when a system of quantity licensing for the PSV industry was first introduced. Following subsequent legislation on this and other matters there was a consolidating act 30 years later, the Road Traffic Act, 1960, in which the licensing system was brought forward without alteration in principle. Subject to numerous subsequent amendments and additions to the procedure which were aimed at relaxing controls under certain circumstances, the system of licensing both bus and long-distance coach services and excursions and tours remained until the Transport Act, 1980 replaced many of the provisions relating to public service vehicles.

The British system of licensing

It was the 1980 Act which abolished quantity licensing for the longer distance coach services, made it easier for applicants to obtain licences for local bus services and strengthened the quality licensing arrangements by the introduction of PSV operators' licences. However, the provisions of this Act were subsequently consolidated in the Public Passenger Vehicles Act, 1981. Following that, the Transport Act, 1985 swept away all quantity control (except in Greater London for the time being) and de-regulation day was 26th October, 1986. At the same time, this Act further strengthened the quality control arrangements.

Details of the British PSV quality licensing system and the machinery necessary for implementing it follows.

The operator

Unlike the other aspects of control, operator licensing is a more recent innovation and is something that came originally through membership of the European Economic Community. The Public Service Vehicle Operators (Qualifications) Regulations, 1977 gave effect to the EEC Council Directive 74/562 on admission to the occupation of road passenger transport operator and the requirement became embodied in the Transport Act, 1980. This was subsequently brought forward into Sections 12–21 of the Public Passenger Vehicles Act, 1981 as is now amended by Sections 24–31 of the Transport Act, 1985.

As has been explained, traffic commissioners are responsible for the issue of public service vehicle operators' licences and without this no PSV as such may be run. Before so doing they are required to satisfy themselves that the applicants are suitably qualified. In accordance with Section 14, potential PSV operators must show that:

1. They are of good repute.
2. They have appropriate financial standing.
3. They are professionally competent or they employ a manager who is of good repute and professionally competent.

Professionally competent means that they are qualified through one of the appropriate professional institutes or they have passed a special examination conducted by the Royal Society of Arts and have thereby gained a certificate of competence.

In respect of such applications, traffic commissioners must also give regard to:

1. Previous conduct involving operation of vehicles.
2. Arrangements to ensure that the regulations concerning drivers' hours (to be considered below) are observed.
3. Facilities for proper maintenance.
4. Manner in which the vehicle is to be used.

Section 25 of the 1985 Act adds a Section 14A to the 1981 Act which gives the police and local authorities the power to object to the grant of operators' licences in cases where they consider that any of these requirements will not be met.

In accordance with Section 13 of the 1981 Act, PSV operators' licences may be either standard or restricted. A standard licence authorizes the holder to use any description of public service vehicle and may be issued either for national only or national and international operations. The restricted licence applies to vehicles with not more than eight passenger seats; a figure which may be increased to 16 if the vehicle is not used as part of a passenger-carrying business.

Applications are made to the traffic commissioners in whose area the operating centre is situated. Undertakings can (and often do) have two or more such centres and if they are in different traffic areas then licences must be obtained from all of the traffic commissioners concerned. Once a licence is obtained an operator may run the vehicles concerned anywhere in Great Britain.

Traffic commissioners will, *vide* Section 16 of the 1981 Act, specify the total number of vehicles that may be operated. However, the 1985 Act amended the 1981 Act to the extent that in the case of a restricted licence, except in any prescribed case, the maximum number will not exceed two. They may also stipulate the maximum number of vehicles within different descriptions and conditions for restricting or regulating the use of such vehicles including stopping places. Their decisions are subject to the right of appeal.

Operators are under an obligation to run the services that they have registered (*see* below) in an acceptable and responsible manner as passengers must be protected from any unscrupulous operator who might make false promises by publishing timetables to which little or no effort is made to observe. Section 26 empowers traffic commissioners to attach conditions to the operators' licences of those who behave in this way which would in effect prohibit them from providing local services. Furthermore, *vide* Section 28 they may revoke a licence and disqualify the former holder from obtaining a PSV operators' licence where they consider that the conduct justifies this course.

The driver

Drivers of public service vehicles must hold an appropriate licence obtainable from the traffic commissioners (except in the Metropolitan Traffic Area where they are issued by the Commissioner of Police) *vide* Section 22 of the 1981 Act. The issue of such a licence is subject to the applicant showing that he is a fit and proper person and he must also prove himself competent to drive a vehicle of the appropriate type. A PSV driver's licence is not a substitute for a normal driving licence which is still necessary. The issue of a PSV driver licence is accompanied by a badge which must be worn whilst on duty.

In the interests of safety, limitations are imposed on the hours which drivers of public service vehicles may work. The principle is not new. Such restrictions were contained in the Road Traffic Act, 1930 with similar requirements brought forward into the Road Traffic Act, 1960. Section 96 of the Transport Act, 1968 as amended by the European Communities Act, 1972 gives the details.

The theory behind the drivers' hours regulations is straightforward. Passengers' lives should not be endangered by a driver who has been dulled by fatigue. The sort of things which the regulations enforce are the number of consecutive hours that a man may drive, overall driving time in the course of a day, length of spreadovers, minimum periods of rest per day and per week, etc. Unfortunately, the principle is the only straightforward thing about it because the subject has become extremely complex. The confusion is compounded because European Economic Community conditions are partly superimposed on British law which means that they apply under certain circumstances. Community regulations are more onerous on the employer, for example under British law 10 hours driving is permitted per day but under EEC law only 9 (10 twice a week), and the EEC specifies a 90 hour driving limit in 2 weeks whereas British law has no such restriction. The British rest-day period required is 24 hours once a fortnight but the EEC calls for a rest of 45 hours each week (which may be reduced subject to compensation within the following 3 weeks).

Whilst this gives a broad picture of some of the main considerations of the drivers' hours regulations let the reader be warned that there is very much more detail to it than that.

British law as is contained in Section 96 of the 1968 Act as amended applies to drivers engaged on 'domestic' operations, being:

1. Public passenger transport services where the length of the route does not exceed 50 km (31 miles).
2. Vehicles equipped to carry 16 or less passengers on any type of service anywhere in Great Britain.

Otherwise EEC law applies in Great Britain to vehicles equipped to carry more than 16 passengers, and this means:

3. Public passenger transport services where the length of the route is more than 50 km (31 miles).
4. Occasional and shuttle services (this means mainly private hire and excursions and tours).

If groups (3) and (4) are confined to Great Britain they are known as 'national' operations but if they travel beyond the UK they become 'international' operations. A vehicle does not have to be a PSV to be covered by the EEC regulations except that they do not apply to vehicles constructed to carry eight or less passengers. In British law, as far as passenger vehicles which are not PSVs are concerned it is only those that have a capacity for more than 12 passengers with either employee drivers or owner drivers who drive in the course of their business (i.e. not for pleasure) to which the 1968 Act applies.

It is not appropriate to incorporate the vast amount of detail regarding drivers' hours in a work of this kind. It is sufficient here for the reader to be advised that such regulations exist. Complete information is contained in *Road Transport Law* by Kitchin, and it is important that operators acquaint themselves with and observe the detailed requirements.

Records are required to be maintained in respect of drivers' hours of work and rest when working under Community rules (which means international and national work journeys but not domestic and remember it includes vehicles with more than eight seats on international journeys and with more than 16 seats on national journeys—and the vehicles do not have to be PSVs).

There are three types of records used: (1) the service timetable and duty roster; (2) individual control books; and (3) tachographs fitted to the vehicles. Method (1) applies only to regular timetabled services and drivers are required to carry a copy of the relevant information with them. Method (2) is a written form of record showing hours of work and rest but it is method (3) (the tachograph) which is the generally adopted way of maintaining records and is compulsory fitting on all vehicles used on community regulated work other than on vehicles used on national regular services. Even then it is frequently used. Note that although specific records as described are not necessary in respect of domestic work, the drivers' hours regulations must, of course, still be observed and if drivers are working on both types of services during the course of the day then complete records must be kept.

The vehicle

The basic requirements for public service vehicles are stipulated in The Public Service Vehicles (Conditions of Fitness, Equipment, Use and Certification) Regulations 1981 and also in The Road Vehicles (Construction and Use) Regulations 1986, the purpose of which is to ensure that they are constructed within statutory dimensions and to acceptable standards. They also set out the requirements for maintenance and use, since vehicles must remain roadworthy and not become a source of danger. In the case of public service vehicles that carry more than eight passengers, because of their capacity and the need for precaution, Section 6 of the 1981 Act requires that a public service vehicle will not be used as such without either a certificate of initial fitness issued by a certifying officer, or a type approval in accordance with Section 10 of the 1981 Act. To qualify for such certificates, a vehicle must comply with the Public Service Vehicles (Conditions of Fitness, Equipment, Use and Certification) Regulations, 1981. A decision of the certifying officer is subject to the right of appeal. A requirement for subsequent testing of PSVs was contained in Section 34 of the Transport Act, 1980 which extended the application of Section 44 of the Road Traffic Act 1972 (which requires test certificates for motor vehicles) to PSVs. An annual test is now required by regulation *vide* the Motor Vehicles (Tests) Regulations 1981 and the Motor Vehicles (Tests) (Extension) Order 1982. Furthermore, Section 8 of the 1981 Act empowers certifying officers or public service vehicle examiners to inspect such vehicles at any time.

Further reference to construction and use regulations is contained in Chapter 3.

There is of course also the vehicle excise licence to which reference was made in Chapter 2. However, buses and coaches come within the Hackney Carriage classification which—*vide* Section 38 of the Vehicles (Excise) Act, 1971—is defined as a mechanically propelled vehicle which stands or plies for hire in any public or private yard, premises or street. This is a very wide definition and embraces not only PSVs but also taxis, hire cars and minibuses. Unlike private cars, the rate varies, being based on seating capacity. For small vehicles so classified the cost of this licence is substantially less than that of a private car whilst even for a 78 seater double-deck bus it is not a lot above the private car rate.

The service

The licensing of the service is basically quantity control which no longer applies in Great Britain where road service licences are not now necessary (except for a limited period in Greater London). There is, however, an element of quality control as far as the services are concerned and it is appropriate, therefore, to discuss the statutory framework that encompasses bus services in Great Britain as a result of the Transport Act, 1985.

The services provided by PSVs (buses and coaches) in Great Britain are termed 'public passenger transport services', and Section 63(10) of the 1985 Act defines these as services on which the public rely for getting from place to place other than by private facilities of their own or by services (except those for the elderly or disabled) provided under a permit (to be explained). Section 2 introduces 'local public passenger transport services' (local services) which are, in effect, the local bus services. They are those public passenger transport services which carry passengers by road at separate fares for journeys of less than 15 miles (24 km) measured in a straight line. Whilst even the local services do not now require road service licences, the distinction is necessary as certain of the administrative (*see* below) and financial (*see* Chapter 11) arrangements are different.

Within the terms of their operators' licence, outside Greater London operators are free to run whatever services they choose but Section 6 of the 1985 Act requires any such person who wishes to operate a local service (other than in replacement of a railway service which has been temporarily interrupted) to register that service with the traffic commissioner of each traffic area where there is a stopping place—and note that only those who hold a valid operators' licence (or permit or who propose to use a school bus—*see* below) may so register. The registration will contain details of the route, timetable, vehicles and stopping places and in so far as the local services are concerned, Section 7 empowers traffic commissioners at the request of a traffic authority to impose at their discretion traffic regulation conditions where they consider that this is necessary to prevent danger to road users or reduce severe traffic congestion. In so doing they will take into account not only the views of the traffic authority but also the interests of the registered operators, the passengers and those who are elderly or disabled. If conditions are imposed they may take the form of detailing roads that may be traversed, stopping places that may be observed and the time that vehicles may wait at those stops. They are effected by attaching conditions as appropriate to the relevant operators' licences or permits and are subject to the right of appeal.

This, then, is the essence of the control over bus and coach operation in Great Britain. The services are known as public passenger transport services and those that are 'local' have to be registered. The real control lies in the quality issues, and it is the need to possess an operators' licence that ensures satisfactory standards. Without this no PSV may be operated. But not every vehicle that carries passengers as part of a public service is regarded as a PSV and when they are not so regarded they do not have to conform to the requirements that have just been described. The exceptions will now be considered.

Permits

Sections 19–21 of the 1985 Act make provision for buses to be used for carrying passengers for hire or reward under certain circumstances with a permit which exempts them from the PSV operator and driver licensing requirements. Buses running under a permit will be used only for purposes connected with education, religion, social welfare, recreation or other activities beneficial to the community and by bodies involved in these activities. They will not be available to the public generally and will not be run for or in connection with any profit-making activities. Conditions as considered appropriate may be attached to permits including limiting the passengers carried to specific classes.

Permits may be issued by traffic commissioners or, for small buses only (as defined in Chapter 3), by designated bodies. Such bodies are appointed by the Secretary of State, they must be involved with the activities as described and their powers may be limited as defined by order. Within these parameters they may issue permits both to themselves and to other bodies involved in the eligible activities. If it is a large bus (also defined in Chapter 3), traffic commissioners may issue permits to bodies that assist and co-ordinate the work of other bodies concerned with the activities defined except that in this instance recreation is excluded. In so doing traffic commissioners will satisfy themselves regarding vehicle fitness and maintenance arrangements.

Whilst permits are not vehicle specific, only one bus may be used under any one permit at any one time but an eligible body may hold more than one permit. The driver and, if it is a small bus, the fitness of the vehicle are subject to regulation but the permit holder need not possess an operators' licence and the driver need not have a PSV licence.

Community buses

Another device for avoiding the full severity of PSV licensing is the concept of the community bus which was first introduced by the Transport Act, 1978 but now contained in Sections 22 and 23 of the 1985 Act. In accordance with the provisions of these sections, traffic commissioners are empowered to authorize community bus permits for local services using community buses. The following conditions apply:

1. The vehicle must be a small (single-deck) bus (i.e. of a capacity of more than eight but not more than 16 passengers) and must fulfil prescribed conditions in this respect.
2. The applicant must be concerned with the social welfare needs of the community. It is not necessary to hold a PSV operator's licence but as a local service it must be registered in the normal way.
3. The service must run without profit.
4. The driver must be an unpaid volunteer who need not be the holder of a PSV driver's licence but if not, must fulfil any prescribed conditions.

Traffic commissioners may also authorize the use of a community bus for any other non-local service (subject to any conditions) should they consider it reasonable in order to provide financial support for the community bus service. In all cases traffic commissioners must satisfy themselves that arrangements for the maintenance of the vehicles concerned are adequate. Although community bus permits are not vehicle specific, only one bus may be used per permit but a body may hold more than one permit.

The advantage of the community bus concept is that it means freedom from PSV licensing (other than registration) and hence some of the rigours of quality control that go with it.

School buses

Section 46 of the 1981 Act provides that a local education authority may use a bus that is providing free school transport also for the carriage of fare-paying passengers and additionally a school bus which belongs to the education authority may be used by that authority to provide a local service when it is not employed on free school transport. Here again there are relaxations from the PSV licensing regulations. The following do not apply:

1. The requirements regarding the certificate of initial fitness.
2. Inspections by certifying officers or PSV vehicle examiners and the prohibitions which can be applied to PSVs in respect of the vehicle.
3. The need for an operator's licence in respect of the education authority.
4. The need for a PSV licence in respect of the driver.

However, as local services school buses must be registered in the normal way.

Taxis and hire cars

The 1985 Act makes provision for taxis and hire cars to be used under certain circumstances for the carriage of passengers for hire or reward at separate fares without the application of the PSV licensing laws. But before these arrangements can be considered it is necessary to explain briefly the system for licensing taxis in their conventional form.

Taxis are licensed under the 'Taxi Code' which is defined in the 1985 Act as provisions made under any enactment which apply when the vehicle is hired by a single passenger for his exclusive use. Any enactment includes the Town Police Clauses Act, 1847 (England and Wales); the Metropolitan Public Carriage Act, 1869

(London); and the Civic Government (Scotland) Act, 1982 (Scotland). Every taxi and every taxi driver must be licensed and the licensing authority is the appropriate district council (in London it is the Secretary of State or as designated). These authorities may make by-laws relating to general conduct, fares, taxi stands, etc. and the vehicles are subject to annual testing. The taxi licence (i.e., authority to operate) refers to the vehicle and can be transferred to a new owner. This brings in an element of quantity licensing as the authorities have been able to use discretion on the number of taxis that they are prepared to license. However, Section 16 of the 1985 Act qualifies these powers to the extent that licences may now only be refused if there is satisfaction that there is no significant unmet demand. Section 30 of the 1985 Act prohibits a PSV adapted to carry more than eight passengers to be used on a road plying for hire as a whole.

Hire cars are in effect taxis which if pre-booked do not therefore ply for hire. As such they are not subject to the Town Police Clauses Act, 1847, etc. They operate under a hire car code which is defined as what applies under any enactment when the vehicle is hired by a single passenger.

So much for the classic taxi operation where a cab is hired on the street for exclusive use and for the pre-booked hire car for exclusive use for specific journeys. But the 1985 Act makes provision for these vehicles to play additional roles where potential traffic is insufficient to justify the operation of large buses. Arrangements are therefore made for taxis and hire cars to carry passengers at separate fares subject to adequate quality controls which means with properly licensed vehicles.

Section 10 enables schemes to be introduced whereby taxis may be used by passengers paying separate fares whilst they are still subject to the taxi code and without becoming PSVs. Such schemes will be devised by the appropriate licensing authorities (as already defined) in areas where at least 10% of the holders of taxi licences so wish. Authorized places where taxis may be so hired will be designated and fares and any other conditions may be set. Section 11 provides for taxis and hire cars to be hired *en bloc* again whilst continuing to be subject to the taxi (or hire car) code by passengers who have agreed to share and pay separate fares. Under these circumstances vehicles must be booked in advance. But it is Section 12 that has the greatest relevance to bus operation. Here, holders of taxi licences may apply to the traffic commissioner for a special restricted PSV operator's licence under the 1981 Act to provide local (bus) services. This may be done without the need to comply with Section 14 of the 1981 Act (i.e., good repute, adequate financial standing, professional competence, facilities for maintenance, etc.) but conditions can be attached which will include the requirement that every vehicle will have a valid taxi licence and that it will be used only for a local service (and this does not include an excursion or tour). When a taxi is running under these circumstances as a PSV, drivers do not require a PSV driver's licence (only a taxi driver's licence is needed) but they must comply with the drivers' hours regulations for domestic services. When a taxi is being used under a special restricted PSV operator's licence the taxi code will not apply but it will revert to the taxi code when not running as a PSV. The maximum of two vehicles applicable to a restricted operator's licence does not extend to the special restricted operator's licence but the number of vehicles allowed will not exceed the number for which the operator holds taxi licences.

One final point regarding the use of taxis and hire cars with eight seats or less for conveying passengers at separate fares in the course of a passenger carrying business is that it is permissible without the vehicles being classified as PSVs under circumstances as contained in Section 1 and Schedule 1 of the Public Passenger Vehicles Act, 1981. The conditions are:

1. The making of the agreement for the payment of separate fares are not initiated by the driver or owner of the vehicle or any other person with a vested interest.
2. There is no previous general advertisement.

If these conditions are met then there will not be an involvement with the PSV licensing machinery.

Car sharing

It was said at the beginning of this chapter that the definition of a public service vehicle (*vide* Section 1 of the Public Passenger Vehicles Act, 1981) was that it carried more than eight passengers for hire or reward or, if not so adapted, at separate fares in the course of a passenger carrying business. In other words, this excludes from the PSV licensing system vehicles carrying eight or less in which passengers are conveyed otherwise than as part of a passenger carrying business. This, of course, covers private cars. It follows therefore that motorists may receive contributions from their passengers as part of a car sharing arrangement for social or other similar purposes provided that:

1. Their vehicle is not constructed or adapted to carry more than eight passengers.
2. Their passengers are not being carried in the course of a passenger carrying business.
3. The total contribution received for the journey does not involve an element of profit and the arrangements were made before the journey began.

Subject to these conditions being met there will be no involvement with the PSV licensing machinery and Section 61 of the Transport Act, 1980 amends Section 148 of the Road Traffic Act, 1972 and extends insurance in respect of the private use of vehicles to cover use under car-sharing arrangements.

Quantity licensing

This, then, is an outline of the application of quality licensing to bus and coach operation in Great Britain. But a vestige of quantity licensing still remains and that is in London. Being only one place in one country and at that may not last very much longer, a lengthy discussion on this particular issue cannot be justified but a review such as this would be incomplete without at least a passing reference.

Other than for services operated by a subsidiary of or through an agreement with London Regional Transport, the 1985 Act requires the grant of a London local service licence before a London local service may be run. The licence is granted at the discretion of the traffic commissioner either as requested or in a modified form to holders of PSV operators' licences or permits who so apply. Applications are published and are subject to objection by interested parties. The traffic commissioner is required to grant the licence either in total or as modified unless he is satisfied that to do so would be against the interests of the public. In so deciding he will take into account the transport needs of the area, any relevant plans or policies of the borough councils and any objections or representations. The decision is subject to the right of appeal.

The foregoing describes very briefly the essentials of a quantity licensing system which for 50 years applied throughout Great Britain. It is now reduced to services in the London area and then only those that are outside the recognition of London Regional Transport. The extent of such applications is therefore small and even this is liable to disappear. Section 46 of the 1985 Act empowers the Secretary of State to repeal by order the provisions for quantity licensing in London. Circumstances in Great Britain which gave rise to the declared need for a revival of the old competitive spirit and hence the demise of quantity control were touched upon at the end of Chapter 4. In some other parts of the world the system still exists in some form or other which brings things back to the opening paragraphs of this chapter. Wherever they are in force, operators must acquaint themselves with the local requirements relative to the running of buses and coaches in whatever situation they might happen to find themselves.

Trams and trolleybuses

Even though Great Britain now has very few trams and no trolleybuses in public service operators must understand the legal complexities that govern this form of transport, particularly as there may well be a partial comeback of one or the other to British transport. It was said at the beginning of this chapter that a tram is not a public service vehicle. A trolleybus now is (or would be) a PSV although this has not always been the case. Re-classification came with the Transport Act, 1980. But the provision of its specialized way is still subject to a similar legal process as applies to tramways. That is why reference to the trolleybus appears within both the bus and tram sub-sections. However, as trams are not classified as PSVs and are not therefore subject to the laws that govern PSVs they are not involved with PSV operators' licences, etc. Nevertheless, they are by no means above the law. They are, in effect, in precisely the same situation as that which applies to the railway and to which mode of transport trams and trolleybuses are, in many respects, legally a part. In short, the construction of a tramway or trolleybus system or the conversion from one to the other requires the authority of Parliament. There is a close relationship between the two modes and there is no clear demarcation between a tramway and a railway.

In Great Britain trams began to proliferate in the second half of the nineteenth century and to facilitate what was in effect a succession of requests from tramway promoters for authority to construct, some easement to what was a cumbersome and expensive procedure was necessary. The resultant Tramways Act, 1870 was introduced for this purpose and became the basis for subsequent local acts which authorized the construction of individual lines. Briefly, the act states that any persons or bodies are free to apply for provisional orders to construct a tramway and it then details the procedure to be followed. Such orders, if granted, would specify, *vide* Section 10, the traffic to be carried, the fares and such regulations as are considered necessary by the minister. Here, of course, lies the control; the contents of the order being contained in a local Act. Section 25 requires the route to be inspected and certified as fit for public traffic before it is brought into use. There are limitations on what the promoters may do to the surface of the road and Section 28 requires them to maintain not only the track but also the road extending up to 18 in on each side. It is Section 43 which enables local authorities to purchase the system after 21 years as was referred to in Chapter 1. A resemblance of PSV licensing lies in Section 48 which gives local authorities the same licensing powers in regard to the trams themselves (i.e. the vehicles) and their drivers as they already had with hackney carriages.

There is, therefore, ample framework for statutory control of trams (and trolleybuses), much of which is (or, more correctly, would be if the occasion arose) the responsibility of the railway inspectorate.

Section 9 of the Transport Charges etc. (Miscellaneous Provisions) Act, 1954 empowers the Minister to make regulations regarding the numbers of passengers carried on trams (and trolleybuses). A small point on fares, however, is worthy of note. It has just been said that Section 10 of the 1870 Act made provision for, *inter alia*, the fixing of fares. With the passing of time, these original orders became somewhat remote and not being PSVs, fares on trams and trolleybuses were not subject to the jurisdiction of the traffic commissioners. This anomaly was remedied by Section 2 of the Transport Charges etc. (Miscellaneous Provisions) Act, 1954 by putting such fares under the control of the traffic commissioners. However, Section 65 of the Transport Act, 1980 repealed Section 2 of the 1954 Act and—like buses and coaches, therefore—fares are not now subject to control.

Conclusions

The law of business and carriage is a subject in its own right, and no attempt has been made in this one short chapter to discuss its many ramifications. Only regulatory and safety matters have been considered which means that the study has been confined to a review of the main features of the more important statutes which affect bus and tram operation in Great Britain. It has not been an exhaustive coverage and it can, therefore, do no more than offer a guide on the sort of controls which exist and where to seek the details.

Enough, however, has been said to show that even this one part of the subject is complex. It is made more so by the fact that at least in Great Britain new legislation has been partly superimposed on old and that successive layers of exceptions, permissions and even administrative arrangements have been introduced without always replacing everything that has gone before. The result tends to become a somewhat formidable maze of legislation.

What has not been contained in this chapter are references to the financial arrangements in Great Britain for meeting the deficits incurred by those local services which have little or no commercial value but meet a social need. This is a matter for Chapter 11.

6 The planning process

Introduction

Planning is an all-embracing term. Reference was made in Chapter 4 to the different functions within a transport organization and it will be recalled that planning was one although few undertakings have a separate planning department. The primary functions must, of course, all plan ahead. The engineer must plan his future fleets and where to house them, the accountant will prepare his budget estimates and the operator will consider service revisions to keep abreast with ever-changing demands. A well-run undertaking should at least do this even though some might work from day to day jumping from one crisis to another meeting (or failing to meet) problems and circumstances as they arise. But this is all short-term planning and calls for no specialist planning department.

It is the newer breed of public transport planner that has particular relevance here. He uses what has become a conventional planning technique which was imported from the United States in the 1950s. It is not proposed to consider this aspect of planning in depth as it is essentially a study in its own right and specialized books are available on this subject. A useful example is *Principles of Urban Transport Systems Planning* by B.G. Hutchinson. Even so, an indication of the way in which the subject is tackled is useful background information for operators and a brief mention follows.

A longer term planning exercise involves first the definition of the area to be studied and its division into geographical zones for analysis purposes. Account is taken of the existing public transport system which is detailed for computer analysis. Within each zone a series of nodes is created which collectively forms a network, the nodes representing the centres from which all trips (by public and private transport) are generated or are attracted to. The next stage is to produce a series of models which simulate the way in which people behave under varying sets of conditions and what their responses would be to changes in basic assumptions. To do this, trip generation figures are compiled which estimate the total number of trips there would be into and out of each zone. From this is developed a trip distribution over the whole network and trip matrices (one for public and one for private transport) prepared which indicate the number of trips passing between each of the zones. The division between public and private transport is referred to as 'modal split'. All of this work is based on data produced in respect of a base year; at the distribution stage there will be revised numbers of trips and different modal splits according to the different assumptions fed in for the design year in question. To assess what the future modal splits might be, a weighting factor is used, the most important inputs of which are the travel time whilst actually on the move and in the case of public transport walking, waiting, changing, etc. together with a monetary cost. Trip assignments are then compiled which relate the specific number of trips to each main road in the case of private transport or to each bus route or railway line in the case of public transport. Alternative policies are by this means evaluated to show the effect of building a new road or providing a new train service or bus route. Different options produce different predictions, all of course worked up on the basic data plus the range of assumptions that have been used.

This transport planning process is a specialist technique and not something that is a supplementary job for the operator although managements are able to provide a valuable input to such studies. To the operator, it could still seem that notwithstanding the degree of sophistication that is attained, the fact must remain that much of the input is based on assumptions and that what comes out of a computer can be no more accurate than what is put in. Bus managements might, therefore, sometimes be excused for putting faith in their own instincts and intuitions when considering development projects for public transport and if they do they could on occasions be at variance with what the planners predict.

Reference to long-term planning beyond what has already been said will here be confined to the land use concept together with certain other factors which have a direct bearing on running buses. Much more elaboration will be given to 'operational planning'. This looks at service development in the shorter rather than the longer term (this year, next year rather than sometime, never, 10 years hence and the turn of the century) which is something closer to the operator's work. This is not to decry the principle of long-term planning which can only be built up on facts as are available plus the application of trends and assumptions and other outside influences, known or estimated with the whole being constantly updated with the passage of time. Whether responsibility for shorter term traffic planning is actually allocated to the planning function as discussed in Chapter 4 or to the traffic department is a moot point. But a short-term planning exercise such as route network rationalization (the aim of which is to match bus services to demand by looking at the route structure as a system instead of route by route) also involves a complicated and time-consuming process if it is done manually. There is, therefore, a case here to take advantage of the sophisticated planning techniques whereby a large number of alternative solutions can be rapidly designed and evaluated including use of optimization skills which suggest improvement measures. Even without specialized planners on their staff operators can obtain the benefits of such facilities by engaging the services of consultants as and when the needs arise. One such possibility is the use, for example, of the computerized tool for network analysis developed by VTS Transportation Systems Corporation, a consultant company in the Volvo Group.

Transport and land use

Attention was drawn in Chapter 1 to the haphazard way in which the older established towns developed and this has resulted in undesirable operating conditions in some areas which have been created as a result of uncontrolled growth. The remedy is organized planning, and in Great Britain local authorities have for some years now been required to produce overall structure plans and local development plans which organize among other things the parallel development of land use, transport and related factors with a view to the achievement of optimum benefits from what are, in effect, separate disciplines. The design and location of residential areas, for example, in relation to industrial estates and commercial and shopping centres have a strong effect on the pattern and hence the cost of the provision of local passenger transport. Much unnecessary expense has arisen in the past to bus operators because of the unsatisfactory layout of built-up areas, and on this reasoning it is good sense to allow transport to be at least one of the dictates of land use. The corporate planning concept takes into account the requirements not only of all vehicular traffic but also of pedestrians and the environment. This could, however, militate against the proper penetration by buses of, say, shopping centres. Those responsible for the provision of transport facilities are very conscious of the fact that this is a service industry and that their passengers should always be carried to the places where they want to go and not to where it happens to be convenient to take them. The more sophisticated approach to town planning is therefore welcome providing the basic philosophy continues to make this possible and an anti-bus lobby is not allowed to predominate. Organized planning and the resultant controls meet with resistance in some quarters where it is seen as placing yet one more restriction on life generally. Nevertheless, population grows whilst the total land mass does not and in countries (such as Great Britain) with relatively dense populations some sort of orderly development which makes the most of limited resources is desirable.

Modal split—public and private transport

Reference was made in Chapter 2 to the private car in relation to bus priorities where it was recognized that people want cars and that politicians are not likely to be anxious to impose restraints without very real justification. To do so would be an unwarranted intrusion into personal liberties and would in any case jeopardize the future support of the electorate. Bus managers themselves are probably also motorists. Their staff certainly are as witness the requirement for car parks at garages. In their professional capacity, however, busmen would like to be rid of the congestion on the roads which cars create. On the other hand, and this point was also made in Chapter 1, they would not wish all of the 'drive to work' fraternity to leave their cars at home and seek conveyance by bus. This would place an impossible strain on peak hour resources and the additional heavy surges of traffic would also be costly to accommodate. If the cars once left at home were used in the daytime instead of the bus, the diseconomies would be compounded with even more accentuated peaks. Financial stability calls for a levelling out of the peaks and it is extra traffic in the slacker periods when vehicles and staff are already available which is constantly sought.

To summarize, therefore, the case has been made for bus priorities. Cars delay buses and abstract their traffic but in urban areas some of that abstracted traffic would not be economic to carry anyway. In short, there are times when the bus needs preferential treatment over the car but only in very selective circumstances would it be wise to annihilate it. Looking at the overall transport picture, i.e. including also the highway input, there might be a case to accept the cost of a heavy peak on the buses as there could be compensation through the elimination of some of the expenditure on roads together with all the related problems. In this

Figure 6.1 Small vehicles when present in large numbers can be self congesting, particularly taxis which pick-up and set-down indiscriminantly and make U-turns at will, all in busy thoroughfares. This scene in Oxford Street, London, is indicative of the situation that can arise. It does suggest that politically bus fares should not be too high, otherwise when three or four people are travelling together there is the danger that the taxi will become cost effective and this, together with its added convenience, will exacerbate what are already very congested conditions.

case, however, there are as has been seen political reasons why this principle is not likely to be pushed too far.

At this stage it is worth considering exactly what is public and what is private transport, and there is a stage when distinction becomes blurred. Consider the following:

1. Private car.
2. Contract hired car.
3. Hired car with driver.
4. Taxi.
5. Car sharing, social car scheme or 'jitney'.
6. Demand responsive bus.
7. Bus.

Note: A 'jitney' is a slang term to describe a large taxi style vehicle which follows bus routes on an unscheduled basis and picks up passengers as required. The practice is prevalent in some urban centres overseas, various towns in the USA, Mexico City and Tel Aviv in Israel are examples. The nearest approach in the UK is a shared taxi, and they are particularly well organized, even on the 'jitney' style, in Belfast where they parallel bus routes.

At the extremities of the scale—(1) and (7)—there is no doubt in which camp they lie; (4)—(7) are all available for anybody who is on the spot and might wish to

Figure 6.2 With private transport limited to motorbikes and bicycles, public transport is in demand in Guangzhou (formerly Canton), one of the larger towns in the south of China. Both buses and trolleybuses are available, some of which are of the articulated variety. Here an articulated trolleybus is seen crossing the Zhongshan Road/Jiefang Road intersection in the commercial centre of Canton.

utilize their services but the writer does not accept that this is necessarily the definition of public transport whilst (3) is also often a freely available facility, and all except (1) represent services which are provided for the public at large to move around without the need to purchase a vehicle. Those in classifications (1) and (2) produce the same parking problems and those in (1)—(5) are all extravagant in road space whilst on the move. Once a taxi (4) has been engaged, the occupant is just as much a part of private transport as is the owner–driver or the passenger in a chauffeur-driven car. It is submitted that the borderline comes with the demand-responsive bus (dial-a-bus), a mini- or midi-bus carrying passengers within a defined area but in accordance with their specific requirements. Nevertheless, there is controversy on what can be regarded as public and and what as private transport just as there is no universal definition of a bus as was discussed in Chapter 2 in connection with bus priorities. The writer suggests that highway and planning authorities should for their purposes classify the taxi, in fact everything from (1) to (5) as private transport and formulate their proposals accordingly. The only real justification that the author can see for the inclusion of the taxi in the public transport sector apart from the absence of parking problems is when it is running as a PSV under a special restricted operator's licence, or when it assumes the role of a feeder to long-distance transport. In the knowledge that taxis are available at the extremities of the journey a person might be willing to travel by public transport throughout. In the absence of such a facility he could well elect to go all the way by car.

Operational planning

Services provided

It has been said that operational planning is very much a borderline issue between the planning process and commercial practices. The standard of service provided and the criteria for service provision which is to be considered shortly certainly reflects commercial policy. Furthermore, the operating department cannot be divorced from this issue as that is where responsibility lies for implementing the proposals and the chances are that it is the operating manager, being the employing officer, who will have to agree the resultant time and duty schedules with his platform staff. Nevertheless, that is an organizational problem. For this purpose, here is a convenient point at which to consider shorter term planning which must be preceded by a brief review of the types of services provided.

To produce another order of progression, the following shows the different groups of services which collectively constitute a road passenger transport network:

1. Local town services.
2. Special works and school services.
3. Orbital services.
4. Rural services.
5. Inter-urban services.
6. Medium distance limited stop services.
7. Long-distance express services.

Between them they cater for many different types of traffic but the distinctions are more apparent in some areas than in others. A small town might not even be large enough to support separate local services, what short-distance traffic there is being catered for by inter-urban services. On the other hand, a very large urban (plus suburban) agglomeration could produce some long and complex local routes and the inter-urban facilities, i.e. facilities to neighbouring urban areas, probably on the other side of a tract of open country, become at least limited stop but often closer to the long-distance express category.

Although even a small pocket of population might support an odd bus running around locally, it is not until a built-up area reaches upwards of, say, 40–50 000 people that a discernible network of town services begins to emerge. At this stage, the local system tends to become more self-contained (although not necessarily under separate management) and passengers become selective between the short- and the longer distance services. This distribution of traffic is often encouraged by protective minimum fares, at least in the out-town direction on the inter-urban (trunk) routes, a practice that is considered further in Chapter 7. Town services may be: radial (terminating at the centre and proceeding outwards like the spokes of a wheel); cross-town (linking places on the opposite extremities of the built-up area but routed via the centre); and orbital (circular or part-circular services without touching the centre). Superimposed on these regular services are likely to be special facilities for works and schools which do not conform to the regular pattern and which run in accordance with specific rather than general requirements.

Cross-town routes have particular relevance when discussing urban transport. They are advantageous compared with separate services which radiate out from the centre in that they provide a useful facility for people who wish to travel either within but across the central zone or from the outer suburbs through to the other side, even if only for a short distance. In other words, it becomes possible to have a direct bus between many more pairs of points, thereby providing a more attractive and useful service. Operationally there are disadvantages as will be considered in Chapter 10 where it will be seen that for control purposes there is an advantage in routes that do turn in the centre. A compromise would be to run only a short distance to the opposite boundary of the central zone; an idea that the writer does not support.

Consider the diagrams in *Figure 6.3* showing services converging at a town centre from six separate neighbourhoods. In (i) all turn at the centre, in (ii) they are linked to run across the town and in (iii) they are projected to give a limited cross-centre facility. The advantages and disadvantages are:

1. In the case of example (iii) additional mileage is incurred in the most heavily congested part of the town and this is likely to be unacceptable on the grounds of traffic congestion, particularly as the resultant facilities would be inferior to that provided by example (ii).
2. The extra mileage of (iii) would involve additional schedule costs in the form of vehicles and staff, again with inferior facilities compared with (ii). On the other hand, example (ii) saves stand time in the centre which is 'dead' time and can, therefore, only reduce schedule costs, not only compared with (iii) but also with (i) as well.
3. Example (iii) does not remove the disadvantage of (i) that standing space must be found in the busy central area where space is likely to be scarce anyway. Example (ii) requires no such facility.

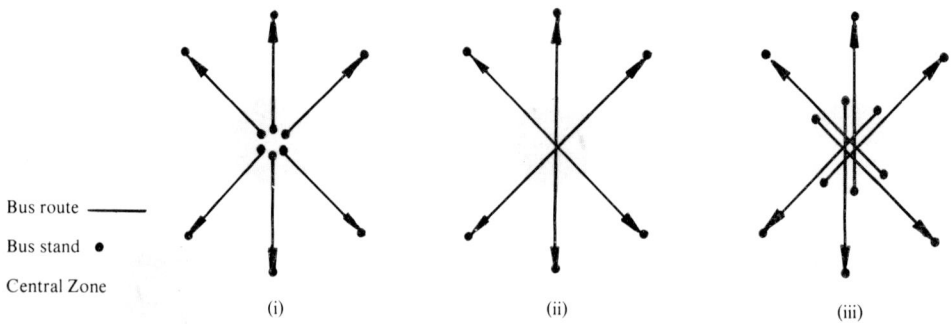

Bus route ——
Bus stand ●
Central Zone

(i)   (ii)   (iii)

Figure 6.3 Alternative types of local town services.

Certainly for local services in a closely knit urban area, cross-town services provide a useful facility and have much to commend them.

A rural service is one that is usually regarded as radiating outwards from an urban centre into the surrounding countryside to serve various villages and hamlets. Rural communities may also be served by the main trunk inter-urban routes depending on geography and whether a village happens to be conveniently located for this purpose. It is quite usual for the trunk routes to make limited deviations for this purpose but there needs to be a balance between the demands of the through and the intermediate riders. Other devices for serving sparsely populated areas take the form of postal buses and other vehicles designed for the carriage of both goods and passengers, community buses, etc. These different types of operation are considered later.

En route diversions of trunk routes to serve what would otherwise be isolated rural communities are more likely to be tolerated if through traffic is also catered for by a faster parallel limited stop service using a direct route. Urban limited stop services are also not unknown, being designed to cater for blocks of traffic which regularly travel between given pairs of points. Not only is a faster journey time more attractive to passengers, it is also more economical in terms of vehicles and staff if more trips can be worked in the same overall time. This is particularly valuable in the peaks when any saving of vehicles and crews has a marked effect on total operating costs. In practice, however, there are also disadvantages which again is a matter for Chapter 7.

The final classification, being the express services or, in other words, the coach business, caters for the longer distance rider, usually on a pre-booked basis, with vehicles expected to have a higher standard of comfort. Even here, some services are faster than others and it is those routes that utilize the motorway network that have the greatest premium on speed.

Criteria for service provision

The criteria that determine what, where and how much bus service will be provided are rapidly changing. Remember what was said in Chapter 1. Transport was pioneered by private enterprise. Speculative bus and railway managements set up in business and earned their livelihood by providing facilities that the people needed. They created demands and they met demands. The more responsible elements within the bus industry accepted that they were providing a service which was essential to the new-found life of the community and they offered comprehensive facilities within what they had come to recognize as their operating territories. Some routes were profitable, others were not, but overall there was a financial surplus. The criteria for service provision was clear; the undertaking as a whole had to pay its way. Within this overall constraint maximum facilities were provided, distributed according to need whilst endeavouring to ensure that nobody was unreasonably isolated. Up until the 1950s it was possible to give a service by allowing these economic forces of supply and demand to follow their course. Traffic managers were able to use their discretion and everybody could be satisfied as much as the public ever can be satisfied on matters of this kind. But times have changed. Although there are now many routes that cannot be run on a commercial basis, there are not enough good routes with which they can be counterbalanced. If therefore they are deemed to be meeting a social need they have to be subsidized but once this happens, then gone is the economic indicator and gone also is the long-established criteria for service provision. However, what is to take the place of judgement by commercial viability remains a very big but unanswered question. The problem is not as much one for the operator as for the third party which provides the subsidy and which in Great Britain is passenger transport executives and county councils. The operator, regardless of the form of ownership, must still pay his way and in the absence of subsidies, unprofitable routes just have to be withdrawn. But the elected representatives who spend public money to support public transport require some sort of measure to determine the level of service which should be provided. It is to this body of people that the criteria for service provision has particular interest.

If some bus services are to be partially paid for out of rates and taxes then those ratepayers and taxpayers resident in the more sparsely populated areas will not respond kindly to a refusal to provide a service on the grounds that there will not be a sufficient number of users to justify it. The theoreticians will no doubt seek a formula to determine whether any particular bus service should be provided but the production of such a formula produces a host of imponderables. Even so, the need for some sort of guidance on service provision when one side of the equation (i.e. revenue) is no longer an adequate measure must, nevertheless, be acknowledged.

A basic criterion is, of course, demand, but if the only consideration is numbers of passengers then the more thinly populated areas where loadings could never be heavy would not qualify for a service. Once a facility is instituted, however, demand, if only by trial and error, can set the frequency but only down to a certain level, below which the timetable could become too unattractive to be worthwhile. Sometimes it is not the individual service that is for consideration but the route network and its density, particularly in urban areas. It must then be decided, for example—if the overall vehicle provision and hence the quantum of service is set—whether a large number of different roads within a residential district should be covered by relatively infrequent services or whether a lesser number of roads should have much higher frequency services.

All of this indicates a need for some pre-determined standards. Consider the following parameters:

1. Distance which a person may be expected to walk to a bus stop.
2. Minimum frequency.
3. Minimum load factor.
4. Length of wait if first available bus has no accommodation.

If (1), (2), (3) and (4) could be quantified then surely at least some standards will have been set and hence progress made towards determining criteria for service provision. The evaluation of these factors, however, can only be subjective as different people will have different interpretations on what might be regarded as reasonable. In 1973 the British government issued guidelines (*Bus Operation in Residential and Industrial Areas*) which included one of these aspects. It was suggested that housing estates should be designed so that the maximum walking distance to a bus stop is 400 m which represents a walking time of about 5 minutes.

It is not sufficient, however, just to quantify these suggested four component parts as they have a bearing on each other, one can influence another and furthermore, standards may have to vary according to circumstances. The distance to walk to a bus might be acceptably (and usually has to be) longer in the country than in town or perhaps longer if the terrain is flat but not so far if it is very hilly and a higher load factor might be expected in the peaks than at midday or in the evening. Items (1) and (2) throw back to network densities already mentioned. Minimum acceptable frequencies certainly vary between urban and rural areas. The town dweller is not timetable conscious, at least for local journeys. He wants only to walk to the bus stop and wait for one to come. He does not want to walk very far and he does not want to wait very long and this means for the first vehicle which has available accommodation. The writer is of the opinion that the suggested maximum 400 m walk could prove over-generous in application even in urban areas as it might produce a very dense network, in which case, either frequencies or load factors would fall below acceptable levels.

Figure 6.4 shows a hypothetical road layout in a housing estate with alternative possible bus routes. Option (i) provides for maximum coverage; option (ii) shows maximum concentration on a centre spine road. What is an acceptable load factor has not yet been considered but for the time being, suppose that whatever it is, the traffic generated by the local residents is sufficient to support six buses per hour or, in other words, a 10-minute headway on the one route as shown in option (ii). If alternative (i) was adopted, the resources would be fragmented and instead of a 10-minute headway on one route there would be three separate routes each with a 30-minute frequency. In this case, it is certainly true that some people would not have to walk as far to and from the bus but it is submitted that the resultant frequencies could be unattractive, passengers would have to be timetable conscious and in the event of late running or cancellations stop selection would become a matter of chance and intending passengers might see a bus pass, perhaps only a few yards away, but not at the point where they are standing. There could also be selective inadequacies (for example, waiting for the next bus because it goes nearer to home and then there is no room on it) and timetables could give rise to complaints (such as, who is to be favoured with the last bus out of town).

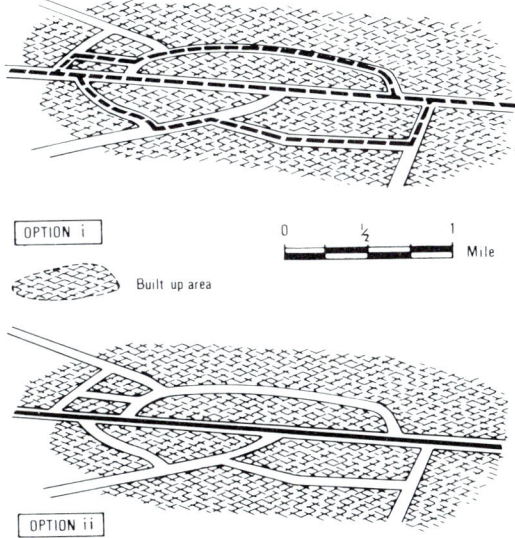

OPTION i

0   ½   1
Mile

Built up area

OPTION ii

Figure 6.4 A hypothetical road layout in a housing estate with alternative bus routes. Every household would be within approximately 1/4 mile (½ km) of a bus in option (i) and within about ½ mile (1 km) in option (ii), but the frequency of the service in option (ii) would be three times that of those in option (i).

All of this suggests that the writer is somewhat critical of those systems that cover as many roads as possible with a lot of relatively low frequency services. But there is, nevertheless, a limit on how far one can go the other way; the limit being the distance that a passenger might be expected to walk to the bus. And whilst on the subject of frequencies, try to have a headway with timings that are repetitive each hour, e.g. every 10, 15 or 20 minutes. Headways such as 13, 18, 22 minutes, etc. never did anybody any good. Nobody can remember when the bus is coming.

Consider now factor (2), the minimum acceptable frequency, which is allied to but nevertheless distinct from factor (4) which is what might be regarded as an acceptable wait for the first bus with available accommodation. Common with factors (1) and (3), the standards adopted are bound to be influenced by the density of population in the area concerned but assume for the moment that the services in mind are running through high-density residential districts. The question is, how frequent should the buses run to qualify as an acceptable facility; that is, a service that is convenient to use without pre-planning? At busy periods, frequency is not the only consideration; what is more important is how long a person must wait before he is able to board. This comes back to the distinction between peak and off-peak periods. As far as the all-day service is concerned, if an acceptable standard is to be maintained then the frequency should not fall below a certain minimum even if, arithmetically, all passengers could be accommodated with a wider headway. It is in the peaks when additional buses must be provided and when load factors are acceptably higher that the maximum wait becomes critical and sets yet another standard.

There remains to consider factor (3), the minimum number of people that should be on a bus, below which its justification becomes a matter of doubt. Once again, there is a distinction between peak and off-peak periods but there are further complications. The normal traffic pattern of an urban bus service which radiates out from a town centre is a general pick-up of passengers progressively through the central zone, a maximum point not far beyond the periphery of the centre and a gradual set-down right through to the outer terminal. It would seem that the place to measure loadings is at the maximum traffic point but even this will not give the complete answer as demand could justify only some of the runnings proceeding through to the extremity of the route with others turning short. Another feature is that some journeys will be popular; others might be very lightly used, but if they were not operated the minimum frequency criterion would not be met. Loadings will, therefore, probably need to be averaged out over all journeys before a satisfactory conclusion can be reached.

This, then, is the more practical background to setting the criteria for service provision. Little of what has been said so far, however, will assist those responsible for spending public money in deciding just what sort of a service they should support. This applies particularly in those countries where government policy is to subsidize networks as opposed to individual services and also where there is power to fix fares as well as services and their frequencies. Because of this, what follows now has less relevance in Great Britain. It must be read in the context of the network principle and as a background to systems planning. As far as fares are concerned, this section is more appropriate for readers in those parts of the world where public transport is treated as a network not only for planning but for finance purposes as well rather than looking at individual services and subsidizing only those that cannot be provided commercially. The question of fares is something that also impinges on Chapters 7 and 11 which deal with the commercial aspects of rate fixing and the various methods of determining subsidies respectively. The three factors (standard of service, amount of subsidy and fares) are inter-dependent and their respective values cannot be set in isolation. More is said about this in Chapter 11. For the moment, remember that those responsible for meeting the bill can only get what they pay for. They have, therefore, to balance what they want against what they are prepared to pay and to do this they must determine their own criteria according to needs and preferences. But still the big question remains—how to quantify those needs and preferences.

Many existing bus networks are still much as they were built up and even if new criteria were introduced it would not always be easy to implement as people are creatures of habit and seldom take kindly to new arrangements. This in itself is a lesson for operators. Do not attempt to make changes without good reason—

passengers are not likely to be impressed. Service revisions in the interests of economy, efficiency or to meet changing demands or public requests are one thing. But playing around with routes and route numbers just to comply with a new philosophy dreamt up by an enthusiastic traffic development officer to keep the system and the records nice and tidy is quite another. But this is digressing. To get back to the point, thoughts on criteria for service provision are most likely to be put into practice where a rural area is intensively developed and there comes into being a large new housing estate or a new town to be served for the first time. Under these circumstances it is appropriate that there should be some criteria for service provision.

Suppose now that an attempt is made to quantify the suggested factors (1)–(4). Begin with some arbitrary price tags which look about right. It has already been suggested that there will have to be different standards for urban and rural areas. For a working example, therefore, concentrate on urban areas (suburban would be a better term as that is where most people live) which could be defined as those that have a population density of, say, not less than 10 000 per square mile. For territory of this type, on weekdays (the situation is likely to be different on Sundays) the following standards might be reasonable:

1. Half a mile to walk to a bus.
2. Minimum regular frequency not less than every 12 minutes.
3. Minimum load factor 25% increased to 95% in the peaks if there is more than a 12-minute service.
4. An actual wait in the peaks of up to 10 minutes if and after the first bus has departed full. (This assumes that buses are on time and are not delayed by traffic and are 'bunching'.)

These are suggestions only. The next step is to see whether they are practical in application. Implementation on these lines could result in over-provision and excessive cost and it would be helpful to have an overriding governing factor. One possibility lies in total population figures. In Great Britain in 1983 a population of some 54.8 million was served by about 45 000 buses which averages out over the country as a whole at about one bus for every 1200 people. It is accepted that this is an arbitrary figure interpreted from information drawn from *Transport Statistics* (HMSO, London). It is based on total vehicles in the public sector plus 20% of vehicles in the private sector or 65% of the total bus and coach figure. It is, therefore, only a guide but it is a good guide. As a matter of interest, on the same basis of calculation, of a total of 21 European countries including Great Britain and 4 in the eastern bloc the figure becomes 1 bus for every 1100 people which is reasonable as some of the countries involved have a lower than average level of car ownership. Those concerned will wish to fix their own levels and demand will in any case be influenced by fare scales and by car ownership, both of which vary from area to area. Even so, buses per unit of population does give a basis on which to start. If this figure, whatever it might be, but for the present 1200 is recommended, becomes a fifth dimension (5) superimposed on (1)–(4) above, the criteria would then become sufficient to develop a realistic exercise. In other words, services meeting the criteria laid down in (1) to (4) could be designed within the overall constraint of (5). At the first attempt things will probably not work out that way and one or more of the specifications will have to be relaxed, being more buses or lower standards, determined, as has already been indicated, according to local circumstances and preferences. It must be reiterated, however, that a network exercise such as this is only feasible when planning for a new town or the like although the standards as determined should be suitable for application when changes are required within established systems.

Route planning

Route planning was partially covered by the previous subsection which dealt with the criteria for service provision and where the difficulties involved in keeping rigidly to a pre-determined standard were seen. The subject will be considered here not from the angle of placing everybody within a short walk of a bus but planning a route which for the passengers achieves maximum benefit for the greatest number of people and for the operator attracts as many people as possible on to the bus.

Consider again the types of service provided as listed (1)–(7) earlier in this chapter. All are designed with specific traffic flows in mind. Most services follow a fairly progressive route between a pair of terminal points although this is not essential. What is important is that in taking people where they want to go, too many other passengers are not involved in riding on a bus which follows an unnecessarily circuitous route which is both irritating and time consuming. Routes can, however, be of the devious kind as, for example, those that follow the course of an arc, if there are alternative direct facilities for through passengers who are not therefore required to travel the long way round. Other services may follow a circular route or adopt loop workings at terminals. It was noted earlier that a full service is not always required right through to the end of the journey. This point is often met by the introduction of bifurcations at the outer ends where routes split in the form of a fish-tail giving a choice of less frequent services to different places. These different route patterns are considered in greater detail in Chapter 8.

Except for the orbital and special services, most routes are likely to penetrate the centre of at least one town and this can perhaps be regarded as the key to route planning. Consider the places to which most people want to go: shops, commercial centres, places of employment, places of recreation, etc., or in other words, the traffic magnets. Remember also the role of the bus as a feeder to train. But operators must not be too concerned about any thoughts that might emanate from the planning arena, as 15 years ago road/rail co-ordination and the systems concept was in Great Britain being hailed by some almost as the panacea for all transport ills. Certainly the bus is an essential and effective feeder to rail but it also has its own established traffics and large numbers of passengers should not be inconvenienced if only an occasional person wishes to transfer to a train. At times there is a case to divert a route via the station but such consideration can be, like the computer analysis system, very much a desk exercise, the findings of which are not, in the event, always substantiated by passenger use. Operators need to be circumspect when introducing devious routes for special purposes. Sometimes occasional journeys are so diverted to serve railway stations, works or schools where there is an established and heavy demand, which is quite acceptable, but the practice can become confusing to both passengers and staff if taken too far. Even so, if routes do pass a railway station where there is a transfer movement, try to make reasonable connections if at all possible. It will save a lot of public irritation and complaint. But with all of the other factors it must be accepted that trains must sometimes come at the bottom of the priority list.

Next consider the traffic affinity between major centres. There is likely to be a movement to and from neighbouring towns, and the resultant inter-urban services can often perform a dual role by catering for both intermediate and through riders. This introduces an important concept in route planning. It has already been said that radial services pick up in the centre and then gradually set down in the environs with perhaps only a very few people riding right through to the end of the journey. Even if the bus started with a full load, the chances of seats becoming vacant on the way and not being refilled are virtually certain. A similar process takes place in reverse when travelling towards town. The routes with traffic magnets only at one end must have a 'thin end' at the other with seldom the chance of good loadings all the way. On the contrary, services that have traffic magnets at each end are more likely to start picking up again as the first batch of passengers begins to alight. To that extent, therefore, inter-urban services have a natural advantage in terms of passenger loadings and they are often the mainstay of many of the provincial networks. If, therefore, an operator is faced with the need for a new route with a thin end—look beyond and see what is over the horizon. Try to stimulate a two-way movement. This is a part of traffic development.

Another important aspect of route planning is any physical difficulties such as weight restrictions in the form of sub-standard roads or overbridges, height limitations caused by underbridges, trees, etc., narrow or tortuous roads or any other factor that might preclude the operation of a standard-type bus. It also pays to ensure that the roads concerned have been adopted by the local highway authority. If they have not it is politic to obtain an indemnity from the owner (probably a private developer) against any damage to the surface which buses might cause before a service is inaugurated. A recent and more deliberate obstruction to buses and one to which reference was made in Chapter 2 is the now-fashionable concept of segregating pedestrians from vehicular traffic or, in other words, pedestrianization. It was said that it might be very nice for shoppers to wander in a traffic-free environment decorated with ornamental street furniture but those same people do not take kindly to walking further to the bus stop with heavy baskets. Neither do through riders appreciate a twisting, longer and more costly route if that is what it means in order to avoid a closed street. Certainly the bus can be a large vehicle, and inevitably there are limitations on where it can run; but the artificial restriction of pedestrianization is something that could be avoided. There are numerous examples where shopping streets are made available and restricted to buses only and the Government circular *Bus Operation in Residential and Industrial Areas* indicates that British official policy is quite open to such an arrangement. It is one way of ensuring that the natural advantages of the bus are not lost. It is not surprising, therefore, that bus managements press for an extension of this practice when proposals for pedestrianization are produced which involve serious disturbance to established routes without any satisfactory alternatives.

Stops and stands are also important issues to be determined and here the operator is to some extent in the hands of the local highway authority. The subject was considered in Chapter 2. In areas of new development, bus stop sites are often predetermined, hopefully after consultation with bus managements, but generally there is a common objective by all concerned which is for vehicles to stop in the most convenient places for passengers subject to physical considerations. Once again, however, there seems to be a desire by planning authorities backed by government policy to segregate pedestrians from vehicular traffic as witness the networks of footpaths which appear in some of the newly developed housing estates. Whilst it is no problem for the bus operator to stop at points suitable for these footpaths and what happens to passengers after they have alighted is not his responsibility, the writer does consider it unfortunate that such policies are being pursued which could in due course lead to requests from passengers for buses to stop elsewhere. Touching now on Chapter 12, it is a fact of life that violence, robbery and other undesirable behaviour is increasing and this should be recognized. Many women are now nervous of using narrow and lonely footpaths and it is often unsafe to do so. To avoid this, some pedestrians take unauthorized routes which sometimes involve walking along and crossing roads, including those that are used by buses, which are not designed for that purpose. This is not a satisfactory arrangement.

It is the opinion of the author that unless applied very selectively, segregation of foot and vehicular traffic in whatever type of area—be it commercial, residential or industrial—will, in the long run and for various reasons, make no net improvement to either convenience or personal safety and as a matter of general policy should be reconsidered.

These, then, are the principles that need to be observed in route planning. Clearly, the operator is not the sole arbiter of where his buses will run. Neither can he expect to be, as he is only one of many users of a shared way and he is not the highway authority. But there are ways in which planning authorities could assist. Of particular importance is the fundamental requirement that buses should be afforded proper penetration into commercial, industrial and residential areas and such access should not be prejudiced by traffic management or pedestrianization schemes. The priorities must be right and this applies in more senses than one.

Special services

The types of services discussed so far are those that provide continuous all-day facilities for general purposes and cater for the predominant traffic flows. Special services cater for specific traffics which require something different to what the basic network provides. They are introduced when there is sufficient demand to warrant the provision of buses solely for this purpose and the routes either serve places which do not otherwise have a bus or they permit a through journey to be made which otherwise could be undertaken only by changing vehicles. Routes of this type run mostly to factories and schools.

Rural services

The rural services are most in need of outside assistance, and the criteria for service provision has a particular application for this type of operation. The bodies that meet the deficits (in Great Britain the passenger transport executives and county councils) must again determine standards but unless an astronomical amount of money is to be spent in moving empty seats along country lanes then, whatever the locals might think, very different standards have to be set compared with what might be applied in urban areas. In rural districts the criteria for service provision is much more directly related to specific needs and the degree of hardship which would arise if no service at all was provided. Country dwellers (at least those without private transport) have long since adjusted their way of life around occasional bus journeys which might run only once or twice a week although even this limited provision is likely to be costly.

Particularly apposite to rural services is the reference to thin ends made earlier in this chapter. A route which on leaving town gets into the country, serves a few hamlets and finishes up on the edge of a field never had much chance of commercial viability, even if it did run only on market days and bank holidays. Remember what was said in respect of inter-urban services. They have infinitely better opportunities and the rural areas which are located astride or close to such routes can be served much more economically. The places that lie away from these main arteries pose the problem, and the ways and means of serving these otherwise isolated rural communities will be discussed.

The particular difficulties associated with the provision of services for rural areas arise from the paucity of the population which means that demand can never be consistently good. Even if a work or shopping bus might carry some people there is unlikely to be a demand sufficient to make proper use of vehicles and staff throughout the day. Traffic cannot easily be spread as workers, shoppers and schoolchildren as groups, village by village, are all likely to require transport at about the same time. The problem of the peak is just as real in the country as it is in the town.

If rural services are to be provided, then once again it must be decided what can be regarded as reasonable facilities. Works traffic will need to be catered for five days per week and shoppers perhaps twice a week, say market day and Saturday. Schoolchildren create a problem but one which must be shared if not borne by local education authorities. The need for maximum economy in operation is paramount for work of this kind and various methods of achieving greater efficiency are often advocated although they are not always practicable.

The seemingly obvious step of eliminating the conductor and introducing one-man operation has in all probability long since been done. Even so, an odd journey might sometimes fit into a space in the crew schedule (assuming there is a crew schedule) and if so there would be every justification to work it this way. The next consideration is the timetable and the route. To get as much work as possible out of one bus and driver some staggering might be necessary with the result that the times will not be ideal for everybody but there is a limit as to how much can be done. There is, however, likely to be a greater tolerance in the country areas of circuitous routes designed to serve as many villages as possible on a single journey. If the alternative is nothing at all these passengers might well accept a longer ride if in the end they are taken to where they want to go. Perhaps the greatest clamour for economy lies in the type of vehicle which is used on country routes, that is if the criticism levelled at operators when double-deck buses are seen working on rural services carrying negligible traffic is anything to go by. But this introduces the subject of mini- and midi-buses which are becoming so fashionable not only amongst passengers but with operators as well that these types of vehicles now warrant a separate sub-heading.

Mini- and midi-buses

Whilst many passengers and armchair critics have over the years suggested the use of small buses as a more appropriate vehicle for lightly trafficked routes, until recently the professionals have resisted this type of operation for very good reasons. Certainly, a 12-seater minibus is cheaper to buy and will use less fuel, remembering always that the smaller van-type vehicle will have a shorter working life than a larger conventional type bus. But the real test is adequacy in terms of capacity. Certainly for most of the time loadings could be depressingly low but if at some point in the working day there is a sudden burst of traffic, perhaps on a school journey or at a factory break, then all of the accommodation of the large bus might be taken up, albeit for only a short distance. Immediately this happens the use of the large bus is justified. It would be uneconomic to use it only for such sporadic occasions and then substitute a smaller vehicle at other times. It would be equally uneconomic to keep the smaller bus and duplicate at times of heavy demand. The cheapest way is to keep the one bigger bus and use it all of the time. Having said that, there is nevertheless a place for mini- and midi-buses, and that place comes for example in cases where there is no heavy influx of traffic as described and when, for physical reasons, a larger vehicle cannot be used.

To make it easier for small vehicles to be used as service buses the British government did even before de-regulation relax certain of the licensing regulations. Details of the various ways in which small buses may be operated without the need to conform to the full PSV licensing procedure are contained in Chapter 5. One outcome is the community bus, the inauguration of which requires local initiative and the availability of volunteer drivers; but where this is possible, otherwise isolated communities can have a service. Another practice sometimes adopted is the use of dual-purpose vehicles carrying passengers on a parcels service. One stage further and there is the post bus whereby vehicles used for the delivery of mail, which must run in any case, are also used for the conveyance of passengers. The system is not widespread as so often the delivery routes are too circuitous even for a rural bus and the Post Office must let mail take precedence over the needs of passengers, which also means that times might not be the most convenient. Nevertheless, there are places where such a system is practicable, in which case a useful facility can be provided.

But the situation in Great Britain, aided and abetted by de-regulation, is now approaching a minibus mania. With comparative freedom of entry into the bus business, both established operators and newcomers are weighing in with fleets of minibuses for use in selected urban and suburban areas. In many cases they are replacing larger buses and at the same time giving a more frequent service and better penetration into residential estates. Whilst it is accepted that these are attractive features, with such small maximum payloads the economics must be doubtful. On the other hand, if with their lower initial costs and running costs they are sufficiently attractive to enable a bus service to be maintained at reasonable fares (or, if subsidized, with minimum strain on the public purse) then the principle is to be applauded.

There are circumstances when the midi-bus could be a less costly form of operation. Chapter 4 indicated that the bus-driving fraternity is a part of well-organized labour with wage agreements (including penalty payments, etc.) and agreed conditions of service which are expensive to the employer. At the same time the standard of service which the platform staff give in return sometimes leaves something to be desired. Midi-bus drivers need not necessarily be drawn from the ranks of the conventional busmen, they do not have to share the established wage rates and conditions and they might be stronger for service. However, the midi-bus timetables might well not cater for all of the traffic all of the time. There might not be any early-morning or late-evening journeys or a service on Sundays when traffic is light. Penalty payments to staff would not therefore apply anyway. If only a limited clientele is sought—such as daytime shoppers and those such as housewives who by using the service could avoid their need for a second car—then, with drivers on lower basic rates with no frills other than a guaranteed wage, the project could be viable.

Such facilities might be highly convenient for those for whom they are intended but in no way would they be a substitute for the service which until now has been a characteristic of the bus and on which the life of the community has relied. The writer still maintains that the midi-bus is not the ideal vehicle for moving the masses, and if small buses are allowed to proliferate in busy urban centres they will become self-congesting. Gone then will be much of the advantage of the bus in terms of economy of road space and hence its valuable contribution to traffic fluidity. The writer would like to think that the large-capacity double-deck bus will continue to be used on those routes where passenger demand is sufficient to justify an acceptable frequency and that the minibus does not become another panacea for all public transport ills.

Modal capacities

One further feature that remains to be considered as part of the planning process is modal capacities. Although this is a book on bus and coach operation, the point has already been made that public transport planning involves networks, and networks include not only buses but also fixed-track systems as well and this goes beyond street trams and trolleybuses. The bus may be only a contribution to a planned network, albeit an important one, and in considering its contribution it is necessary to have some idea of the potentials of each of the modes. In order, therefore, to put some measure of relativity on the bus, as far as this particular topic is concerned, reference will be made to the entire spectrum of urban public passenger transport. But like setting down criteria for service provision, it is virtually impossible by any rule-of-thumb method to determine maximum capacities in terms of passengers per hour on any one type of system. Whatever the declared maximum there is usually room for one more. Another passenger could crush into a railway coach; another bus could find its place on the public highway. What follows, therefore, constitutes generalized observations more than scientific fact based on formulas compiled to interpret specific situations. The thoughts are presented only to give a measure of perspective and must be treated accordingly.

Buses and trolleybuses

Although technically different, excluding the extra-large capacity double-deck buses, buses and trolleybuses have similar characteristics in so far as their passenger carrying ability is concerned. Remember that buses share the public highway with all other vehicles, passenger and goods, that might care to use it. The amount of traffic that can be moved by a conventional bus service is not, therefore, determined by the qualities of public transport as such but by the highway on which it runs. Highway capacities are governed by such things as width of road and number of traffic lanes, general speed of traffic and obstructions to progress such as conflicting vehicle movements, traffic lights, pedestrian crossings, parked vehicles and the like. If a busy shopping street is compared with a motorway the differences become apparent. It goes without saying that the capacity that a bus service can provide is governed by the size of the vehicle and the frequency. As far as vehicles are concerned, the capacity of a conventional type bus is finite, that is, it is limited to the number of seats plus a few standing which can easily be controlled. For a standard double-deck this is usually about 80 but large double-deck or articulated crush loading vehicles can carry more than this. To ascertain what is the maximum capacity that such a service can provide it is necessary to know how many vehicles can actually use the road in question and that is the figure that is elastic and depends on circumstances. If, for example, with standard double-decks there was a 30-second headway or 120 per hour (and that is a lot of buses) then nearly 10 000 people could be moved in that hour providing they were evenly spread as any peak surges within that hour could not be accommodated. Apart from highway capacities, the provision of stops and facilities for queueing could also become a serious problem. A service of this level would be better with a segregated bus lane. If this in turn provided an exclusive uninterrupted flow—i.e. grade separated junctions, etc.—and if such a facility was provided for the full length of the route then it gets into the light rapid transit class (LRT does not have to be of the fixed track variety). The principle can be taken one stage further by the use of large double-deck or articulated buses which can accommodate up to about 150 or 160 people (under crush loading conditions) and, like the 80-seater double deck, still with just a one-man driver. This puts the theoretical potential capacity up to about 18 000 people per hour. This figure, however, like the previous one represents the extreme; they are not likely to be reached in practice and in the case of the articulated bus would at the same time

Figure 6.5 An example of the 'large double-deck', in this instance a three-axle Leyland Olympian bus of Kowloon Motor Bus Company seen in Chatham Road, Kowloon (Hong Kong) on Route 5 proceeding from Choi Nung to Star Ferry. This vehicle has a total capacity for 164 passengers (74 on upper deck and 30 plus 60 standing on the lower deck). It is one-man operated with the farebox type of fare collection with a flat fare and no change given. Whilst the flat fare system is general throughout Hong Kong, Kowloon and the New Territories, the actual fare varies route by route according to its length.

produce a very uncomfortable way of travel. Again the traffic must be evenly spread although over a complete hour this is not likely to happen. There is usually a peak within a peak and the crucial factor is more what can be moved within the maximum quarter hour. To be realistic, in any one hour some capacity is invariably wasted and a sustained 30 second headway without some form of delay is super-optimistic. A practical figure for hourly capacities attainable, certainly on the normal public highway, might be more in the region of, say, 5000 for standard double decks and 7000 for large double-deck or articulated buses (or about 1250 for minibuses!). This is substantially less than the theoretical maximum quoted but here there might be a little more room to accommodate short additional bursts of traffic. Furthermore, with the one-man articulated bus, fare collection problems arise. On the conventional double-deck the driver is either able to collect fares or check tickets in the way which is to be described in Chapter 9. Not so with the articulated bus if passengers board at more than one entrance and this is a feature that needs to be considered further.

Trams

A street tramway is perfectly feasible as is proved in a number of heavily trafficked urban areas in Europe and North America. Although the tram is at a disadvantage compared with the bus in terms of cost, it can have a greater capacity. Whilst the articulated tram, like its bus counterpart, can carry up to about 150 or 160 people, albeit in discomfort, the double-deck tram of Blackpool Transport Services Ltd. (*see Figure 3.37*) has 100 seats. Together with a permitted 24 standing (which could probably be increased if necessary) its potential is not far short of that of the articulated vehicle but offers relative comfort for the majority to go with it. If the track is on a mainly segregated right of way with vehicle conflict only at controlled crossings and possibly on other short stretches where lack of space precludes any other arrangement, there would seem to be no reason why such trams should not be coupled in pairs with one driver. A double unit of this type running every 30 seconds would give a theoretical hourly capacity of about 30 000 people. However, like the buses, a regular 30-second service, even on a partially segregated system, is unlikely to be attained. With such fine precision, a slightly extended wait at a stop whilst passengers are boarding and alighting or even at traffic lights would result in a block back from which it is difficult to recover and would lead to yet wider gaps in the service. But based on a 60-second headway the theoretical capacity could still be 15 000 per hour and if this was accompanied by complete grade separation in the form of light rapid transit the figure becomes yet more realistic.

Further reference to the capacity of trams as well as buses and trolleybuses is contained in Chapter 11.

Heavy rapid transit

To avoid getting too far beyond the scope of this book it is sufficient to say here that a heavy rapid transit system, completely segregated and grade separated, represents the ultimate in mass transit. The movement of trains is governed by a signalling system, generally automatic, and by judicious spacing of block lengths, 7–10-car trains can travel at speed between stations say a mile apart or even less with down to about a 90-second interval between them. A system such as this can provide for about 30 000 passengers per hour but a feature of heavy rail rapid transit is that it does have an overload capacity and hence the ability to meet sporadic heavy surges of traffic and the equivalent of 60 000 passengers per hour for short periods becomes physically possible and is certainly not unknown. The fare collection problems of high-capacity buses and trams do not arise as with purpose-built stations, controlled entry and exit can be enforced. This does, of course, sacrifice the casual but more frequent stops which are convenient to passengers in terms of length of walk to board the vehicle, hence the need for systems of this type to be supported by feeder facilities.

Statistics

Statistics of various kinds are required by all branches of management in the daily conduct of the business. The engineer will want to know, for example, how many miles his buses will run for each gallon of fuel, how frequently breakdowns occur, how many miles are lost due to engineering causes, etc. Similarly the operating manager will seek information on miles lost through staff and traffic reasons, etc. All of this information is readily obtainable. Those responsible for service development require information on the number of passengers carried and financial viability, route by route, as it is the information produced by the examination of the trends of these figures when comparing one period with another which is the first indicator that something might need attention. Although details of passenger loadings are not always readily available, information regarding cash taken by conductors and one-man drivers is and the total divided by the mileage, service by service, produces statistical data in terms of receipts per mile (RPM). However, whilst at one time this information was a valuable tool for short-term traffic planning, with the increasing use of season tickets and the like it is becoming useless.

Whilst a blanket subsidy to maintain services and hold down fares will affect revenue collected by platform staff and hence produce lower RPM figures, for statistical purposes this is not serious if such revenue support is applied evenly across the system and a common albeit cheaper scale is applied to all passengers. For various reasons, however, which are partly political and partly operational, this is now tending not to be the case. Politically there is a call for cheaper fares for certain classes of people, notably the elderly. This coupled with the growing popularity of 'anywhere' type period tickets means that the accuracy of the RPM has gone as it no longer reflects the number of people who are using the service. Passengers who pay nothing at all at the time of travel are not necessarily recorded and if some pay less than the normal fare then again cash receipts cannot be translated into traffic volumes. Furthermore, if a farebox type fare collection system is used as is described in Chapter 9 (this is another way of overcoming problems of one-man operation) and buses move from one route to another in the course of a day, cash collected cannot be allocated to specific services unless a special recording apparatus is attached. In any case, waybills are not as explicit as they were at one time, and all of these factors militate against the production of a record of route receipts which are of sufficient accuracy to be of any value. Certainly these features can now be overcome by the sophisticated albeit expensive electronic equipment which is considered in Chapter 9.

When the RPM barometer becomes suspect or useless, some alternative data are required if services are to be properly developed and that alternative can only be passenger loadings. But just as the RPM cannot be calculated when circumstances as described prevail, neither can this information be obtained from ticket sales if some passengers do not buy tickets on the bus at the time of travel. From a fare collection aspect this subject is dealt with in some depth in Chapter 9 but an alternative is to count physically. To do this will give total passenger journeys but to obtain passenger miles then the numbers boarding and alighting at each point must also be known unless an average length of journey is accepted. To obtain this information manually in respect of each passenger on high-density services is unrealistic; the cost would be tremendous and beyond contemplation even if the necessary manpower could be obtained. This must immediately reduce the exercise to a sample. However, to keep costs within reasonable limits, the sample must be a small one but the smaller the sample the less reliable it becomes. It might, in fact, have to be reduced to something like once or twice a year and then maybe only on the less frequent services could on-bus point-to-point loadings be recorded. On the busier frequent routes passing loads at the maximum traffic points might have to suffice which, for traffic planning purposes, is something less than ideal. In the light of these circumstances it is worth reflecting on how many bus managements and certainly those without an electronic revenue control system know with any degree of accuracy how many passengers they are carrying, in total or service by service, and how many could refine those figures to passenger miles. Depending on circumstances such as fare collection methods and travel concessions, the answer might be not very many. But how many managements would admit that they do not know how many passengers they are carrying? The answer again is not very many. Their reticence is understandable and in any case they all actually produce these figures; they appear in published statistics.

They are of course estimates—but estimates based on what and how accurate are they? Such figures as are available are adjusted according to local circumstances. It will be known how many pre-paid anywhere and elderly persons tickets are issued. Some special sample census might help to establish how many rides per week and where are made per ticket. Different types of ticket issuing machines produce varying amounts of statistical data and fleet figures must be built up on whatever information is available. And the fleet figure might be somewhere near the mark but it is hardly an adequate basis on which to start to think about timetable changes.

All of this only poses the problem, it does not answer it. What is needed is some means that produces passenger loading figures and people left behind, journey by journey, stop by stop, at least for a period in the summer and another in the winter and more frequently if possible, all without incurring excessive cost. This information properly summarized will indicate where there is over-provision and where strengthening is necessary. The only other source of information is inspectors' observations as mentioned in Chapter 10. Electronic equipment described in Chapter 9 goes some way but even that will not tell management how many people are left behind and how long they have to wait before they are eventually able to board.

Surveys

Although the need to obtain traffic statistics as has just been discussed is important, this in itself is still not sufficient when there is reason to believe that the route pattern is not right. Furthermore, when changes are being contemplated, even on-bus loadings as recorded by supervisors or staff appointed for that specific purpose or statistics produced by electronic ticket issuing equipment are inadequate. Special investigations into not only the requirements of the passengers but also the potential demands of the local populace are necessary. This is the meaning of market research. It is of no small importance that the services provided are in accordance with what the people want, and there must be genuine attempts to ferret out those needs. It is not sufficient just to daub on a new name such as 'marketing' to an old established function and with lip service thus done, take no further real interest in the matter. This is a world of change and a dynamic management must constantly trim, adjust and supplement as the case may be. As long as it is somebody's job to do this, it does not really matter what he is called.

The basis of a survey of this type is usually pre-printed questionnaires which ask for complete details of the passenger's overall journey or, in other words, origin and destination. They can be distributed on the vehicles but that only catches existing passengers. A household survey is more representative but the magnitude of the task must confine the information to a sample. Such surveys could take the form of a personal interview with answers to questions filled in on the spot, or cards could be completed by householders at their leisure and returned through the post in pre-paid envelopes. Questions will, of course, be designed in accordance with whatever project might be in mind but if people are to answer and if what they say is to be meaningful, there must not be too many questions and they must be short, to the point and free from ambiguity. Preferably the answers should be one of several alternatives which requires only a tick in an appropriate box. As not everybody will answer, and this applies particularly to postal surveys, the resultant evidence will be only a sample of a sample. Nevertheless, it is still likely that a mass of information will become available for processing. The individual responses will need to be put into a summarized form before they can be properly considered and a computer is appropriate for work of this kind. This of course must have a bearing on the design of the original questionnaire and specialized techniques have been developed. Smaller undertakings which do not employ staff with particular qualifications and training in this field might, therefore, find it more convenient to engage the services of an outside firm which undertakes this sort of work on the occasions when specific projects are in mind. Back, therefore, to the computerized tool for network analysis to which reference was made at the beginning of this chapter.

7 Commercial practices

The commercial function

The commercial manager is responsible for promoting and selling the service. His particular designation, how he fits into the organization and his relationship with other functions were considered in Chapter 4 and are not important in this context. The smaller bus undertakings are unlikely to have a separate commercial department. The work is then normally part of the responsibility of the operating side although it is quite distinct from the daily task of actually controlling movement. In fact, under these circumstances it is common practice for this function to become known instead as the traffic department with the traffic manager or traffic superintendent in charge of both running and selling the service. In popular jargon, marketing is a frequently used term for the same subject. The writer feels that when 'market' is used as a verb, it is more appropriately applied to merchandise than to a service. Nevertheless, the fact that the subject has had sufficient thought and attention to bring about a re-christening is not a bad thing. The subject which the name describes has just been introduced in Chapter 6. It is something more than sales or publicity as this activity attempts only to encourage and help people to use what is there. True traffic promotion (or marketing) adopts the different approach as was described. It first seeks what the people want and what they are most likely to use. Market research techniques are used and publicity is the natural supporting follow-up. The principle of this is, of course, very good. It is right and proper that passengers should be provided with what they want. On the other hand, such exercises take time and money and there must not be heavy expenditure just to prove something that any experienced traffic man should know in any case.

It is the commercial or traffic people who must supply the raw material for schedule compilers to turn into workable programmes for implementation on the road by operating personnel. The schedule process is explained in Chapter 8 and it is an advantage if the traffic staff have some knowledge of scheduling principles. This will enable them to prepare realistic specifications, which is the subject under discussion now.

Just as the schedules staff work to the requirements of the traffic department, the latter is, in turn, developing the policy which has been laid down at the basic planning stage. This was covered in Chapter 6 and the final sections of that chapter which covered operational planning lead directly into what is now being considered.

Facilities

Review of the different types of services and provisions

Route planning and timetable specifications are developed from the basic parameters as determined by the criteria for service provision. Unless, however, the system becomes essentially a social service with a high percentage of income coming from places other than passengers at the time of travel, it is unlikely that there will be a pre-determined and laid down set of standards which has to be rigidly followed. It will be there but more likely subconsciously in the manager's mind and commercial decisions will be made accordingly as the different issues present themselves. Whatever the background, however, there will be a policy on route patterns, service frequencies and load factors and it is on this that the network will evolve.

The different types of service were listed (1) to (7) in Chapter 6. Factors now to be considered are:

1. Route.
2. Frequency.
3. Timetable.
4. Stops.
5. Stands.
6. Type of vehicle.

Each is important and none can be considered in isolation. One has a bearing on another and all will be influenced by general policy. Much of this will be based on preferences and opinions. The treatment of this particular topic is, therefore, to some extent subjective by nature. The thoughts that follow will reflect the commercial practices of some undertakings and not others. Those who work differently will have their reasons, even though the author might not necessarily agree with them.

Figure 7.1 Truck buses of Bangkok Mass Transit Authority can command a higher fare not because of any extra comfort but because they are able to weave through traffic faster than the larger conventional vehicles and hence complete their journeys more quickly. This vehicle is seen operating in Bangkok, Thailand.

The relationship between route network and service frequency was fully considered in Chapter 6. There might also, however, be a relationship between the route and the type of vehicle. In a country (and Great Britain is in mind) where available headroom on public roads of 16ft 6in (5 m) is accepted as a national standard, the writer is of the opinion that that advantage should be fully exploited by bus operators. A double-deck bus can carry either a larger payload than its single-deck counterpart, which means it is more economical, or, depending on the design of the single deck, the double deck will carry a similar number but in much greater comfort. In other words, the double deck will give everybody a seat whilst the single deck will be a standee-type crush loader. To follow this thought through, the author is suggesting that as a basic principle, on routes where there is sufficient traffic justification to warrant something more than a small bus, double-deck vehicles should be used unless there is some special reason why this should not or cannot be done. On very short inner-city services, passengers are unlikely to wish to climb to the upper deck and crush loading does not really matter for such short distances. Even so, although it seems to be the preferred option if the alternative is being left behind, people do not really like being herded in to a confined space to stand in what are most uncomfortable conditions and what might be grudgingly accepted on local railways (underground or otherwise) is not tolerated on buses. Custom and practice may be one reason but the fact that steel wheel on steel rail gives a smoother ride which makes standing less arduous is certainly another. The other reason in support of single-deck buses is physical obstruction but even here a diversion to avoid a height or weight restriction might be justified. Much depends on any alternative routes which are available.

Whatever the policy, bus routes must be devised so as to provide the greatest good for the greatest number. Most people put some value on the availability of a public service, even though they may want it only when their car is not available and preferably on the next road rather than their own but only a short walk away. As far as stops are concerned, not outside their own house; several doors away at the very least. What this is really saying is that route determination does sometimes have complications even after an otherwise ideal way through has been found. This applies particularly to residential neighbourhoods on the outer fringes.

The foregoing applies to all types of services except the long-distance coaches and which run to a pre-determined and published timetable from point to point at standard speeds. For special circumstances, variants must be considered. Possibilities include guaranteed journeys, limited stop services (which is why stops were mentioned as one of the considerations) and customer orientated anywhere to anywhere or fixed point to anywhere, frequently referred to as dial-a-bus. All are devices to give more attractive facilities and/or reduce costs and hence improve viability.

A guaranteed journey is a method of providing a service for which there is a specific demand but which would otherwise be quite uneconomic. It could apply, for example, to an additional journey on an established service, perhaps before the first or after the last bus. The idea is that the vehicle would operate as a normal service bus with normal fares charged and available for anyone to board who might care to do so. The only difference is that the guarantor would underwrite any shortfall between costs and receipts, which means that the greater the number the passengers the less would be the subvention. It is an alternative to a contract.

A device that might reduce costs and give a more attractive service at the same time is the provision of limited stop journeys. The theory of this principle is sound although unfortunately the practical arrangements are difficult and often not a success. It could be a special service or just selected journeys with distinctive blinds of an otherwise normal stopping service which run fast. If the running time is less, there is greater productivity. If the saving is sufficient to move a greater number of people say by working an extra trip with the same resources, then there is an economy. At the same time, the facilities should become more attractive. In the event, however, things do not always work out like that and that is why the practice is not widely adopted. With traffic congestion the level that it is (and it is at its worst at the very time that the limited stop journeys will be wanted, being in the peaks) speed is often dictated more by the general traffic flow than the need to stop for passengers. It might so happen that there is a section of motorway that can be used. If not and the faster timetable is not realistic there is no great benefit. But there is something more fundamental than that. Although there are certainly some stops that are much more heavily used than others, it is customary for there to be pick-ups and set-downs at frequent points all the way along the route. Indeed, it is this door-to-door facility that is a characteristic of the bus and which gives it an advantage over other modes. There is, therefore, the very real possibility of buses with empty seats passing stops where people are waiting; and if they have to wait long, the writer regards this as a very bad operating tactic. The resources of most undertakings are strained in the peaks. Queues form and waits are sometimes extended. If, under these circumstances, buses are running around (that is, in the appropriate direction) with surplus capacity, then, as a general principle, it is the view of the writer that something is badly wrong and the runnings need to be rearranged.

Long-distance express services

For the final classification in the list in Chapter 6—the long-distance express service—there are rather different considerations.

There will probably be only one centralized pick-up/set-down point in any one urban centre, and the precise spot will not be quite as crucial as it is for local bus services. Although passengers will want a reasonably convenient location, the journey is likely to be an infrequent occurrence, and a further conveyance to the ultimate destination is likely to be required in any case. A terminal with amenities such as covered accommodation where arrivals can be met and access to feeder services (buses or taxis) or a car park are therefore of more importance than the sort of things that a local bus passenger would look for.

As the nature of the service is 'town to town' rather than 'door to door' and with an emphasis on speed, the most direct route will be sought depending to what extent intermediate centres are to be served. It is the construction of motorway networks which has revolutionized longer-distance coach travel. On these highways, speeds of 60 mph (100 km/h) can be scheduled compared with say 25 mph (35 km/h) on orthodox roads where stop–start traffic and parking are permitted. Substantially shorter journey times, therefore, are possible where suitable motorways exist but it must be remembered that many coach services are in direct competition with the railway, and new railway technology has also enabled faster train speeds to be attained which road transport still cannot rival. The competitive power of the coach must therefore rely on fare levels but abstraction of traffic from the railway is not necessarily permitted. As was seen in Chapter 5, there is no such inhibition in Great Britain, but elsewhere many governments do not allow competition by road along those routes where there is a direct railway facility.

Sometimes, road and rail between them provide a co-ordinated 'inter-city' network, perhaps under common ownership. In South Africa, for example, the railway administration operates a comprehensive network of long-distance road services which complements the railway and provides facilities for journeys where the train is not available. But this is digressing. To get back to routeings, the use of the motorway is really for end-to-end traffic (and it is this type of traffic which predominates). However, it is not only the large towns that need to be served by express coaches; there will be some justification for serving also some of the intermediate smaller but nevertheless important centres which means that not all express coach services will be of the motorway variety. Indeed, it could even be that on some rural sections where a local bus could not be sustained, the coach could be used for this purpose and carry the few passengers who would not otherwise have a service for short local journeys. Where 'non-motorway' express services are provided, there might be a case to duplicate with non-stop (motorway if available) journeys at the busy times. The only halts necessary for coaches on motorways are at service stations where refreshment and toilet facilities are available. Even these stops can be eliminated if such facilities are made available on the coaches themselves—and this is the current trend. But refreshments mean hostesses, and they must not occupy accommodation that passengers would like to use.

Unlike most bus services, the timetables of express coach services will probably be limited to two or three trips per day, some of which will be seasonal. Timings must be arranged for optimum passenger convenience which means that morning departures must not be unacceptably early and evening arrivals not after a time when many people would not be prepared to be around (or when all local transport has ceased to run).

Types of vehicles, including those for use on express services, were considered in Chapter 3. The writer maintains that the comments made on the use of double-deck buses for local services apply equally to express services but whereas there is a trend to introduce smaller buses on the local services there is now a considerable veering towards the use of double-deck coaches of the type shown in *Figure 3.22* on the express services. More and more coaches are being equipped with toilets and many have arrangements for refreshments, including hot drinks. In fact, everything is done for the passenger's entertainment including the installation of video-cassette players! However, the vehicles used do not have to be purpose-built for express work only. The need for duplication at busy periods has already been noted, and this occurs mainly at weekends, particularly in summer. As this is the time when the requirements of the local services are likely to be less it could be convenient and economic to use the same vehicles on local and inter-urban work during the week and as coaches at weekends. Hence the case for the dual-purpose vehicle as was described in Chapter 3.

Finally on this discourse on express services, a further distinction is that many operators have adopted a system of pre-booking. It is a policy decision whether pre-booking should be instituted but if it is, and it does give passengers peace of mind regarding the availability of accommodation, then a whole range of complications and costs are introduced. Pre-booking calls for a ticket selling organization, which means the appointment of agencies (travel agents and sometimes even newsagents are suitable for this purpose). But agents will look for commission, and tickets sold by them will therefore be at a discount (although it does of course save operators what would otherwise be the prohibitive costs of setting up their own ticket sales points). Then there is the process of reservations. A place on any one coach could be booked at a multitude of different selling points and operators must therefore maintain a charting room to collate bookings and confirm availability of accommodation.

Further reference to ticket sales by agencies is contained in Chapter 9. The purpose of the discussion here is to consider from a commercial viewpoint the need or otherwise for a system of pre-booking. It depends very much on the general availability of spare seats, remembering that the express coach is not like the bus where an unfortunate passenger can usually wait for the next one or the train which can invariably take just one more, albeit in no very great comfort. The capacity of a coach is finite and passengers left behind could be stranded. Advance purchase of a ticket on a coach might guarantee a seat (although no specific seat—this would be nice but too complex to administer) which is a selling point over the railway which (at least in Great Britain) usually charges for its seat reservations. But the system can inhibit travel by coach, particularly as some operators insist on the return journey being booked at the time the sale for the outward journey is made.

In order to ensure that potential passengers are not turned away unnecessarily, even with a pre-booking system drivers should be equipped to collect fares and issue tickets on the spot to the extent that accommodation is available. In Great Britain, most of the longer distance services are subject to pre-booking but some of the more medium-distance routes are run in the same manner as conventional one-man buses, i.e. pay as you enter. In the USA, Greyhound Lines, for example, whose vast network spans the entire country, does not have a pre-booking system. In the main towns passengers purchase their tickets from a booking office in the bus station (on the railway principle) or if there is no bus station maybe from an agency prior to departure, but otherwise those boarding intermediately are able to pay the driver.

This, then, covers the main commercial aspects peculiar to express coach operation. As far as operators in Great Britain are concerned, remember it is a free market (subject to operator's licence, etc.) and is highly competitive both within the coach industry itself and with the railway. In some cases it also competes with air transport. The weapon is price (which means that costs must be kept as low as possible) coupled with a guaranteed seat. However, the need to book in advance (and certainly the return journey in advance) does make travel arrangements much more difficult. As coaches usually have the edge on price compared with other modes it could be thought that they are catering for the lower end of the market, hence the provision of facilities that are considered to match the taste of the clientele. But it is not everybody who appreciates what has been provided. What pleases some offends others as some passengers prefer peace and a scenic view to a television screen with the blinds drawn, and this certainly includes visitors from overseas who like to travel by road and see the country. In such a competitive environment relative trivialities can become important selling points. An enterprising operator in Great Britain would get some grateful customers if he came on the scene with a blaze of publicity promising such things as no compulsory viewing of raucous videos, hostesses who will not make excessive claims to the popular seats in the front, drivers (and passengers?) who will not smoke and thereby pollute the atmosphere, coupled with the issue of open-dated return tickets—features that, sadly for some, are lacking on most of the present services. Until that time, however, many of those who would like to go by coach will continue to travel by train where all of these requirements are met. People so wishing may or may not be in the majority. Gimmicks may be a good thing. Too many might be bad. Better staff behaviour can only succeed. But regardless of all this, the thoughts are there and these are the sort of things which must be considered as part of any sales drive in the coaching business.

Demand activated systems

It was said in Chapter 1 that the tram played a significant role in urban development. Residential and commercial areas flourished along its fixed routes and there was a self-perpetuating process whereby public transport both controlled development and created traffic sufficient to support a frequent service. But the private car has changed all that. No longer need the dormitory areas be centred around public transport routes. The journey can be made by car no matter how diverse the travel requirements might be. Of course, this has led to problems in other directions; congestion, cost of road space, need for car parks, plight of those without cars and perhaps in due course the need for economy in the use of fuel. Hence the approach as indicated in Chapter 6 that public transport should be a function of land use. Nevertheless, residential districts have already grown up in the more affluent areas both in Great Britain and overseas, particularly in North America, where either development is too dispersed or there is no adequate through road which means that it is difficult or impossible to provide a viable public transport service.

It is places such as this where the dial-a-bus concept (a colloquial but apt term used to describe a special demand-responsive bus service) might be suitable. The principle is that a mini- or midi-bus would be made available between any pair of points within a defined zone upon receipt of a telephone call. Alternatively it could run to and from a central point (shops, local railhead, etc.) on a many to one/one to many basis. In this case, only the forward journey would need to be by prior arrangement. A control office is, of course, essential with two-way radio between controllers and drivers and optimum routes must be devised immediately requests are received to minimize both excessive mileage and passenger waiting times. It has been established that in the right places, a service of this kind is popular and serves a useful purpose. The question of viability, however, is another matter. The economics of small buses was discussed in Chapter 6, and the dial-a-bus concept cannot alter the situation. Indeed, the higher mileage covered in order to meet specific requirements can only worsen the position.

Another factor for consideration, however, is the effect on the public transport system as a whole. If the bus is used as a feeder to rail then it might encourage people to go this way instead of by car. If a free car park at the station is provided and passengers use their own cars it might be cheaper, but once in the car, they might be tempted to stay in it all the way to town. Conversely, dial-a-bus could abstract traffic from normal bus services which might otherwise be more profitable. If, for the reason already stated, it is impossible or very costly to provide normal buses to what could be fragmented development then this is a practical alternative, and it is the nearest approach to the convenience of the private car. It is this latter situation where thoughts could most usefully turn to a demand-responsive system.

Services for the disabled

Reference was made in Chapter 3 to vehicles specially adapted to carry passengers in wheelchairs. Remember they can be standard single or double-decks which are equipped with lifts (or ramps) and with space on the lower deck to park and anchor the chairs in which the disabled passenger remains seated during the course of travel. As far as the actual construction or adaption of the vehicles is concerned there is no particular problem, and with this knowledge representations are made occasionally by various associations of disabled people for at least some service buses to be suitably equipped for their purpose. Several years ago the government of the USA took a lead on this issue and required buses on urban routes to be fitted for the carriage of wheelchairs in order to qualify for grant aid. Such an approach has not been followed elsewhere, but what arrangements if any should be made for the conveyance by bus of passengers in wheelchairs will now be considered in the commercial context.

In saying this, let the terms of reference be clear. This discussion is about the carriage of passengers who are fit other than for the fact that they are confined to a wheelchair. The requirement is therefore distinct from an ambulance service and in this context there is no involvement in the carriage of passengers to such places as hospitals for out-patient treatment or day-centres for the elderly. They are matters for the local health or welfare authorities and are not a part of this review. But it remains for consideration whether provision should be made for the conveyance of otherwise healthy people in wheelchairs to the shops, places of employment or wherever, bearing in mind that they can be pushed or even propel themselves to a bus stop and then go about their business after they have alighted.

Although it may be a deserving case, operators cannot help but recognize the problems with which they will be confronted in providing for this type of traffic. Consider the following:

1.   Although buses can be fitted with lifts, such a conversion is expensive.
2.   Space left for wheelchairs significantly reduces the seating capacity.
3.   Wheelchairs must be negotiated in and out of the bus and securely anchored to the floor during travel which means that an attendant conductor must be carried.
4.   Boarding and alighting times will be considerably extended.

All of this of course spells cost—big cost. Apart from the more expensive vehicle and added maintenance requirements, the payload is reduced, the running time is increased and one-man operation is not possible. Maybe the bus could be used as a standee when there are no wheelchairs being carried or perhaps some form of tip-up seats could be provided, but either way normal passengers could be at a disadvantage. Operationally, if only some buses on a regular service were so equipped as is sometimes suggested, the delays at stops would mean that the bus behind would catch up, there would be bunching (even more than usual!) and headways would become ragged. For these reasons alone mixed operation on any one service would be far from ideal.

Although the writer has every sympathy with those who are confined to wheelchairs, these are the inescapable facts and as far as the provision of facilities for them is concerned they give no cause for optimism. Although there are a lot of disabled people they still nevertheless constitute only a small minority of the potential traffic. With, therefore, the delays at stops and loss of seats it is inevitable that the many would suffer for the few. This coupled with the costs involved means that it is not something that operators are likely to provide without some financial help. It would not be viable.

Nevertheless, the needs of the disabled are very real and such facilities could give them links with the outside world instead of being virtual prisoners in their own homes. Local authorities and welfare organizations might therefore be sympathetic, and if they are prepared to meet the deficits, there is no reason why some special services should not be provided. Indeed, in Great Britain in some places they are provided. If it is a shopping facility that is required, a most satisfactory method is to equip two or three single-deck buses for use in any one urban centre and run them on a pre-scheduled, timetabled and advertised basis, routed through different neighbourhoods on each successive day of the week to run into the main shopping areas or wherever. Such services can then be used by chairbound passengers in the same way that normal passengers use conventional buses and the administrative arrangements can be dealt with through the normal tendering procedure.

Excursions and tours

The operation of excursions and tours may be an ancillary activity of what is primarily a bus operating company, it might be the main business with just a small amount of regular service work as well or it might be the sole specialized function of a coach undertaking. Similarly, there is a wide variation in the types of excursions and tours that can be provided. Consider the following:

1. Short trips.
2. Day excursions.
3. Extended tours (domestic).
4. Fantail tours.
5. Foreign tours.

Short sightseeing trips are run in the larger towns which have a particular commercial or historical interest with the routes passing and probably waiting a while at the popular tourist attractions. This of course involves parking which in congested areas can be difficult—an alternative idea practised by some operators in London, for example, brings the 'tour' only one stage removed from a conventional bus service. Here, one of the tour options is a service running to a regular set frequency on a typical tourist circuit with passengers being allowed to board and alight at will for a defined period of time with one ticket. Other types of short excursions might be arranged, for example in the evenings to places of interest or entertainment, maybe on a travel and admission basis. Whilst luxury coaches are frequently used on excursions of this kind, conventional double-deck buses are suitable for the sightseeing tours, and if the weather is fine open-top buses are popular.

Day excursions are likely to include trips from inland towns to the coast or from main centres to places of particular interest and again could include combined travel and admission. Double-deck buses could be popular for this traffic but touring coaches are also used.

It is the extended tours, etc. (classifications (3), (4) and (5) on the list) which require somewhat complex and scrupulous planning as they are likely to be all inclusive; that is, providing the entire input to a complete holiday. This means the arrangement of not only coach travel but also hotel accommodation, *en route* stops for meals, etc., possibly admissions to places of interest and for an island country such as Great Britain, a short sea crossing utilizing roll-on roll-off ferries in the case of foreign tours. A tour such as this may be for 2 or 3 weeks' duration and may take the form of a circular trip covering a particular area with short breaks here and there or a direct route to a destination with the holiday spent there but with the stay punctuated by local excursions (this is what is known as the fantail tour).

Like all other aspects of the coaching business, the market is highly competitive, and price and quality are the critical factors. But it is not only the coach travel (the vehicle, the driver and the courier) in which passengers are interested. They will judge their holiday also on hotel standards, meals, etc., over which the operator has no direct control—all reasons why tour planning and operation is a job for the specialist.

For extended tour work, purpose-built coaches should be allocated but again they may be either double-deck or single-deck. Unlike the normal scheduled services, however, it is suggested that the sale of numbered seats is justified even though the booking system becomes more complex. Indeed, the front seats of the upper deck could even command a premium fare. The coach ride is part of the holiday and passengers should be able to select their desired positions in the vehicle in the order in which they book and not as the result of a push and a scramble at the original boarding point. Some operators like to rotate their passengers through different seats over the period of the tour. But then there are some seats in which some passengers are not prepared to travel and they, therefore, require the option of booking early and getting (and keeping) what they want or not going at all.

Excursions and tours can be very remunerative. Unlike regular services where vehicles are not necessarily in continuous operation and advertised journeys must run even if there are only a few passengers, the touring coach is fully utilized all of the time. It would not be operated in the first instance if it was under-subscribed. But if the business is to be viable and prices kept at an acceptable level, resources in terms of vehicles must be kept fully employed. Intensive utilization of this kind does, however, produce difficulties in the event of unavoidable delays which can happen, particularly on foreign tours.

If a tours programme develops to this extent, the work becomes very specialized and distinct from bus operation as such. This is why some companies deal exclusively in tour work and those bus undertakings that do cater for this type of traffic generally organize the activity within a separate department. But regardless of how it is organized, part of the success lies in sufficient imagination in planning the tours programme and selecting the itineraries and the hotel accommodation. On the commercial side this is what is needed. Having prepared the plans the customers must be satisfied and reference to the operational complexities is contained in Chapter 10.

Private hire

The term 'private hire' is used in the bus industry when a vehicle and driver is let out or chartered to a private party for a special occasion. Excursions and tours (which have just been discussed) lie somewhere between the regular service and private hire. They are something which the operator plans, advertises and sells individual tickets for. In the case of a private hire, the vehicle is chartered as a whole by the hirer to comply with an itinerary which he has requested and the public at large has no knowledge of or interest in the transaction. The bus will be running under a contract. Colloquially, it is the regular private hires that are regarded in the industry as contract work such as with an education authority for schools traffic and to playing fields and swimming baths or with a factory management for works journeys. One further variant is when a vehicle is hired by another transport undertaking to run a public service on their behalf. This could be by another bus or coach company at times when their own fleet is insufficient for the traffic that they have to carry, by a railway administration when trains are temporarily interrupted or even by an airline when flights are diverted through reasons beyond their control to different airports and passengers have to be conveyed by road to their true destination.

Like excursions and tours, private hire work is attractive to bus and coach operators (i.e., operators who run regular services) because it is nearly always profitable. The reason for this is that they need only accept such work when it is convenient for them to do so. In other words, vehicles can be used when otherwise they would be idle. It is not quite so easy for the firms who specialize in and rely on this type of work. They will have established their own clientele in this particular field and in consequence will not lightly turn away customers and lose goodwill. This is an example when sub-contracting comes into play with one operator hiring vehicles from another.

To conclude this sub-section, therefore, private hire of buses and coaches may be a business in its own right but to the regular service operator it is something that the commercial department can organize and produce some useful additional revenue for the company by utilizing vehicles at times when they are not otherwise required.

Ancillary services

Parcels

Reference has already been made to the carriage of passengers on a parcels service in remote areas where demand is insufficient to support a separate facility. This is the exceptional case. What is more usual is for parcels to be conveyed on passenger services. On town services there is little scope for the carriage of unaccompanied parcels but on the less heavily used inter-urban and rural routes, some operators have developed quite a considerable subsidiary business in this traffic.

Systems have grown up based on a series of collection and delivery points being either the company's own enquiry offices or suitable shops appointed as agents. Consigners deliver their parcels to and consignees collect them from these agencies. A scale of charges is likely to be based on weight without the application of a distance complication although this could also be taken into account if required. Conductors would call at these agencies to collect and deliver. Alternatively, consigners could hand packages direct to conductors who would collect the fee and issue a special parcel label in the form of a receipt. One half of this ticket would be attached to the parcel and the other half handed to the consigner. Similarly the consignee could meet the bus rather than utilize the services of the agency. Over recent years, however, the increase in one-man operation has inhibited the operation of a parcels service in all but the very rural areas. Drivers cannot easily leave their vehicles to collect and deliver parcels, particularly as they have cash and tickets in the cab. In any case, for them to look after parcels when there are heavy surges of traffic on double-deck buses is expecting a lot, just as it is of the intending passengers who would have to wait for the driver to attend to this duty before they could board. Nevertheless, where operating conditions are right it has been possible to preserve a useful facility which at the same time earns additional revenue at little extra cost.

Left luggage

Provision for passengers to deposit their luggage for short periods is a facility that has been provided at some bus stations for many years. It is not a service that is likely to bear a high charge and can, therefore, really only be provided in conjunction with some other activity, such as a parcels or lost property office. A more recent innovation is the provision of lockers activated by coins in a slot. Unaccompanied baggage, however, is becoming a serious security risk and the small amount of additional revenue that is forthcoming is of doubtful justification if there is no other parcels traffic on the premises.

Catering

The provision of a restaurant, cafeteria or snack bar is a popular and hopefully remunerative sideline at the more important passenger transport terminals, and this may be done either directly or through an outside contractor. Where food is served in the vehicles themselves—and in Great Britain it has been seen that there are examples of this on some long-distance express services—the hostess will be an employee of the company. Even here, however, one option is for them to receive only a nominal wage and use their own initiative on the purchase and sale of food, keeping whatever profits are made. But the biggest business is at bus stations and garage staff canteens. The use of outside contractors is suitable under these circumstances, and the operator will receive money through granting the concession. In this context it is of note that in Great Britain the trend is for bus stations to be owned by third parties such as passenger transport executives or local councils, in which case those bodies must determine the catering arrangements rather than the operating companies. Even if public restaurant or buffet facilities are difficult to justify in their own right, many of the larger companies provide their staff with subsidized canteen facilities. Bus crews are often scheduled for meal reliefs at bus stations in which case there is a need for a staff canteen. It is then but a small step to provide separate facilities for passengers, all based on the same kitchen.

Other miscellaneous activities

All that has been mentioned so far refers to facilities which are subservient to the main business of carrying passengers. In providing such conveniences, goodwill is promoted with some additional revenue to go with it. Transport undertakings do, however, often engage in other activities. The larger ones might have a separate consultancy business which is of particular value to overseas clients. The smaller firms frequently run their buses alongside a garage repair business and petrol filling station, possibly also with self-drive cars and even minibuses for hire. The larger ones might offer garage space for parking purposes for other operators or they might undertake repairs and overhauls of other heavy vehicles either on a regular or casual basis. Some bus undertakings, both large and small run travel agencies, quite lucrative in themselves but sometimes producing the ironical situation of providing booking facilities for not only their own services but also for those of their competitors.

Commercial advertising

One further way in which a public transport undertaking can earn revenue other than through selling transport is commercial advertising. The exteriors and interiors of buses and trams provide valuable advertising sites, the announcements of which will be seen and read by hundreds of thousands of people. Bus shelters and other public places in the ownership of public transport undertakings also offer potential revenue earning possibilities in this way. Some administration is, of course, involved although the entire job could be placed in the hands of a contractor. Remember also from Chapter 2 that some advertising contractors will supply shelters free of charge (Adshel for example) in exchange for advertising rights. However, at least in Great Britain, responsibility for bus shelters is being assumed increasingly by local councils which means that it is the ratepayers rather than the bus company that benefits from the free shelter arrangement. Some will say, and the author accepts the point, that commercial advertising on vehicles has an aesthetic disbenefit. This is particularly so in the case of the complete allover advertising in which some buses are dressed. But when finance is difficult money must come from somewhere. The more that is earned through advertising the less will need to come from public funds—money that people have paid in rates and taxes—and environmentalists or no, any saving in taxes must be a welcome relief. It is important that advertisements are kept in good condition—this helps to keep up appearances—and for this reason they are sometimes painted on by signwriters instead of using paper stickers.

Figure 7.2 Single-deck buses have less scope for exterior commerical advertising than the double-decks. However, Citybus Ltd. which has a predominance of single-decks spares no effort to maximize their advertising potential. Pictured here is one of its vehicles in the centre of Belfast, Northern Ireland, UK.

Figure 7.3 Commercial advertising is a useful source of additional revenue. Particularly so the all-over advertising although it does nothing to enhance the appearance of the vehicle and it destroys any corporate identity. Even so, if it helps to hold down fares it can't be bad. This bus of Luton and District Transport was earning yet further revenue when pictured at Great Yarmouth, Norfolk, UK. It was a summer Sunday and an excursion to the coast produced a full load at a time when the bus would otherwise have been idle.

Fares and charges

Basic rates

In a commercial setting it is the responsibility of the fares and charges officer to fix his rates at a level sufficient to cover costs and service capital in accordance with the financial structure and requirements of his undertaking. If by political necessity or whim there is a declared social need to bolster up the system with monetary support then clearly not all of the costs will have to be recouped through fares but there could, nevertheless, still be a target according to whatever dictates may have been issued. Further reference to this aspect will be made later in this chapter. Whilst, therefore, the different methods of charging as are to be described are certainly valid when economic fares are required, the principles could also be applied when part of the revenue appears in the form of a subsidy. First, however, must be considered the economic theory of rate fixing in a competitive market.

A logical base on which to fix charges is cost plus profit. This is something that can be and is done by, for example, the smaller road hauliers when asked to quote for a specific job. (The cost of an excursion or tour, incidentally, could also be costed and charges fixed in this way.) But to continue the theory, apply the same concept to large-scale enterprise and it becomes impracticable to cost individually any one item. The sheer magnitude and complexity of a national railway system to take another example clearly makes it impossible to identify in a meaningful way the extra cost involved in the carriage of one particular consignment. An alternative method is to charge not on the cost of the service but on the value of the service (that is to the customer), and the principle of charging what the traffic can bear is something that is steeped in railway history. At the same time, the concept is ever present, consciously or sub-consciously, in people's minds, and this applies to their own personal movements as well as when they are seeking transport for their goods. Furthermore, this thinking applies regardless of the mode and as far as the users are concerned, the bus passenger will be just as interested in its effects as will be the person who is sending merchandise by rail.

To expand a little on transport economics, note that the function of transport is to move goods or passengers from where they are to where their relative value is greater or where they would prefer to be. In the case of people this could be for a variety of reasons of an economic or personal nature such as travel between home and work, the places being dictated by house prices and district appeal on the one hand and availability of work and salary levels on the other; or for shopping where prices might be cheaper or there might be a wider range of goods to justify travel, or even for pleasure where the cost is set against some alternative pursuit. Although this process will not be undertaken by the individual with mathematical precision, it is nevertheless very real. For example, a man might be prepared to spend £1 per day in travelling between home and work. He might not be prepared to spend £10 a day. It follows, therefore, that somewhere between these two points—the point where it is no longer 'worth it', and that means where he is beginning to spend more than he is getting in return—he will have no alternative but to change his habits. The options open to him might be to move his home, change his job, walk, buy a bicycle or whatever. If no option is open to him and hardship arises or if the adoption of one of the options, say, becoming a private motorist, carries a disbenefit to the community at large, then there might be a case for political intervention with subsidies but that is another matter. The point being made here is that on economic factors alone there is a limit (undefined) above which fares cannot go. If they do, then fewer people will use the service and it will have to be withdrawn.

The parameters for rate fixing, therefore, are that at the lower limit revenue must be sufficient to cover costs and at the upper limit must not be above what the traffic can bear. These limitations should, as far as possible, be applied collectively taking one journey with another and possibly one service with another. If an established operator is protected from competition on the busier and more lucrative services through a system of quantity licensing or whatever and in consequence he is required to meet the needs of the territory as a whole, some cross-subsidization is likely but in the final accounts the undertaking must remain solvent.

There are various methods that may be adopted for the formulation of a charges scheme just as there are means of collecting those charges, which is the subject of Chapter 9. Fare fixing is a commercial activity but fare collection is an operating responsibility. The former can, however, materially help or hinder the latter depending on the method and scale adopted and the two functions should not, therefore, be considered in isolation.

Basic fares may be determined in accordance with any of the following principles:

1. Rate per mile.
2. Rate per mile with a taper (i.e. the longer the journey the lower the mileage rate).
3. Flat rate.
4. Flat rate within a geographical zone.
5. Flat rate within a time zone.

Superimposed on this could be special concessions designed either to maximize revenue or to facilitate fare collection.

Dealing first with the basic structure, option (1) which produces a graduated scale of charges is simple in theory but does not always lend itself to rigid application. It is for consideration whether fares should be charged to the nearest whole mile, half mile, quarter mile or whatever. Also, suitable fare stage points must be selected. In the case of limited stop bus services this is pre-determined by the location of the stops. With normal bus services, however, (as with trams and trolleybuses) stops are frequent, they cannot all be fare stages and there is a choice. Stage points could nevertheless still be frequent or they could be widely spaced and this is one of the differences between a fine scale and a coarse scale. The fewer the number of stages the greater is the likelihood that the correct fare will be charged and a coarse scale is a help with one-man operation. The siting of fare stages is also important regardless of mileage. If a fare expires at a little-used stop just short of a popular setting-down point, overriding can be anticipated. Geography as well as distance, therefore, should help to determine stage points. One other difficulty in adhering strictly to a rate per mile policy is if two or more services link pairs of towns via different routes. The combined timetables would be designed so as to provide an adequate facility for through traffic. Such provision would be satisfactory subject to a spread of traffic and by the law of averages, other things being equal, this would happen. If, however, there was a difference in mileage with a corresponding difference in fares, the chances are that traffic would not spread. Instead, the shortest route would become overloaded because it was the cheapest and there would be surplus accommodation on the other which could not be altered because of intermediate traffic. The solution is to equate the fares but this can only mean that either the shorter route is priced at a higher scale (which might not be desired) or that fares on the longer route become substandard. Once substandard fares are introduced, however, there must be care not to introduce anomalies. An anomalous fare is one which, by the process of re-booking, enables the journey to be made at a cheaper rate than the advertised through fare. To avoid this, one substandard fare, particularly if on an intermediate section of route, can hold down another and a ripple effect is created. Consider the following example where fares are based on a standard '6' per mile (in units of whatever money) with a stage every half mile (see Figure 7.4).

In the specimen farechart (i) (which is an example of a fine scale), '3' is charged for each half-mile fare stage but for some reason the fare between Stage D and Stage G which is worth '9' is held down at '6'. This, however, causes anomalies. The correct fare between Stage D and Stage I, for example, is '15' but by re-booking at Stage G it could be done for '12' and there are numerous other similar instances. To avoid these anomalies there is a ripple effect on the other fares and the resultant farechart is as shown at specimen (ii). In farechart (i) the anomaly is circled. In farechart (ii) the fares reduced by the ripple effect are circled. One further point before leaving the rate per mile system and that is to facilitate collection, it is helpful if fares could be reasonably compatible with coins of the realm. Reference is made in Chapter 9 to the time-consuming process of giving change, and in Great Britain, for example, a fare scale of say 20p, 30p, 40p etc. would be good for fare collection purposes. Of course this cannot always be and in times of inflation, even if it is attained, it will be only until the next fares revision. What really should be avoided, if at all possible, are fares like 24p, 32p etc. which in British currency require at least three coins for the correct fare but as passengers often pay for more than one person and the fact that fares tend to change (upwards) rather frequently anyway the ideal becomes impossible. Even so, if help yourself coin in the slot machines are in use it is something that cannot be disregarded.

Farechart (i)

Stage A

3	Stage B							
6	3	Stage C						
9	6	3	Stage D					
12	9	6	3	Stage E				
15	12	9	6	3	Stage F			
18	15	12	(6)	6	3	Stage G		
21	18	15	12	9	6	3	Stage H	
24	21	18	15	12	9	6	3	Stage I

Farechart (ii)

Stage A

3	Stage B							
6	3	Stage C						
9	6	3	Stage D					
12	9	6	3	Stage E				
15	12	9	6	3	Stage F			
(15)	(12)	(9)	6	6	3	Stage G		
(18)	(15)	(12)	(9)	9	6	3	Stage H	
(21)	(18)	(15)	(12)	12	9	6	3	Stage I

Figure 7.4 Hypothetical farecharts to illustrate a fares anomaly.

The tapered scale—option (2)—has similar characteristics to the true mileage scale and is the system which is in more common use in the UK. One justification for a taper is that it can be argued that the major cost lies in providing a vehicle for somebody to board with all the overheads and administration which that entails. The distance travelled has less significance. If, in support of this theory, an imaginary split in the fare is applied to distinguish between a standard boarding charge and a mileage charge then the taper will appear. The specimen farechart (ii) above has actually had a taper forced into it for a different reason. The system does give a means of relief to the longer distance rider and it might, therefore, encourage travel and overall it can be regarded as a sensible commercial practice. However, for local services where journeys are not particularly long, the effect is not great.

Option (3), being a flat fare, is the simplest of all both to prepare and to implement and is the very antithesis of the graduated system. It consists of just the boarding charge, no more, no less, and for that money, the passenger can go as far as the bus goes. If he has to change vehicles then he pays another boarding charge (unless a transfer facility is available) and if the fare is compatible with a coin in current circulation, nothing could be easier. Statistics are also easily obtained. For passengers carried just divide the total revenue by the flat fare. It is a practice which is very common in North America but is less widely adopted elsewhere.

The disadvantage of the flat fare is that the longer distance passengers get a cheap fare whilst the short-distance riders are penalized and could be discouraged from travelling. Those passengers who can complete their journeys only by means of two short trips on two different buses are at a disadvantage and it is here that a transfer facility is particularly welcome. Furthermore, such a facility could avoid demands for a direct service which might be costly to provide. Whilst it need not necessarily be the case with local urban services, for longer inter-urban routes the flat fare is likely to become impracticable. Even in the large conurbations it produces serious inequalities to the extent that it cannot be tolerated and it is the zonal system—option (4)—which achieves a degree of compromise between the flat fare and the graduated scale.

As its name suggests, the zonal system involves the division of the operating area into two or more fare zones which might take the form of a series of concentric circles radiating outwards from the centre, although there could, of course, be any suitable geographical base. In its simplest form, there is a flat fare within each zone and passengers travelling in two zones, for example, pay twice. This puts a burden on those passengers who wish to travel only a short distance into the second zone and a still greater burden on those whose journey is short but crosses a zonal boundary. Sometimes special fares may be put in to accommodate these particular trips but it does rather complicate things. Again, the North Americans are used to this system and it works well with fareboxes even without tickets as will be considered in Chapter 9.

Option (5), the time system, is sometimes found in Europe. Holland is a good example. It is, in effect, a flat fare for a defined period, say an hour, and can be used in conjunction with fare zones. It involves the issue or cancelling of a ticket from a special machine which is capable of recording the time. It has the advantage of allowing free transfer between vehicles without any further recording but would seem a little hard on passengers travelling on vehicles which are delayed through traffic congestion or for any other reason.

A further aspect of rate fixing is a premium fare for a superior service. Very occasionally buses can be found with a separate compartment for superior class travel, perhaps in the developing countries, but what has a greater potential is to apply higher fares on premium type services such as those of the faster limited stop variety. In Bangkok in Thailand higher fares have been charged on certain small buses, not because of any additional comfort but for faster journey times as a result of their ability to pick their somewhat hazardous paths through heavy traffic more quickly. It depends again on what the passengers are prepared to pay and it must certainly not result in empty seats with a parallel standard bus becoming overloaded.

Passenger resistance is an important factor when considering charges and has particular significance when preparing fares revisions. It is for this reason that the additional yield cannot be predicted by a straight arithmetical calculation. An allowance must be built in for those passengers who decide either not to travel, to travel less frequently or to make shorter journeys. A widely accepted measure of resistance is that a 10% fares increase might produce a net yield of only 7%, but this is only a guide; a more precise estimate must depend on local circumstances and the type of traffic involved. Those making essential journeys will remain captive for a little longer. In other words, the elasticity of demand has a strong bearing on the matter. It is also important when considering special promotional fares as will shortly be seen.

Closely allied to higher fares are minimum fares which are sometimes applied on certain sections of longer distance services. The purpose of this is to protect passengers for whom the service is intended from being crowded out at the main boarding points by short-distance riders who have alternative facilities available to them. It is, of course, only necessary to do this in the out-town direction as on the inwards journey the passengers who are being protected are already on the bus. Such application is entirely a matter of local circumstances. It could hardly be justified if, for instance, it meant empty seats whilst local passengers had an extended wait; but to apply the system to isolated journeys in the peaks does tend to be confusing.

As well as the variants of the basic farescales there are promotional fares to maximize revenue. These include such things as return and season tickets. However, the encouragement to travel, although important, is not their only purpose. They can also aid fare collection which on buses, as will be seen from Chapter 9, is also a crucial issue. Nevertheless, fare concessions must be commercially sound (unless they are otherwise subsidized) and it is appropriate, therefore, that they should be considered here.

Sales promotion

Traffic promotion is very much a part of fares and charges as traffic can be promoted by the availability of special fares. There are also sub-standard fares for social reasons. Here, however, will be considered the offers that are made as a commercial venture and not because of a political decision. The latter are discussed later in this chapter and in Chapter 11.

Sales promotion through the pricing mechanism is a practice that is widely followed in the retail trade and just as business can be stimulated by attractive offers so can passengers be encouraged to use buses by the availability of travel bargains. Vacant seats on public transport services are highly perishable. Once the journey has been completed they have gone for good and can never be sold. If those empty seats can be filled, however, there is additional revenue without any significant increase in costs. On the other hand, if the offer of an attractive facility results in the available accommodation becoming over-subscribed and the service has to be strengthened or the net result is that existing ordinary fare-paying passengers instead become cheap fare-paying passengers, the exercise would not be an economic success. The elasticity of demand is involved and in this case any special facilities are directed at those whose demand is elastic, being those who do not have to travel but who might be encouraged to do so. It is the job of the commercial manager to plan any such schemes with these factors in mind.

However, schemes must be simple in application; indeed it is helpful if any such concessions have the added advantage that they facilitate fare collection on the road.

The sort of promotional fare schemes that might be offered are:

1. Day returns, sometimes confined to the off-peak.
2. Period returns.
3. Day tickets for unlimited travel within a defined area.
4. Period tickets for unlimited travel within a defined area.
5. Weekly 10 journey tickets.
6. Prepaid multi-journey tickets.
7. Tickets available for unlimited travel within defined areas on the services of more than one undertaking, including the railway.

Some of the facilities mentioned lend themselves to the sale of tickets off the vehicle and prior to travel. If this is done, then the driver has only to check the ticket and sometimes there is a machine to do that. In any case, a cash transaction at the time of boarding is avoided which will materially assist one-man operation. Where there is free competition and more than one operator on a service, the special facilities (1)–(6) could be a means of encouraging passengers to use the services of one particular undertaking. In other words, as money is spent in excess of what is required for immediate travel, passengers are committed to use the services of that particular operator. The writer feels that this is not the most desirable state of affairs as far as passengers are concerned. It would be more useful if the various services were properly co-ordinated and tickets inter-available which is government policy in some countries. Even then there is still a case to issue these types of tickets. The need to encourage traffic remains because there is still the very strong counter-attraction of the private car. The ultimate is facility (7) and in Great Britain this type of ticket is issued in London and in some of the major provincial centres. However, with the British now veering towards less co-ordination and more competition there could be a trend away from this type of facility.

Operators may be aware that railway administrations often have a multitude of different promotional fares. Care, however, must be taken before introducing similar facilities on buses. A train is a large unit. It has already been noted that it can usually take one more and without extra cost. A too-large influx on the bus and the journey has to be duplicated or it leaves behind. Discounts on group travel are, therefore, more suitable for the railway (unless, of course, the group likes to hire a bus which has already been discussed). The principle is, as has been said, to try to fill those seats which would otherwise be empty with people who would not otherwise have travelled. Also, railway charges tend to become very complex and more than what a one-man driver could be expected to contend with. However, a man with a wife and family might not afford to take an optional trip unless some relief is obtained by allowing the children to travel at a cheaper rate. Those on a pension similarly might not go. Thus comes the justification for offering special concessions to specific classes of people even on a commercial basis.

Whilst on the subject of display tickets, great efforts are made today to identify the holder with the ticket in his possession by the inclusion of a card containing a photograph, usually at the passenger's expense. All this is to help enforce the 'not transferable' regulation which prohibits a multi-journey ticket being used by anyone other than the person who bought it. The author wonders whether this is really necessary. One ticket has been paid for and one seat is occupied and whether it is the same or somebody else's posterior on that seat can have little effect on costs. Very occasionally it might make the ticket more attractive, say if the wife works on days and the husband on nights, but such cases are few and hardly worth the elaborate safeguards. Certainly if a queue of people are boarding with season tickets which are not subject to journey cancellations a person who has boarded could hand out his ticket to another person in the queue but in the opinion of the writer this is trivial and there are some misguided priorities here. No strong views are held on this point but it is worth a thought. Concessionary or free tickets issued on a personal basis to elderly people or staff etc. are, of course, quite another matter.

Private hire

One further matter on rate fixing is the formulation of charges for private hire, particularly in the case of a bus company which undertakes this work as a subsidiary activity. Marginal costing is considered in Chapter 11. Suffice to consider here whether the charge for a private hire at a time when spare vehicles are available and otherwise idle (such as at a weekend) should be based on the actual costs incurred—drivers' wages, fuel, tyres and a proportion of maintenance—or whether it should include also a full proportion of overheads which, in this case, must be incurred anyway. If the former course is adopted then the quotation would be more attractive and hence more competitive. On the other hand, overhead expenses must be met and it is difficult to see why everything should be allocated to the regular Monday to Friday services, thereby allowing the weekend outing to escape its legitimate share. This is a policy decision for the commercial manager who in the event may not adopt a rigid scale but exercise discretion according to circumstances and prepare his quotations in a way that will maximize business (and revenue) for his company.

Selling the service

Publicity

Publicity can be either indirect or direct. Indirect publicity is provided automatically by the efficiency of the undertaking itself, by the degree of service afforded by its staff, by the sight of vehicles well maintained in a suitable livery of smart appearance and by the mere existence of bus stops. Also, special reports in the local and national press or trade journals and the display of films etc. can do much to further the interests of the service.

It is, however, the direct publicity with which this subsection is particularly concerned. Direct publicity is produced to stimulate demand and to make known new facilities to which traffic must be attracted if it is to be profitable. There must, therefore, be advertising to publicize existing facilities, which is done in two ways. First and most important is the publication of timetables and maps. The issue of a system map is the ideal way of conveying to the public the extent of the services and the value and interest of the map is enhanced if it is true to scale and contains other more general features as opposed to a diagrammatic plan of the routes concerned. A production along these lines is in popular demand. Having reached the masses it does bring home to all who may care to see the existence and details of the system, even if the map was not acquired originally for that purpose. Most transport undertakings do in fact publish a map of some kind of their services in many cases as an insert contained in their timetable booklets. One of the best examples is that produced by London Regional Transport in respect of the bus routes operated by London Buses and other undertakings with whom there is a working agreement. On a map measuring no more than 25in by 21in (63.5 × 53 cm) conveniently folded for pocket use is contained all of the bus routes including the names of the roads served within an area of approximately 1200sq miles (3100 km²) and also showing place names, route numbers with terminal points, all railway lines which are open for passenger service, parks and open spaces etc., all with remarkable clarity. If a system of this magnitude can be plotted successfully in such a concise form, few undertakings should experience difficulty in this respect and the resultant publication has substantial advertising value.

Also very desirable (except possibly where services run at frequent intervals) is the issue of a timetable. No matter what the form of transport, users must be able to ascertain by easy reference the exact times of operation, and for this purpose the availability of a timetable is essential. The tables themselves should be presented clearly to be readily understood by the layman unfamiliar with operational techniques, supported by an index to places served. At this point the writer is at odds with many in the passenger transport industry by expressing his dislike of the 24-hour clock system of presentation which is so dear to the hearts of publicity officers and the like. A public timetable is for passengers to read and readily understand. They should not be subjected to a mental arithmetic exercise before ascertaining the time by their own clock of the next departure. Many people cannot do this calculation and others who think they can get it wrong. It is ironic that in North America where long-distance services do cover a 24-hour day operators adhere to the 12-hour clock in their timetables as does the British Broadcasting Corporation in the *Radio Times*. If there was light type for a.m. and heavy type for p.m. everybody would understand.

It is usual for the timetables to be presented separately for each route or groups of routes as are the specimens in *Figures 8.1, 8.3* and *8.5*. This does of course mean that when a section of route is parallelled by more than one service any one trip necessitates reference to several pages but in cases where a popular journey is catered for by a series of different services, each one of which is relatively infrequent, then the production of a separate summary timetable is useful.

A secondary feature to timetables and maps is the issue of advertising material in either poster or leaflet form regarding special facilities, cheap fares, scenic routes, etc. There is scope for considerable initiative in the preparation of this literature but valuable as it may be, the work and expense of production must not be accorded priority over the timetables for which there is very justification to sell below actual production cost or even given away in leaflet form.

So much for the direct advertising of available facilities. An alternative method of inducing people to travel is by advertising places served, with footnotes indicating how to get there by public transport. Again there is considerable scope for publicity of this nature. Booklets or leaflets could be prepared covering such topics as parks, country rambles, historic buildings with hours of opening, details of popular exhibitions, sporting events, popular resorts, etc., with a view to stimulating travel. As in all business, the product must be advertised if it is to sell and any monopolistic tendencies do not lessen this need. A public transport undertaking which operates under conditions of so-called monopoly has still to compete with private transport and for the optional traveller (i.e. when the demand is elastic) with other forms of relaxation such as television which encourages them to stay at home.

Another important function of a publicity department but not always recognized as such is the provision of signs and the outward display of other written material. It is good advertising to adopt a standard short title for the undertaking (which might be slightly different to the legally registered name), written in a distinctive style and supported by a house symbol for use on all printed matter, on vehicles and property and for all outside display purposes. Over the years, fleet names in all branches of transport have become well-known household terms. Many are based on geographical locations; a few on the colour of the fleet. In Great Britain examples such as Royal Blue, Grey Green, Chocolate Express, Red and White, Green Line, Black and White, and Yelloway, come readily to mind although some have long since vanished and others no longer wear the livery that their name suggests. It is of note, however, that most of these names mentioned refer to longer distance coach services where traffic is more of an optional nature and the degree of competition that much greater. Perhaps there is a connection here with the need to generate public interest and goodwill demanding rather more than a service known only by a geographical reference or the name of the proprietor. It is the opinion of the writer that a company image, providing it is a good image, is important and the identity of the undertaking should instill confidence in the passenger. It is suggested therefore, that a policy of co-ordination can be taken too far if it is allowed to spill over into the publicity arena. It is not only in the retail trade that a brand name stands for something and where it is the label rather than the contents that sells the bottle. If a comprehensive map or timetable is produced advertising a co-ordinated but faceless product (or service) there is the danger that it will lose public appeal.

Whilst on the subject of brand names, the author again sees countless examples of what he regards as misplaced enthusiasm in this respect by the proliferation of descriptive titles given to specific or groups of services. Few ever stick and they do nothing to sell the service. Publicity might implore people to go by 'Wonder Bus' or 'Barnsley Banger' or whatever fancy name tag might be dreamt up but the passengers still see themselves as travelling by train or bus or whatever. They are likely to identify only the name of the operating company which comes back to the point that, in the opinion of the writer, this is the name that should be sold and not a particular facility.

Public relations

The larger the undertaking, the more distant does top management tend to become from both its customers and its staff. The resultant staff problems were discussed in Chapter 4. It is essential that this difficulty is overcome because should management appear to the rank and file as some remote mythical body, team spirit and sense of loyalty will be lost, which can, among other things, damage good staff relationships. Similar problems arise in respect of the customers. Management must take steps to guard against the danger of actions becoming stereotyped and public protest lost in bureaucratic officialdom. Nevertheless, it must be recognized that in a large undertaking it is difficult to preserve the personal touch and it is the job of the public relations officer to maintain the goodwill of the undertaking which he represents. He is the medium through which management speaks to its customers and customers speak to management. The customers' interests are his interests and it is his responsibility to bring public opinion to the notice of other sections of management responsible for shaping policy. But it must be remembered that good public relations does not end with the establishment of a specialized department at headquarters. All staff, and particularly supervisory staff on the road, are ambassadors in their own right and the appointment of a public relations officer in no way lessens the responsibilities of other staff in this respect.

A branch of public relations activities calling for special mention is the press section. All transport undertakings, particularly the large ones, are frequently 'in the news' in the national and local newspapers, both of which can and do influence public opinion regardless of the accuracy of their announcements. Lack of first-hand information usually leads to a misinterpretation of policy and misrepresentation in the press makes bad publicity. Bad news sells better than good news, and unjustified criticism is more likely to be avoided if newspaper editors are given adequate and authentic advice. The publication of such information has a dual purpose, particularly if it relates to the introduction of new facilities, as a suitable column in the press has news value to the publisher and advertising value to the operator. It is the special job of the press officer to maintain friendly contact with editors and keep them fully informed of current events as they effect the undertaking by the preparation of special press handouts. It is the image that counts and it is the job of the public relations officer as well as the publicity officer to help to create and preserve it. If the engineers or the operators fall down then the task becomes difficult; it is always easier to bring a good service to public notice than it is to explain why it is not a good service. Nevertheless, some explaining has to be done, particularly if policies are not likely to be received with general acclaim. Staggering of hours, bus priorities and other such measures that contribute to efficiency or economy take a little bit of public education if opinion is to be directed the right way. The reasons must be pursued through the media, in correspondence and at public meetings. This is not likely to be done satisfactorily without a public relations department even if in a small undertaking the function happens to be one of the many responsibilities of the traffic manager.

Political influence

Commercial implications

Whatever the context, politics tends to creep in but the style of its influence varies according to government policies and, as far as road passenger transport is concerned, to the extent that it is seen as a social service. In Great Britain the current policy is privatization (as has been seen) with minimum revenue support; but, importantly in this context, the emphasis is on small-scale ownership rather than large which certainly does nothing to encourage the network principle. Operators run commercially whatever and wherever they wish and it is only the unremunerative and hence the uncovered parts that are left where local government (passenger transport authorities and county councils) step in and seek tenders to provide financially supported facilities in those areas at political discretion (see Chapter 11). In some parts of the world and particularly in the major conurbations it is a different story and there are many examples where much more public money is spent to support buses and trams, not necessarily with ultra-cheap fares but certainly with fares well within 'what the traffic can bear'. What follows, therefore, has only limited relevance for British operators but as politics tend to change and world-wide there is in some places still considerable political involvement, this book would be incomplete without reference to the subject.

Mention has just been made of fare levels in a subsidy situation. The basis of charging and the cost of travel has a strong bearing on the number of passengers who use the service. It has been seen that it is self-defeating to charge more than the traffic can bear but this in itself is dependent on the purpose of the journey and the person who is making it. The cheaper the fare the more people will be attracted to ride, although seldom would the extra traffic so generated be sufficient to justify commercially any general lowering of fares. But it could, nevertheless, be a political expedient that more people should ride, and if adequate compensation is forthcoming then the operator can be expected to charge lower fares as required. In any case, he is not likely to demur as it can only mean more business for him. If, however, the process is taken to its ultimate conclusion with no fare at all being charged at the time of travel, the bus would then become a purely social service paid for out of taxation either nationally or locally. Although apart from isolated services, special cases or groups of people, there are at present no examples of a free fare system of any significance, the idea has been mooted in various places. If it ever came it would have a profound effect on operating practices and should, therefore, be mentioned. Although in a sense this is somewhat inconsistent with commercial practices, discussion in this context is appropriate in view of its close association with charging practices and revenue receipts. Before so doing, however, there is one other side to the revenue support issue which should be considered, and that applies not to the receiver (the operator) but to those who authorize such an arrangement.

Revenue support

All that has been said so far has been geared to the commercial viewpoint of a bus undertaking. Although the need for revenue support has been acknowledged it has been suggested for operational and customer relation reasons that independent transport managements should not only remain but should be seen to remain in complete control of their businesses, thereby preserving their local identities and public goodwill. But at the same time it must be acknowledged that as it is the responsibility of politicians to determine the extent to which public money will be allocated for revenue support, they will also want to be satisfied that it is spent in the most propitious way. It is reasonable to assume, therefore, that they will expect to do rather more than allow operators to continue in the way they see fit without question and then foot whatever bills might be presented to them. Such an arrangement would be something less than satisfactory for the custodians of the public purse and just as they take professional guidance from their engineers, planners and administrators, so they will wish to have people versed in the provision of public transport to advise them. Hence operators are likely to find themselves in discussion and negotiation with staff of local authorities, etc., whose job it is to implement the policies as laid down by their political masters.

The more that is paid in subsidy the greater will political influence be and it is the social factors and repercussions on highways and land use that politicians take into account. The provision of bus services allows everybody to move around and thereby enables the daily life of the individual and the nation collectively to continue. There are, however, other social benefits which a bus gives. Although public transport cannot match the convenience afforded by private transport and it is not easy to attract existing motorists away from their cars and on to buses, the existence of a bus system does, nevertheless, reduce to some extent the number of private cars that would otherwise be on the road. This is of considerable importance as the bus is far more economical in terms of road space per passenger carried than is the private car. If there was no bus network or it was reduced to such proportions that it could no longer cater for all local travel requirements, then those bus passengers who were able to do so would turn to private transport and more cars are not to be encouraged. Even to the existing motorist, the bus has a social value as not only does it hold down traffic congestion to the extent that he is able to use his own car, the bus is also there as a stand-by service when his own vehicle is for any reason not available.

The social benefits of a bus service may be summarized as follows:

1. It helps to reduce traffic congestion and keeps it at acceptable proportions.
2. It avoids the need for costly roadworks which would otherwise be necessary to accommodate as far as possible an increase in vehicular traffic.
3. It helps to reduce fuel consumption which, in view of the energy situation, can only be an issue of increasing national importance.
4. It reduces air and noise pollution from cars.
5. It avoids the need for more car parks.
6. It makes it possible for everybody to move around, including those who have no access to or are unable to use cars and would otherwise be immobilized.

On the question of spending public money, politicians have perforce to take a wider view of things than does transport management. They need to consider:

1. The value of the benefits as listed at (1) to (6) above and the situation which would emerge if the bus system either disappeared or was severely truncated.
2. Fare levels as they would be in the absence of subsidy and the relationship with price and income levels generally and what the traffic can bear.
3. The desirability or otherwise of subsidizing the travelling expenses of any specific categories of people.
4. Whether cheaper fares attract the right type of traffic to produce overall community benefits.

Furthermore, just as an operator will seek a situation which is most favourable to him, politicians will rightly endeavour to get the most for the least. They will, therefore, try to ascertain what action operators would take if no financial support was forthcoming. For various reasons it would not necessarily mean automatic withdrawal.

If it is decided that a subsidy in some form is justified then consideration must be given to the following possibilities either singly or in combination as a means of helping to determine the extent of that subsidy. It will need to be decided whether there should be:

1. A percentage ceiling on a subsidy in relation to either farebox revenue or total costs.
2. A blanket subsidy or selective by routes.

3. A ceiling on the amount of subsidy per passenger journey (or passenger mile).
4. A ceiling on the amount of subsidy per head of population, either for the area as a whole or a specific part.
5. A subsidy set as a percentage of revenue as a method of assessment.

As well as providing for a service, all forms of subsidy are, of course, also to hold down fares at an acceptable level because to charge an economic fare at what would be an unacceptable level is tantamount to not providing a service at all.

The actual amount of subsidy might be decided after consideration of the values of alternative levels of service. If a blanket subsidy is provided, say to keep fares below or service levels above what could be justified on pure economic grounds, there is little influence over operators or incentive for them to conduct their business with maximum efficiency or economy. At the end of the day they just indicate their shortfall. This is not to suggest that managements would tolerate inefficiency but there are nevertheless no built-in safeguards for those who are paying other than examination or audit to the extent that they are able. Selective support, service by service, particularly if there is a final upper limit would help to eliminate services which are either very poorly used or inordinately expensive to run and the criteria for service provision as considered in Chapter 6 has a bearing here. If the policy is to hold down fares, there could be advantage in compensating for each ticket sold. For example, if a 'commercial' fare of '12' is held down at '9', pay '3' for each '9' ticket sold and so on throughout the range. In other words pay by results and leave service levels to the operator who would be required to answer for any inadequacies. If there are no passengers then there is no money. If the service fails to operate again there is no money. The disadvantage of this system lies in excessive administration, and the difficulties in producing the required figures will be seen in Chapter 9 although the advent of electronics into fare collection does overcome (at a cost) most of the problems here.

A further aspect which must be considered is fare levels in a subsidized system. Under these circumstances there can be no commercial yardstick as such—cost plus profit is not relevant. Politicians motivated by social considerations are likely to profess to be pro-bus, anti-private car (although they themselves may be motorists) and in 'playing to the gallery' might seek very low fares with maximum subsidy. However, all this really does is to turn buses into political tools. It will please some and annoy others, and heavy rate bills can only put the bus companies in an unfavourable light even though they had no hand in determining policy. Furthermore, a study by A. Hay of bus patronage in an area of Great Britain (South Yorkshire) where such a policy was followed from 1975 to 1986 suggests that although bus travel did increase there was little contribution to reduction of traffic congestion and no evidence (indeed evidence to the contrary) of the achievement of any income transfer amongst the resident population. One conclusion was that the subsidy of public transport in this way had a disappointing effect in promoting transport, planning and social objectives. But be that as it may and whilst it is all very interesting, the question of what fare levels should be on subsidized services remains. The writer suggests that fares should be up to what the traffic can bear but this again is rather indecisive and not particularly helpful. Nevertheless, fare fixing has already been discussed earlier in this chapter and even in a commercial environment it was seen that the cost plus profit method could not be applied to individual fares or even to individual services. But fares are fixed and are done so in the knowledge that if they are too high people will not (or could not) use buses.

It would seem therefore that a similar principle should be applied to the services that are subsidized.

Free fares

Although there are very few examples, the concept of a free bus service is not new, even on a commercial basis. There are instances of such facilities being provided for publicity purposes, as a means to induce people to visit certain shops or to encourage recruitment at awkwardly sited factories. Being considered here, however, are the social aspects of a no-fare principle applied to a local network and available for everybody to use. Funding entirely through rates or taxes could be accomplished only by a political decision, and disquiet has been expressed regarding the arguments put forward in support of such a policy. If considerable sums of money are to be spent on revenue support then equally considerable sums must be used for capital expenditure, which might not necessarily be available. If it is not, then to take the extreme case, everyone would have a bus pass but there would be no buses. But more than that. Some money at least would have to come from local rates, and shops and other commercial premises carry heavy liabilities in this respect. This additional burden on the owners could only be passed on to customers and the cost of living would in consequence rise. It is likely that under such circumstances a higher percentage of income would then have to be spent by the lower paid groups than by those who are more affluent with the result that those who would suffer would be the very people whom it was planned should benefit. As a means of reducing traffic congestion by enticing motorists out of their cars and on to public transport, the system is once again of doubtful value. Mention was made in Chapter 6 of the great store that the motoring fraternity puts on the convenience of personalized transport. According to *Transport Statistics* (HMSO, London) between the years 1975 and 1985, because of higher prices the average expenditure per household on private motoring has increased between three and four times. The percentage of household expenditure spent on private motoring has increased from 11.04% to 13.0%. But there was still nearly a 23% increase in the number of cars on the road. This suggests that it will take more than free buses to make much impression on the trend and only car restraints will deal with the congestion issue. There is, however, evidence to believe that many pedestrians would become short-distance bus riders if they did not have to pay but this would only delay the service and make it less attractive. It would not achieve the desired objective.

For various reasons, therefore, a free fares policy is not likely to find widespread support and it must remain a relatively minor issue in any study of transport operation. Nevertheless, a free fares system is a possibility which some politicians have not overlooked. It is necessary, therefore, to consider, albeit briefly, the effects of such a policy on operating practices.

A free fares system might be preceded by a range of sub-standard fares—fares held down well below what the traffic could bear, for political reasons. It could be, for example, that existing charges are kept constant with the effect that in a period of inflation, in real terms, prices fall. If this situation remains then, subject to inflation not abating, the time must come when the cost of collecting fares is greater than the revenue that they produce, in which case there is good reason not to charge anything at the time of travel. There are two aspects of a free fares policy that call for consideration. The first involves the economics of the system in terms of bus operation and secondly there are the operating and other complexities which are bound to arise.

It will be quite clear from Chapters 9 and 10 that fare collection involves cost in terms of both capital equipment and labour. Money has to be collected, tickets issued, cash handed in, coins counted and cash in bulk banked together with a need for all of the supporting administration, audit and necessary security arrangements. Conductors could be dispensed with subject to the vehicles being of a suitable type (most of them now are) but conductors are a disappearing breed anyway and as drivers would still be responsible for passengers it is debatable whether they could ever be deprived of their one-man allowance. A free fares policy, however, is not likely to be a part of any national policy. If ever it did come it would more probably be through a local decision and any local free fare zone is unlikely to coincide with a bus undertaking's operating territory. In other words, some bus routes are always likely to be cross-boundary in local authority terms, in which case they would operate only partly within a free fares area. Those services that did go outside such a zone would still be subject to normal charging methods. This being the case, provision for fare collection and all that goes with it would have to be retained although the equipment would be under-utilized. The absence of tickets within a free fares zone would of course eliminate the need for travelling ticket inspectors, but those officials are likely to be required in any case for control work and other supervisory duties. Nevertheless, some savings in administration could be anticipated and furthermore there would be no loss of revenue through tickets not being issued, fares uncollected, passengers overriding, etc.

Thus far the exercise is straightforward. The savings are quantifiable but variable according to circumstances although they need not be as great as might at first be imagined. The imponderables come when the repercussions on traffic planning are examined and this is where the criteria for service provision becomes of even greater significance. Remember what was said in Chapter 6. Route statistics are the all-important tool for traffic managers to judge whether their services are correctly planned. Trends can be detected and warning lights can spark off more detailed investigations to see whether any adjustments are necessary. With a free fares system, all such statistics have gone, but with a purely social service it does not necessarily follow that a deterioration in demand signals reductions or withdrawals. At this stage buses would come into a similar category to that of other public utilities such as the library service, schools and refuse collection where everybody pays regardless of the extent of use and expects to receive a standard 'product' in return. This could create an entirely new situation and the greater the degree of subsidy, the more remote might the hitherto accepted practices for determining service provision become. Unlike certain other public utilities, the demand for public transport would not be easily predictable as:

1. The journeys to be made vary considerably.
2. The demand for shopping and pleasure travel is not regular and some people do not use buses every day or, indeed, every week.
3. Some people do not use buses at all, in which case it would be a waste to make provision for them even though those concerned might not accept the point.

One final point, of course, is that people with nothing better to do could inundate the system. If a supermarket gave away its goods there would be a queue and the 'customers' would take more than they really required. The same principle could apply to buses, and the formula adopted for the other utilities, e.g. one refuse bin emptied or four library tickets issued, could not be applied to public transport. Also, complete rate support could provoke demands from ratepayers for reasonable (undetermined) facilities to be provided for their use regardless of the numbers of people involved.

Free fares would be the final transition from a commercial to a social service; and if it ever came, planning and service provision would take on a completely new dimension.

8 Schedule compilation

Introduction

This chapter is about the compilation of time and duty schedules.

Scheduling falls into two parts —that which applies to vehicles and that which applies to the staff who man them, i.e. the drivers and conductors. It is the vehicle schedules that must first be prepared and it is here that the compiler must maintain a close liaison with his counterpart who determines service requirements. The latter performs more of a commercial function which was considered in Chapter 7 as was the publication of the timetable after it has been prepared. Not only must the compiler be advised regarding the quantum of service and any set timings for specific purposes which might be necessary; he must also be informed regarding the scheduled speeds, which is a subject of Chapter 10.

It is the predetermined schedules which govern the utilization of vehicles and staff, both of which are very expensive items. An inefficient schedule could cost the undertaking a great deal of unnecessary money and it is imperative that the assets be used to maximum advantage. At the same time there is nothing to be gained by padding out the timetable with journeys of no traffic value only to keep buses moving. Idle time on the part of drivers and conductors is also waste time because they will be entitled to a full day's pay regardless of what they do, which brings in the point that duty schedules must conform to conditions as agreed with the trade union.

The schedules department, assuming that the undertaking is of a sufficient size to warrant a separate function for this purpose, is sandwiched between what is fed into it from the commercial and staff sides and the implementation of its endeavours on the road by the operating staff. For the reason already stated, much of the financial prosperity of an undertaking depends on the skill of the schedule compilers in getting the most out of the least. This applies particularly to duty schedules where there is likely to be a much greater range of alternatives and it is with experience that optimum solutions can be produced. Nevertheless, however much ingenuity might be exercised, if the parameters are set it could be that even the best possible schedule is extremely wasteful. It is under these circumstances that compilers might seek a reconsideration of the specification and a balance must then be struck between service requirements and schedule efficiency.

It is not easy to describe and explain in textbook style the act of schedule compilation. Different undertakings have different approaches to the subject; their method of working varies just as does the way the finished product is presented. Duty schedules in particular are not only very closely associated with staff agreements, the process of preparation and implementation is also one of the main topics of staff consultation. Trade unions have a particular involvement on this issue and schedules do certainly affect the working life of their members as much as anything else. At the same time trade unions tend to be parochial. Whilst, therefore, there are basic principles that can be explained here, the detail becomes more a matter of custom and practice and that is why the successful schedule compiler relies as much on experience as on book knowledge. There is, however, one breakaway from established practice and that is schedule compilation by computer. Such a process has been in the course of exploration and development since the early 1960s and some of the larger organizations do now prepare their schedules in this way. The same basic principles must, of course, apply, but they are programmed into a computer instead of being interpreted manually. What has been said in a few words, however, has meant years of research and experiment and it is not part of this book to become involved in the finer arts of computer programming.

Timetable preparation

The type of service most appropriate for consideration here is that which runs regularly all day at set frequencies (which may, of course, be varied according to the time of day). The essential ingredients for drawing up such a timetable are:

1. The required quantum of service, which may be end to end or with augmentation over certain sections and which is likely to vary according to the day of the week.
2. The speed schedule (which will include intermediate timing points for operating and publicity purposes and which could vary between different periods of the day).
3. Minimum layover periods at each end of the route and any intermediate hesitation points plus any built in recovery time at the termini.
4. Any special instructions such as specific departure or arrival times either as a general requirement or for particular journeys such as factory breaks or connections with other services.
5. First and last journeys.

Armed with this information, preparation can proceed. The important feature as far as timetable efficiency is concerned is the variable at (1) in relation to (2) plus (3). To put it another way, the relationship between (1) and (2) will determine the length of the layover at (3) and the shorter this is (down as far as the declared minimum) then the less will be the stand time, remembering always that vehicles do not earn money when their wheels are not turning.

The following formula is important:

$$\frac{\text{Journey time} \times 2 + \text{stand time}}{\text{service frequency}} = \text{number of vehicles required}$$

In other words, the return journey time plus the stand time must be a multiple of the service frequency. It is the stand time that is the variable and it is this that determines efficiency. To take an easy example, if the single journey time is 26 minutes, the frequency is every 30 minutes and the agreed stand time plus recovery time is 15% of the running time (which would make it eight minutes split between the two ends) then, in accordance with the formula:

$$\frac{26 \times 2 + 8}{30} = 2 \text{ buses}$$

The stand time of 8 minutes is the bare minimum, there is 52 minutes wheel turning time in every hour, and nothing could be more efficient than that.

Imagine now that the running time was not 26 minutes but 31 minutes. The figures would then be:

$$\frac{31 \times 2 + 10}{30} = 3 \text{ buses}$$

As the numerator must be a multiple of the denominator and the only variable is the stand time (now 10 minutes), this figure must become 28 to give:

$$\frac{31 \times 2 + 28}{30} \text{ or } \frac{90}{30} = 3 \text{ buses}$$

If the stand time is split equally at each end, then the bus would run for 31 minutes and then stand for 14 minutes, which would be very wasteful. If the vehicle had to remain manned whilst on the stand, then the waste would be compounded. In fact the three buses could give a 24-minute frequency at no extra vehicle (or staff) cost, namely:

$$\frac{31 \times 2 + 10}{24} = 3 \text{ buses}$$

Whether a 24-minute headway would be acceptable, bearing in mind that the times are not standard for each hour but can be repeated only in every alternate hour, is another matter, but this does lead into a working practice which is usually adopted at the formative stage. If it is accepted that the times need to be repetitive, which means that the service frequency is a factor of 60 (and remember from Chapter 6 that the writer strongly recommends this wherever practicable) then, apart from first and last journeys and those that mark a change in frequency, only the 'specimen hour' needs to be indicated (i.e. 'and then at the following minutes past each hour'). This means that it is the specimen hour that is first considered by the traffic department when the specification is being prepared. It should be noted, however, that the more frequent is the service, the less will be the effect of the relationship between running time and timetable efficiency. When a headway gets down to as little as, say, 5 minutes, wheel turning time can be maximized regardless of the journey time. Note that although in this example the agreed stand time is quoted as a percentage of running time, this does not have to be the case and in reality it is not always as generous as this. Even so there could be an agreed minimum stand time even on short routes.

Consider now some living examples. The timetable of service 261 of London Buses Ltd. (*Figure 8.1*) represents a suburban service in a built-up area and illustrates straightforward 12, 20 and 30 minute headways. By determining the running and layover times and in accordance with the above formula the number

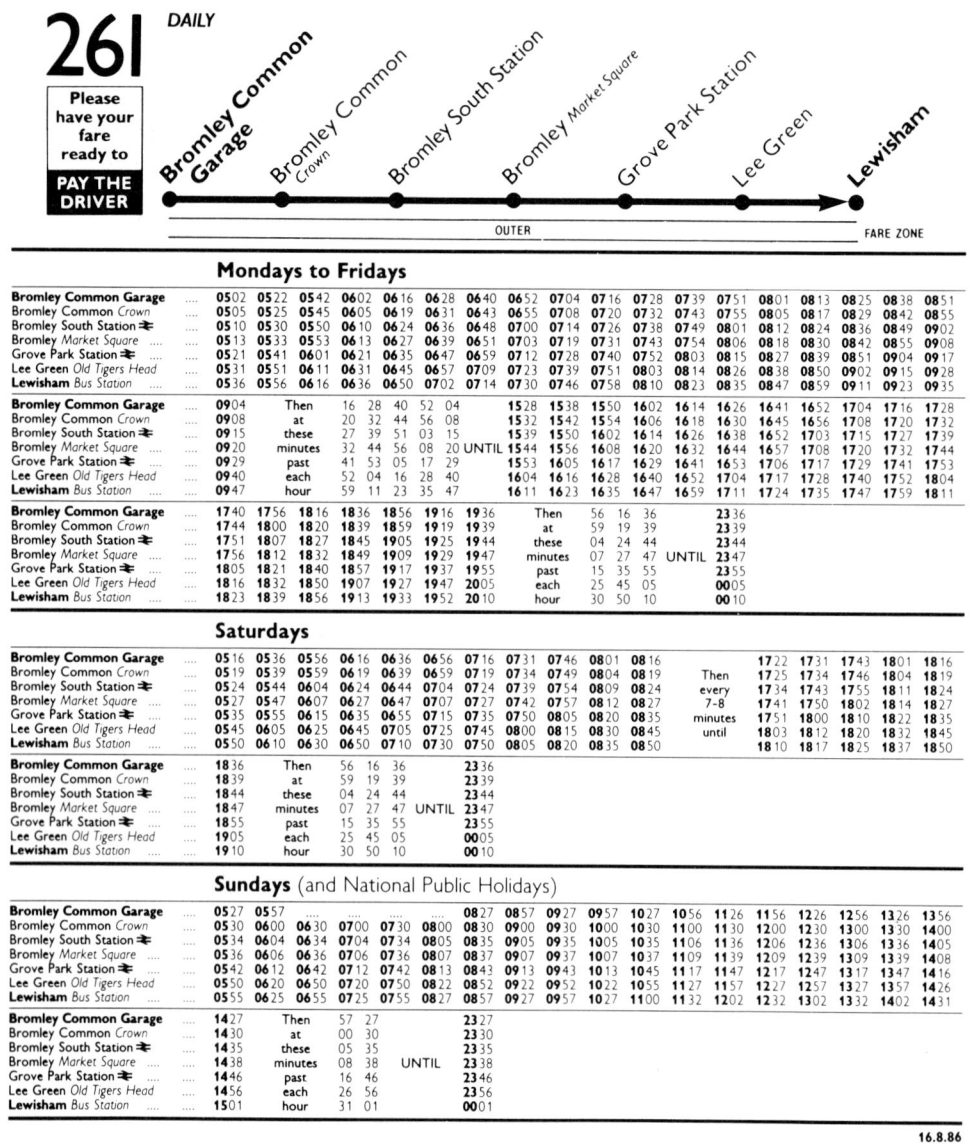

Figure 8.1 Timetable of a self-contained surburban service. (Reproduced by kind permission of London Regional Transport.)

261 DAILY

Please have your fare ready to **PAY THE DRIVER**

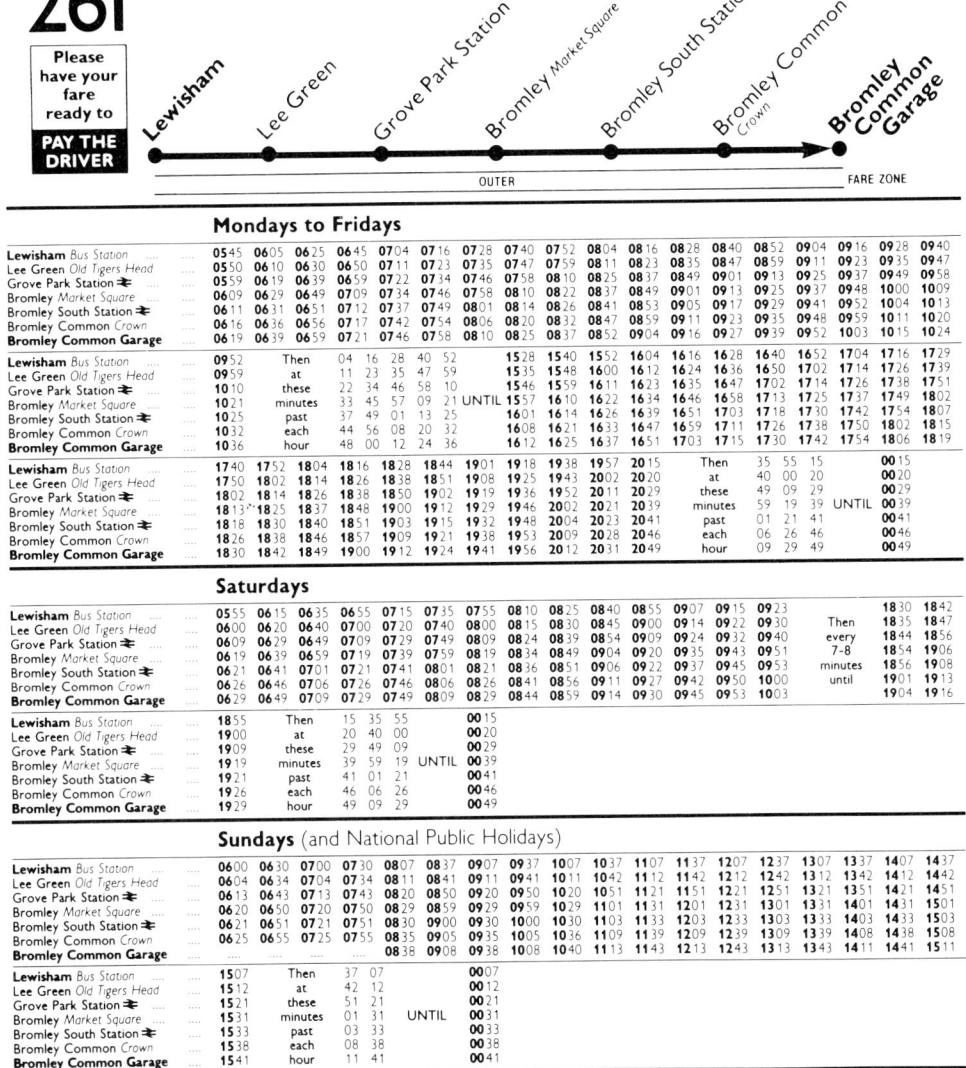

Lewisham — Lee Green — Grove Park Station — Bromley Market Square — Bromley South Station — Bromley Common Crown — Bromley Common Garage

OUTER   FARE ZONE

Mondays to Fridays

Lewisham Bus Station	0545	0605	0625	0645	0704	0716	0728	0740	0752	0804	0816	0828	0840	0852	0904	0916	0928	0940
Lee Green Old Tigers Head	0550	0610	0630	0650	0711	0723	0735	0747	0759	0811	0823	0835	0847	0859	0911	0923	0935	0947
Grove Park Station ≷	0559	0619	0639	0659	0722	0734	0746	0758	0810	0825	0837	0849	0901	0913	0925	0937	0949	0958
Bromley Market Square	0609	0629	0649	0709	0734	0746	0758	0810	0822	0837	0849	0901	0913	0925	0937	0948	1000	1009
Bromley South Station ≷	0611	0631	0651	0712	0737	0749	0801	0814	0826	0841	0853	0905	0917	0929	0941	0952	1004	1013
Bromley Common Crown	0616	0636	0656	0717	0742	0754	0806	0820	0832	0847	0859	0911	0923	0935	0948	0959	1011	1020
Bromley Common Garage	0619	0639	0659	0721	0746	0758	0810	0825	0837	0852	0904	0916	0927	0939	0952	1003	1015	1024

Lewisham Bus Station	0952	Then	04	16	28	40	52		1528	1540	1552	1604	1616	1628	1640	1652	1704	1716	1729
Lee Green Old Tigers Head	0959	at	11	23	35	47	59		1535	1548	1600	1612	1624	1636	1650	1702	1714	1726	1739
Grove Park Station ≷	1010	these	22	34	46	58	10		1546	1559	1611	1623	1635	1647	1702	1714	1726	1738	1751
Bromley Market Square	1021	minutes	33	45	57	09	21	UNTIL	1557	1610	1622	1634	1646	1658	1713	1725	1737	1749	1802
Bromley South Station ≷	1025	past	37	49	01	13	25		1601	1614	1626	1639	1651	1703	1718	1730	1742	1754	1807
Bromley Common Crown	1032	each	44	56	08	20	32		1608	1621	1633	1647	1659	1711	1726	1738	1750	1802	1815
Bromley Common Garage	1036	hour	48	00	12	24	36		1612	1625	1637	1651	1703	1715	1730	1742	1754	1806	1819

Lewisham Bus Station	1740	1752	1804	1816	1828	1844	1901	1918	1938	1957	2015	Then	35	55	15		0015
Lee Green Old Tigers Head	1750	1802	1814	1826	1838	1851	1908	1925	1943	2002	2020	at	40	00	20		0020
Grove Park Station ≷	1802	1814	1826	1838	1850	1902	1919	1936	1952	2011	2029	these	49	09	29		0029
Bromley Market Square	1813	1825	1837	1848	1900	1912	1929	1946	2002	2021	2039	minutes	59	19	39	UNTIL	0039
Bromley South Station ≷	1818	1830	1840	1851	1903	1915	1932	1948	2004	2023	2041	past	01	21	41		0041
Bromley Common Crown	1826	1838	1846	1857	1909	1921	1938	1953	2009	2028	2046	each	06	26	46		0046
Bromley Common Garage	1830	1842	1849	1900	1912	1924	1941	1956	2012	2031	2049	hour	09	29	49		0049

Saturdays

Lewisham Bus Station	0555	0615	0635	0655	0715	0735	0755	0810	0825	0840	0855	0907	0915	0923		1830	1842
Lee Green Old Tigers Head	0600	0620	0640	0700	0720	0740	0800	0815	0830	0845	0900	0914	0922	0930	Then	1835	1847
Grove Park Station ≷	0609	0629	0649	0709	0729	0749	0809	0824	0839	0854	0909	0924	0932	0940	every	1844	1856
Bromley Market Square	0619	0639	0659	0719	0739	0759	0819	0834	0849	0904	0920	0935	0943	0951	7-8	1854	1906
Bromley South Station ≷	0621	0641	0701	0721	0741	0801	0821	0836	0851	0906	0922	0937	0945	0953	minutes	1856	1908
Bromley Common Crown	0626	0646	0706	0726	0746	0806	0826	0841	0856	0911	0927	0942	0950	1000	until	1901	1913
Bromley Common Garage	0629	0649	0709	0729	0749	0809	0829	0844	0859	0914	0930	0945	0953	1003		1904	1916

Lewisham Bus Station	1855	Then	15	35	55		0015
Lee Green Old Tigers Head	1900	at	20	40	00		0020
Grove Park Station ≷	1909	these	29	49	09		0029
Bromley Market Square	1919	minutes	39	59	19	UNTIL	0039
Bromley South Station ≷	1921	past	41	01	21		0041
Bromley Common Crown	1926	each	46	06	26		0046
Bromley Common Garage	1929	hour	49	09	29		0049

Sundays (and National Public Holidays)

Lewisham Bus Station	0600	0630	0700	0730	0807	0837	0907	0937	1007	1037	1107	1137	1207	1237	1307	1337	1407	1437
Lee Green Old Tigers Head	0604	0634	0704	0734	0811	0841	0911	0941	1011	1042	1112	1142	1212	1242	1312	1342	1412	1442
Grove Park Station ≷	0613	0643	0713	0743	0820	0850	0920	0950	1020	1051	1121	1151	1221	1251	1321	1351	1421	1451
Bromley Market Square	0620	0650	0720	0750	0829	0859	0929	0959	1029	1101	1131	1201	1231	1301	1331	1401	1431	1501
Bromley South Station ≷	0621	0651	0721	0751	0830	0900	0930	1000	1030	1103	1133	1203	1233	1303	1333	1403	1433	1503
Bromley Common Crown	0625	0655	0725	0755	0835	0905	0935	1005	1036	1109	1139	1209	1239	1309	1339	1408	1438	1508
Bromley Common Garage					0838	0908	0938	1008	1040	1113	1143	1213	1243	1313	1343	1411	1441	1511

Lewisham Bus Station	1507	Then	37	07		0007
Lee Green Old Tigers Head	1512	at	42	12		0012
Grove Park Station ≷	1521	these	51	21		0021
Bromley Market Square	1531	minutes	01	31	UNTIL	0031
Bromley South Station ≷	1533	past	03	33		0033
Bromley Common Crown	1538	each	08	38		0038
Bromley Common Garage	1541	hour	11	41		0041

16.8.86

of buses required during these regular periods of operation is as follows. By way of explanation the running times in each direction and the layovers at each end have been spelled out separately:

$$12 \text{ min headway} \quad \frac{43 + 44 + 4 + 5}{12} = 8 \text{ buses}$$

$$20 \text{ min headway} \quad \frac{34 + 34 + 7 + 5}{20} = 4 \text{ buses}$$

$$30 \text{ min headway} \quad \frac{34 + 34 + 16 + 6}{30} = 3 \text{ buses}$$

The Greater London area where this service operates is a particularly congested part of the country through high car ownership, even in the outer suburbs between Lewisham and Bromley. Delays are so consistent that contrary to what is said in Chapter 10, London Buses sees fit to allocate extra running time during the daytime on Mondays to Fridays which is when the 12 minute headway is in operation. (It is even greater in the Monday to Friday peaks.) Overall, the timetable provides for 91% wheel turning time and 9% stand time on the 12 minute headway example, 85% and 15% on the 20 minute headway example and 76% and 24% on the 30 minute headway example. The Monday to Friday specimen hour is particularly efficient. It might even be too efficient as the stand time plus extra running time might still not give sufficient recovery time for the service to be maintained. If this was the case then an extra bus would have to be built in to the schedule and the combined stand time of 9 minutes would then become 21 minutes. The extra bus would provide no extra service and therefore earn no extra revenue. If the evening and weekend running times could be maintained in the daytime on Mondays to Fridays then, for a 12 minute headway, only six vehicles would be required with 2 minutes at each end or seven vehicles with 8 minutes at each end. This speaks volumes of the costs to bus operators of traffic congestion. There is also the point to what extent bus crews are prepared to make up time, forgo layovers, etc. Staff attitudes vary not only between companies but also between countries but this is something more appropriate for Chapter 10.

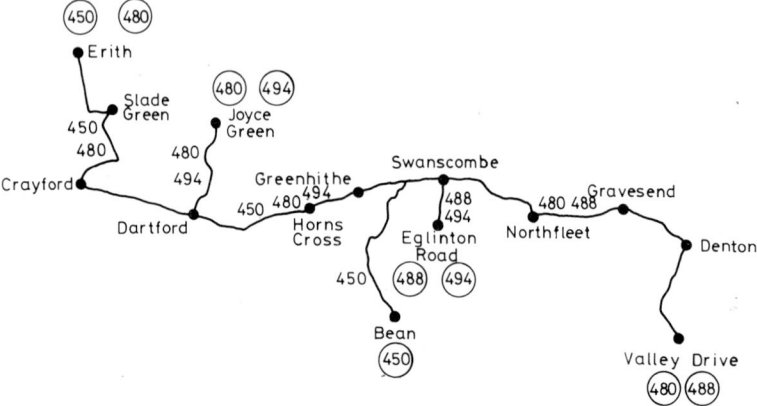

Figure 8.2 Sketch map of Services 450, 480, 488 and 494 of London Country Bus Services Ltd (now Kentish Bus and Coach Company).

The next example—services 450/494 and 480/488 of the Kentish Bus and Coach Company—shows a more complex arrangement with interworkings between services to provide regular headways over common sections of route and also interworking of vehicles between services to produce efficient running schedules.

First look at *Figure 8.2* and see how the different services interwork, particularly along the main road east of Dartford towards Swanscombe where a joint 10 minute frequency is provided. Now consider the specimen hours in *Figure 8.3*. Services 450 and 488 are self-contained like 261. However, 494 has a return running time of 71 minutes which would be grossly inefficient for a 60 minute service. The service 480 timetable could not be efficient either. Furthermore, the 480 specimen hour is more complex than the other services examined and one which the required number of vehicles cannot be calculated by recourse to the formula. However, as the timings cover the complete workings during the course of 1 hour, the totals of the running times and stand times for each direction must be a multiple of 60. For schedule efficiency it is appropriate in this example to interwork vehicles employed on services 480 and 494 (into Joyce Green at 26 as a 494 and out as a 480 at 32 and into Joyce Green at 06 as a 480 and out at 12 as a 494) and the total figures in minutes are as follows:

	Totals
Service 480	
To Valley Drive	
79 + 60 + 60 + 79	278
To Erith/Joyce Green	
83 + 64 + 64 + 83	294
Stand time at Erith	
8 + 8	16
Stand time at Joyce Green	
6 + 6	12
Stand time at Valley Drive	
10 + 10 + 10 + 10	40
Service 494	
To Swanscombe	
31	31
To Joyce Green	
40	40
Stand time at Swanscombe	
3	3
Stand time at Joyce Green	
6	6
	720

The number of vehicles required to work this combined service is obtained by dividing 720 by 60 which is 12.

Another example which involves vehicle interworking but this time not on parallel routes are the services 1 and 39 of South Yorkshire Transport Ltd. Look at the sketch map in *Figure 8.4*. Remember that service 261 ran along a main road through residential suburban areas. The 480 group linked smaller 'country' towns. Now there is an example of local town services in what is a busy and densely populated urban area, being Sheffield. Service 1 is of the radial type (type (i) in

LONDON COUNTRY

Erith to Bean
via Dartford

Service
450

Joyce Green Hospital to Swanscombe Eglinton Road
via Dartford

Service
494

Including Service 480 between Erith or Joyce Green Hospital and Swanscombe

Mondays to Fridays

Service:	480	480	450	480	480	450	480	480	480	450	480	480	494	480	494	480	480	450	480	480	480	494
Erith Bexley Road/Cross Street				0615				0651			0708		0735		0759		0823		0843			
Slade Green Station ⇌				0623				0659			0717		0744		0808		0832		0852			
Crayford Jolly Farmers				0626				0702			0721		0748		0812		0836		0856			
Crayford Bridge ⇌				0630				0707			0726		0753		0817		0841		0901	0909	
Joyce Green Hospital		0605		0622		0641		0657		0717		0748		0809		0832		0852				0912
Dartford Station ⇌	0518	0612	0624	0629	0638	0650	0655	0705	0716	0723	0725	0735	0756	0802	0817	0826	0840	0850	0900	0910	0918	0920
Horns Cross Bull	0528	0622	0633	0639	0648	0701	0707	0717	0728	0734	0737	0747	0808	0814	0829	0838	0852	0901	0912	0922	0930	0932
Greenhithe Knockhall Post Office				0638			0707				0740								0907			
Bean Bramble Avenue				0646			0717				0750								0917			
Swanscombe George & Dragon	0535	0629		0646	0655		0715	0725	0736		0745	0755	0816	0822	0837	0846	0900		0920	0930	0938	0940
Swanscombe Eglinton Road	E	E		E	E		E	E	0739		E	E	0819	E	0840	E	E		E	E	E	0943

Service:	480	480	450	480	480	494		480	480	494	480	480	450	480	480	480	480	450	480	480
Erith Bexley Road/Cross Street	03		23		43			1743		1803			1823		1843		1903		1923	2003
Slade Green Station ⇌	12		32		52			1752		1812			1832		1852		1911		1931	2011
Crayford Jolly Farmers	Then	16		36		56		1756		1816			1836		1856		1914		1934	2014
Crayford Bridge ⇌	at	21		41		01	U	1801		1821			1841		1901		1918		1938	2018
Joyce Green Hospital	these		32		52		12	N	1752		1812		1833		1852		1912		1932	G	1959	
Dartford Station ⇌	mins.	30	40	50	00	10	20	T	1800	1810	1820	1830	1841	1850	1900	1909	1919	1926	1939		2006	2026
Horns Cross Bull	past	42	52	01	12	22	32	I	1812	1822	1832	1842	1853	1901	1910	1919	1929	1936	1949		2016	2036
Greenhithe Knockhall Post Office	each			07				L					1906							
Bean Bramble Avenue	hour			17									1914							
Swanscombe George & Dragon		50	00		20	30	40		1820	1830	1840	1850	1901		1917	1926	1936	1943	1956		2023	2043
Swanscombe Eglinton Road		E	E		E	E	43		E	E	1843	E	E		E	E	E	E	E		E	E

E — To Gravesend

Bean to Erith
via Dartford

Service
450

Swanscombe Eglinton Road
to Joyce Green Hospital
via Dartford

Service
494

Including Service 480 between Swanscombe and Joyce Green Hospital or Erith

Mondays to Fridays

Service:	480	480	480	480	480	480	480	480	480	450	480	480	450	480	480	494	450	480	480	450	480
Swanscombe Eglinton Road																0746					0822
Swanscombe George & Dragon ⇌	0454	0522	0532	0547	0557	0615	0625	0631	0637	0644		0701	0712		0733	0745	0755		0805	0815	0831
Bean Bramble Avenue										0648			0720			0752					
Greenhithe Knockhall Post Office										0654			0727			0759					
Horns Cross Bull	0501	0529	0539	0554	0604	0622	0632	0638	0644	0651	0659	0709	0720	0734	0741	0753	0803	0806	0813	0823	0839
Dartford Market Street	0510	0538	0548	0603	0613	0631	0641	0647	0653	0700	0709	0720	0731	0744	0752	0804	0814	0816	0824	0834	0850
Joyce Green Hospital		0558	0613		0651				0712			0743		0804		0826		0846			
Crayford Bridge ⇌	0546			0621	0639			0702			0730		0754		0814				0834		0854	0900
Crayford Jolly Farmers	0549			0624	0642			0707			0735		0759		0819				0839		0859	
Slade Green Station ⇌	0552			0627	0645			0711			0739		0803		0823				0843		0903	
Erith Bexley Road/Cross Street	0603			0638	0656			0723			0751		0815		0835				0855		0915	

Service:	480	480	494	480	480	450		480	480	494	480	480	450		480	480	480	494	480	450	480	480
Swanscombe Eglinton Road			0846										Y					1846				
Swanscombe George & Dragon ⇌	0835	0845	0855	0905	0915			35	45	55	05	15				1815		1835	1855	1911		1927	2007
Bean Bramble Avenue						0920	Then						20				1820			1916		
Greenhithe Knockhall Post Office						0927	at						27	U			1827			1922		
Horns Cross Bull	0843	0853	0903	0913	0923	0934	these	43	53	03	13	23	34	N		1823	1834	1843	1903	1918	1927	1934	2014
Dartford Market Street	0854	0904	0914	0924	0934	0944	mins.	54	04	14	24	34	44	T		1834	1844	1854	1912	1927	1935	1943	2023
Joyce Green Hospital	0906		0926		0946		past	06		26		46				1846		1906	1922			1953	
Crayford Bridge ⇌		0914		0934		0954	each		14		34		54	L			1854			1936			2032
Crayford Jolly Farmers		0919		0939		0959	hour		19		39		59				1859			1940			2036
Slade Green Station ⇌		0923		0943		1003			23		43		03				1902			1943			2039
Erith Bexley Road/Cross Street		0935		0955		1015			35		55		15				1913			1954			2050

Figure 8.3 Timetable extracts of services to show interworking and a more complex specimen hour. (Reproduced by kind permission of London Country Bus Services (South-East.) Ltd.) (now Kentish Bus and Coach Co.)

LONDON COUNTRY

Erith or Joyce Green Hospital to Gravesend Valley Drive
via Dartford, Swanscombe, and Northfleet

Service 480

Swanscombe Eglinton Road to Gravesend Valley Drive
via Northfleet

Service 488

For complete service from Erith see 450 and 494 and complete service from Joyce Green Hospital via Mill Pond Road see 499

Mondays to Fridays

Service							488			488			488	488
Erith Bexley Road/Cross Street						0615			0651		0708		0735	
Slade Green Station						0623			0659		0717		0744	
Crayford Jolly Farmers						0626			0702		0721		0748	
Crayford Bridge						0630			0707		0726		0753	
Joyce Green Hospital				0605	0622 +		0657		+	0717	+		
Dartford Station	0518			0612	0629 0638		0655 0705		0716 0725 0735			0802		
Horns Cross Bull	0528			0622	0639 0648		0707 0717		0728 0737 0747			0814		
Swanscombe Eglinton Road					+	0657 +	+	0726 0739 +	+	0801 +		0831		
Swanscombe George & Dragon	0535		0629	0646 0655	0705 0715 0725 0735	0745 0755 0810 0822 0840								
Northfleet Leather Bottel	0540		0634	0651 0701	0711 0721 0731 0741	0751 0801 0816 0828 0846								
Northfleet Bus Garage	0443 0458 0525 0540 0555 0611 0621 0636 0645 0653 0703 0713 0723 0733 0743	0753 0803 0818 0830 0848												
Gravesend Stuart Road	0446 0501 0528 0545 0558 0614 0624 0639 0648 0656 0706 0716 0726 0736 0746	0756 0806 0821 0833 0851												
Gravesend Clock Tower	0450 0505 0532 0549 0602 0618 0628 0643 0652 0701 0711 0721 0731 0741 0751	0801 0811 0826 0838 0856												
Denton Milton Ale Shades	0453 0508 0535 0552 0605 0621 0631 0646 0655 0705 0715 0725 0735 0745 0755	0805 0815 0830 0842 0900												
Valley Drive Admiral Beatty	0457 0512 0539 0556 0609 0625 0635 0650 0659 0711 0721 0731 0741 0751	0801 0811 0821 0836 0848 0906												
Valley Drive Mackenzie Way	0502 0517 0544 0601 0614 0630 0640 0655 0705 0717 0727 0737 0747 0757	0807 0817 0827 0842 0854 0912												

Service		488		488			488		488		488
Erith Bexley Road/Cross Street	0759		0843			03		43		1503	1543
Slade Green Station	0808		0852			12		52		1512	1552
Crayford Jolly Farmers	0812		0856			16		56		1516	1556
Crayford Bridge	0817		0901 0909			21		01		1521	1601
Joyce Green Hospital	+	0832	0852 +	+	Then	+ 32	52 +	+		1537	+
Dartford Station	0826 0840		0900 0910 0918		at	30 40	00 10	U	1530 1545	1602 1610	
Horns Cross Bull	0838 0852		0912 0922 0930		these	42 52	12 22	N	1542 1557	1614 1622	
Swanscombe Eglinton Road	+ 0901	+	+ + 0931	minutes	+ +	01 +	+ 31	T	+ 1601	+	
Swanscombe George & Dragon	0846 0900 0910 0920 0930 0938 0940	past	50 00 10 20 30 40	I	1550 1605 1610 1622 1630						
Northfleet Leather Bottel	0852 0906 0916 0926 0936 0944 0946	each	56 06 16 26 36 46		1556 1611 1616 1628 1636						
Northfleet Bus Garage	0854 0908 0918 0928 0938 0946 0948	hour	58 08 18 28 38 48		1558 1613 1618 1630 1638						
Gravesend Stuart Road	0857 0911 0921 0931 0941 0949 0951		01 11 21 31 41 51		1601 1616 1621 1633 1641						
Gravesend Clock Tower	0902 0916 0926 0936 0946 0954 0956		06 16 26 36 46 56		1606 1621 1626 1638 1646						
Denton Milton Ale Shades	0906 0920 0930 0940 0950 1000		10 20 30 40 50 00		1610 1625 1630 1642 1650						
Valley Drive Admiral Beatty	0912 0926 0936 0946 0956 1006		16 26 36 46 56 06		1616 1631 1636 1648 1656						
Valley Drive Mackenzie Way	0918 0932 0942 0952 1002 1012		22 32 42 52 02 12		1622 1637 1642 1654 1702						

Gravesend Valley Drive to Erith or Joyce Green Hospital
via Northfleet, Swanscombe and Dartford

Service 480

Gravesend Valley Drive to Swanscombe Eglinton Road
via Northfleet

Service 488

For complete service to Erith see 450 and 494 and complete service to Joyce Green Hospital via Mill Pond Road see 499

Mondays to Fridays

Service						488			488			488
Valley Drive Mackenzie Way		0507 0522		0550		0606		0619	0636 0645		0700 0712 0722 0732 0742	
Valley Drive Admiral Beatty		0513 0528		0556		0612		0625	0642 0651		0707 0719 0729 0739 0749	
Denton Milton Ale Shades		0517 0532		0600		0616		0629	0646 0655		0713 0725 0735 0745 0755	
Gravesend New Road ★ ‡		0521 0536		0604		0620		0633	0650 0659		0720 0732 0742 0752 0802	
Northfleet Bus Garage	0447 0504 0525 0540 0550 0608 0614 0624 0630 0637 0642 0654 0704 0710 0712 0725 0737 0747 0757 0807											
Northfleet Leather Bottel	0449 0517 0527 0542 0552 0610 0620 0626 0632 0639 0644 0656 0706 0712 0714 0727 0739 0749 0759 0809											
Swanscombe George & Dragon	0454 0522 0532 0547 0557 0615 0625 0631 0637 0644 0649 0701 0711 0717 0720 0733 0745 0755 0805 0815											
Swanscombe Eglinton Road	+ + + + + + + + + 0652 + 0721 + + 0758 + + 0822											
Horns Cross Bull	0501 0529 0539 0554 0604 0622 0632 0638 0644 0651 0709 0720 0739 0753 0813 0823 0839											
Dartford Market Street	0510 0538 0548 0603 0613 0631 0641 0647 0653 0700 0720 0731 0739 0752 0804 0824 0834 0850											
Joyce Green Hospital	+ 0558 0613 + + 0651 + 0712 + 0743 0804 + + 0846 +											
Crayford Bridge ‡	0546 0621 0639 0702 0730 0814 0834 0900											
Crayford Jolly Farmers	0549 0624 0642 0707 0735 0819 0839											
Slade Green Station ‡	0552 0627 0645 0711 0739 0823 0843											
Erith Bexley Road/Cross Street	0603 0638 0656 0723 0751 0835 0855											

Service	488		488		488		488			488
Valley Drive Mackenzie Way	0752 0802 0812 0822 0832		0849 0902 0912 0922		32 42 52 02 12 22		1432 1442			
Valley Drive Admiral Beatty	0759 0809 0819 0829 0839		0856 0909 0919 0929		39 49 59 09 19 29		1439 1449			
Denton Milton Ale Shades	0805 0815 0825 0835 0845		0902 0915 0925 0935		45 55 05 15 25 35		1445 1455			
Gravesend New Road ★ ‡	0812 0822 0832 0842 0852		0909 0922 0932 0942		52 02 12 22 32 42		1452 1502			
Northfleet Bus Garage	0817 0827 0837 0847 0857 0907 0914 0927 0937 0947	Then	57 07 17 27 37 47		1457 1507					
Northfleet Leather Bottel	0819 0829 0839 0849 0859 0909 0916 0929 0939 0949	at	59 09 19 29 39 49	U	1459 1509					
Swanscombe George & Dragon	0825 0835 0845 0855 0905 0915 0922 0935 0945 0955	these	05 15 25 35 45 55	N	1505 1515					
Swanscombe Eglinton Road	0828 + + 0858 + + 0925 + + 0958	mins	+ + 28 + + 58	T	+ +					
Horns Cross Bull	0843 0853 0913 0923 0943 0953	past	13 23 43 53	L	1513 1523					
Dartford Market Street	0854 0904 0924 0934 0954 1004	each	24 34 54 04		1524 1534					
Joyce Green Hospital	0906 + + 0946 1006 +	hour	+ 46 06 +		+					
Crayford Bridge ‡	0914 0934 1014		34 14		1534				
Crayford Jolly Farmers	0919 0939 1019		39 19		1539				
Slade Green Station ‡	0923 0943 1023		43 23		1543				
Erith Bexley Road/Cross Street	0935 0955 1035		55 35		1555				

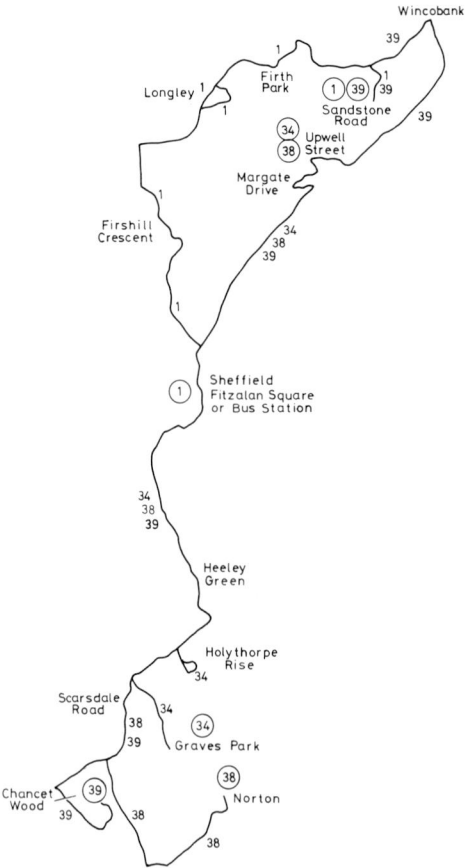

Figure 8.4 Sketch map of Services 1, 34, 38 and 39 of South Yorkshire Transport Ltd.

Figure 6.3). Service 39 (and 34 and 38) are cross-town services (type (ii) in *Figure 6.3*). The specimen hours in *Figure 8.5* show that the Longley 'shorts' on service 1 are conveniently self-contained but the hourly through journeys are not as they have a return running time of 69 minutes. Similar remarks apply to services 34 and 38 which are self-contained but 39 has a return running time of 138 minutes which again is useless for an hourly headway. A round trip with a 60 minute frequency would need a time block of 180 minutes with 3 buses and 42 minutes (or nearly 25%) stand time. But by interworking the buses on 1 and 39 end-on at Sandstone Road it becomes efficient.

Study the specimen hours for 1 and 39 and see that independently they would require the allocation of two and three vehicles respectively. By interworking at Sandstone Road together they need only four as Sheffield–Sandstone Road–Chancet Wood–Sandstone Road–Sheffield becomes a 228 minute cycle leaving the 12 minute stand in Sheffield before going round again. Bearing in mind that every bus requires a driver, the savings become substantial.

SHEFFIELD CITY SERVICE

CITY · LONGLEY · SANDSTONE ROAD

Service **1**

Via Waingate and Nursery Street outwards; (inwards via Chatham Street); Pitsmoor Road, Barnsley Road, Firshill Avenue, Firshill Crescent, Shirecliffe Road, Longley Avenue West, Norwood Avenue, Longley Lane and Longley Hall Road; journeys terminating at Longley returning via longley Hall Road and Longley Lane; Longley Lane, Barnsley Road, Stubbin Lane, **Firth Park**, Bellhouse Road, Primrose Avenue, Bracken Road, Wincobank Avenue, Jenkin Road and Sandstone Road.

Monday to Friday

FITZALAN SQUARE	0655	0725	0753	0825	0849	0925	0945		05	25	45		1525	1601	1630
Firshill Crescent		0708	0738	0806	0838	0902	0938	0958	then at these	18	38	58		1538	1614	1643
LONGLEY, Longley Hall Road	0718	0748	0816	0848	0912	0948	1008	minutes past	28	48	08	until	1548	1624	1653
Firth Park, Bellhouse Road		0753		0853		0953		each hour		53			1553		1658
SANDSTONE ROAD		0801		0901		1001				01			1601		1706

FITZALAN SQUARE	1657	1725	1755		25	55	2225	2255	2315
Firshill Crescent	1710	1738	1808	then at these	38	08	2238	2308	2328
LONGLEY, Longley Hall Road	1720	1748	1818	minutes past	48	18	until	2248	2318	2338
Firth Park, Bellhouse Road		1753		each hour	53		2253		
SANDSTONE ROAD		1801			01		2301		

SHEFFIELD CITY SERVICE

SANDSTONE ROAD · LONGLEY · CITY

Service **1**

Monday to Friday

SANDSTONE ROAD	0640		0740		0840				40			1440			1545
Firth Park, Bellhouse Road	0647		0747		0847		then at these		47			1447			1552
LONGLEY, Longley Hall Road	0652	0722	0752	0818	0852	0912	minutes past	32	52	12	until	1452	1512	1530	1557
Firshill Crescent	0659	0729	0759	0825	0859	0919	each hour	39	59	19		1459	1519	1537	1604
FITZALAN SQUARE	0713	0743	0813	0839	0913	0933		53	13	33		1513	1533	1551	1618

SANDSTONE ROAD		1640			40		2240		
Firth Park, Bellhouse Road		1647		then at these	47		2247		
LONGLEY, Longley Hall Road	1624	1652	1722	minutes past	52	22	until	2252	2322
Firshill Crescent	1631	1659	1729	each hour	59	29	2259	2329
FITZALAN SQUARE	1645	1713	1743		13	43	2313	2343

SHEFFIELD CITY SERVICE

SANDSTONE ROAD · CITY · GRAVES PARK
UPWELL STREET · CITY · NORTON
SANDSTONE ROAD · CITY · CHANCET WOOD

Service **34**
38
39

Monday to Friday

Service No.	39		34	38	39		38	34	39	34	38	39	34	38	39
SANDSTONE ROAD	0906				06			1406			1506			1606
Wincobank, Fife Street	0913				13			1413			1513			1613
UPWELL STREET	0923		45	03	23		1403		1423	1445	1503	1523	1545	1603	1623
Margate Drive	0926		48	06	26		1406		1426	1448	1506	1526	1548	1606	1626
CENTRAL BUS STATION	0945	then at these	07	25	45		1425	1433	1445	1507	1525	1545	1607	1625	1645
Heeley Green	0955	minutes past	17	35	55	until	1435	1443	1455	1517	1535	1555	1617	1635	1655
Hollythorpe Rise, Thorpe House Ave		each hour	23					1449		1523			1623		
GRAVES PARK			35						1535			1635		
Scarsdale Road Bottom	1002			42	02		1442		1502		1542	1602		1642	1702
NORTON, Cloonmore Drive				57			1457			1557			1657		
CHANCET WOOD, Abbey Br. Dr	1016				16			1516			1616			1716

SHEFFIELD CITY SERVICE

GRAVES PARK · CITY · SANDSTONE ROAD
NORTON · CITY · UPWELL STREET
CHANCET WOOD · CITY · SANDSTONE ROAD

Service **34**
38
39

Monday to Friday

Service No.	34	38	34	39	34	38	39	34	38	39		34	38	39	34
NORTON, Cloonmore Drive		0902				1002			1102				02		
CHANCET WOOD, Abbey Br. Dr				0930			1025			1125				25	
Scarsdale Road Bottom		0913		0938		1013	1033		1113	1133			13	33	
GRAVES PARK	0849			0949			1049					1449			
Hollythorpe Rise, Thorpe House Ave	0854		0930		0954			1054			then at these	54			1454
Heeley Green	0900	0920	0936	0945	1000	1020	1040	1100	1120	1140	minutes past	00	20	40	until	1500
FITZALAN SQUARE	0915	0935	0948	1000	1015	1035	1055	1115	1135	1155	each hour	15	35	55	1515
Margate Drive	0928	0948		1013	1028	1048	1108	1128	1148	1208		28	48	08	1528
UPWELL STREET	0936	0956			1036	1056		1136	1156			36	56		1536
Wincobank, Fife Street				1025			1120			1220				20	
SANDSTONE ROAD				1038			1133			1233				33	

Figure 8.5 Timetable extracts of services to show 'end-on' interworking of vehicles. (Reproduced by kind permission of South Yorkshire PTE.)

All that has been said so far relates to services that follow a progressive route, reverse direction at the outer terminal and return the same way. A slight variation on this is the 'fishtail' type service as depicted at route A in *Figure 8.6*. In this example, the full service runs between points U and V but bifurcates at V with probably alternate journeys serving different places at W and X. Providing the running times to each point are similar then the principles regarding timetable preparation as already described remain. But if one leg is substantially shorter than the other and an even headway is to be maintained on the main spine, then an excessive layover will be incurred at the end of the shorter of the two unless the difference in journey time is sufficient to approximate to a multiple of the service frequency. The following illustrates the point:

U		1.10	1.40	2.10	2.40	3.10	3.40
V		1.30	2.00	2.30	3.00	3.30	4.00
	W	1.35		2.35		3.35	
X		↓	2.35 →		3.35 →		4.35
X			1.40	→ 2.40		→ 3.40
	W	1.40		2.40		3.40	
V		1.45	2.15	2.45	3.15	3.45	4.15
U		2.05	2.35	3.05	3.35	4.05	4.35

In this example, the journey times beyond V are 5 minutes to W and 35 minutes to X and the difference is sufficient to maintain schedule efficiency.

If the ends of the 'fishtail' are linked to form a continuous route, so forming a loop working or 'frying pan' type service as depicted at route B in *Figure 8.6* a different situation arises. The size of the loop will determine whether buses need to traverse it in both directions. If it is reasonable to ask a passenger who uses the first stop on the loop beyond the junction at point Y to travel the long way round one way (subject, of course, to no fare surcharge) then there is advantage in going one way only. Resources do not then have to be split and a more concentrated service is possible at the stops in the one direction. All stand time will probably be given at the single terminal, which means that on the 'handle of the pan', the timings in one direction are governed by those on the other and there is no opportunity for adjustment. If a hesitation period is given somewhere on the loop, it can only be to the inconvenience of passengers who need to override that point.

One stage beyond the loop working is the complete circle as shown at route C in *Figure 8.6*, so often advocated by those outside the industry but so rarely having any real traffic value. It is the radials to and from the centre that usually attract the passengers, not the orbitals which tend to keep on going without ever getting anywhere. There are notable exceptions but only when there are sizeable neighbourhoods or industrial areas between which there is a particular traffic affinity. To return to running schedules, if the journey time of route C from Z back to Z is an exact multiple of the service frequency, then the vehicles will keep going without any hesitation, giving 100% utilization. Certainly this is super efficiency in scheduling terms but there would be no recovery time to correct late running; on present-day standards it would be highly unpopular with the staff and so in practical terms the arrangement would be something less than satisfactory. In any case it would be fortuitous if the running time was an exact multiple of the service

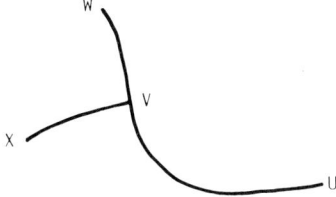

Route A: 'Fishtail' type service

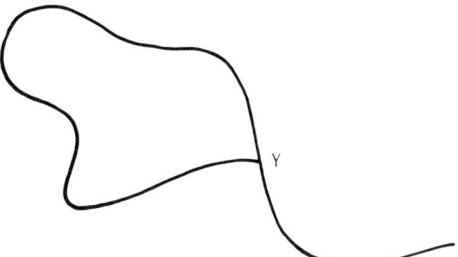

Route B: 'Frying pan' type service

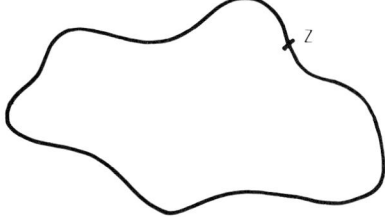

Route C: Circular type service

Figure 8.6 Specimen routes to illustrate different patterns.

frequency and if it was not and repetitive timings were to be maintained then time would have to be lost somewhere. This could only be at a point *en route*, to the irritation of passengers on board.

Time schedules

This discourse on timetable preparation has so far concentrated on the basic all-day services. This, however, is only one part of the subject. Even on these routes it is likely that augmentation is required during the peaks when the timetables might depart from standard timings. But other services of a more specialized nature also come in at these times, often for works and schools but also, perhaps, as variations to the regular routes. There can be no general pattern here on which to calculate vehicle requirements. Such supplementary services have to be superimposed on the basic runnings and worked in the most expeditious way to meet local

SHEFFIELD · HIGH BRADFIELD

Service
62

From Central Bus Station **Platform A** via Paternoster Row, Furnival Street, Arundel Gate **outwards** (**inwards** via High Street, Fitzalan Square and Flat Street); Angel Street, Snig Hill, West Bar, Gibraltar Street, Infirmary Road, Langsett Road, **Hillsborough**, Holme Lane, Malin Bridge, Stannington Road **outwards; inwards** via Loxley New Road, Loxley Road, **Loxley** and Damflask End.

MINIMUM FARES apply between Sheffield and Malin Bridge.

FOR OTHER BUSES between Sheffield and Loxley, see Services 14 and 61;
between Sheffield and Low Bradfield, see Service 61.

Tuesday			Saturday		
SHEFFIELD, Central Bus Station......✦	1000	1420	1000	1600	
Malin Bridge..................................	1015	1435	1015	1615	
HIGH BRADFIELD, Old Horns Inn........	1032	1452	1032	1632	
HIGH BRADFIELD, Old Horns Inn........	1040	1455	1040	1640	
Malin Bridge..................................	1056	1511	1056	1656	
SHEFFIELD, Central Bus Station......✦	1110	1525	1110	1710	

CODE   ✦—Buses pass near Railway Station.

Figure 8.7 Specimen timetable of a rural bus service. (Reproduced by kind permission of South Yorkshire PTE.)

requirements. It is likely that these extra peak hour buses will do more interworking between different routes, often travelling 'dead' (i.e. out of service) after finishing on one and taking up service on another. Specific timings are often important and occasionally it is necessary to resort to dead running on the non-essential sections in order to get a faster run and thereby enable a particular commitment to be met. This is not, however, something that should be practised unless the extra speed is crucial either for physical or duty schedule reasons. Most journeys will carry at least some traffic and it is pointless (and irritating to intending passengers) for an empty bus to pass people waiting at stops without a very good reason. From a revenue point of view, a bus running dead earns no more than one which is stationary on a stand but the cost is there just the same. A similar type of service, i.e. odd journeys at specific times, but one that does not run at the same periods and hence caters for a different clientele is that which meets the shopping needs of the rural populace of hamlets outside the main towns. A typical example appears in *Figure 8.7* (Service 62) which has journeys only on Tuesdays and Saturdays, being market days. Although two journeys are provided in each direction only one is likely to carry many passengers as the movement is from the country into town and then back. In territory of this kind it is inevitable that the base of the bus is at the opposite end of the route to that of the passengers and a return journey must be made for each single effective trip. For a fairly short route this is not particularly serious but if it becomes longer and the journeys more numerous then waste is then a greater cause for concern. This is the reason for the out-station concept referred to in Chapter 2.

The most convenient way of allocating vehicles to services that have only sporadic journeys is to diagram all of the bus runnings on a time basis as depicted in the specimen time schedule which will be described shortly.

A schedule exercise

Preparation

Whilst timetable presentation is quite straightforward and examples of printed specimens have been shown, to explain the preparation of time and duty schedules, rather more material than this is necessary. A small imaginary network has, therefore, been devised on which to base a theoretical schedules exercise and is illustrated on the pages which follow. A fictitious presentation is necessary as for the sake of clarity and to bring out various features the operating unit used as an example is unrealistically small with the timetables designed primarily to illustrate principles. In real life, schedules are bulky documents, and in any case there is no standard method of preparation. For various reasons, therefore, it would not be practicable to include an actual example. Even if it was, the detail would obscure the issues. The explanatory material falls into eight parts:

1. Map of routes (*Figure 8.8*).
2. Speed schedules (*Figure 8.9*).
3. Draft timetables (*Figure 8.10*).
4. Vehicle runnings (*Figure 8.11*).
5. Time schedule (*Figure 8.12*).
6. Duty allocation (*Figure 8.13*).
7. Duty schedule (*Figure 8.14*).
8. Duty roster (*Figure 8.15*).

Everything that follows in respect of this exercise must be read in conjunction with these data.

The map, speed schedules and timetables which represent the basic data are compiled to illustrate what has already been explained and to provide a foundation on which to build time and duty schedules. In this exercise routes 1 and 2/2A form the all-day services. Route 1 is deemed to serve an area of fairly high car ownership which means that whilst a 15-minute headway is needed in the peaks, a half-hourly service is adequate at other times coming down to hourly in the

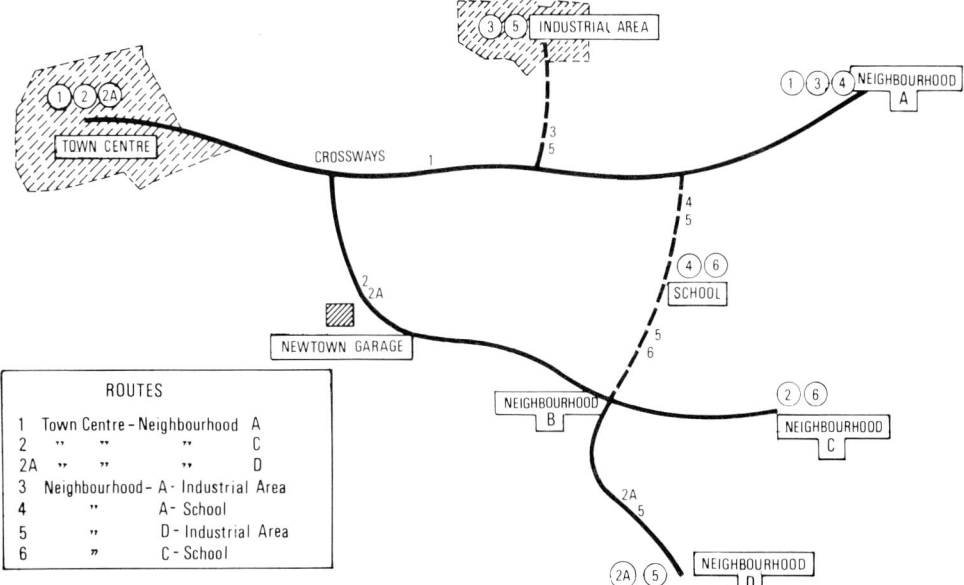

Figure 8.8 Map of routes for schedule exercise.

Speed schedules

Route 1

	minutes	miles	mph
Town Centre			
Crossways	8	1.6	
Neighbourhood A	17	3.4	
	25	5.0	12.0
Walking time			
Crossways to garage	10		

Route 2

	minutes	miles	mph
Town Centre			
Crossways	8	1.6	
Garage	2	0.4	
Neighbourhood B	14	2.8	
Neighbourhood C	10	2.0	
	34	6.8	12.0

Route 2A

	minutes	miles	mph
Town Centre			
Crossways	8	1.6	
Garage	2	0.4	
Neighbourhood B	14	2.8	
Neighbourhood D	9	1.8	
	33	6.6	12.0

Route 3

	minutes	miles	mph
Neighbourhood A			
Industrial Area	14	2.8	
	14	2.8	12.0

Route 4

	minutes	miles	mph
Neighbourhood A			
School	7	1.4	
	7	1.4	12.0

Route 5

	minutes	miles	mph
Neighbourhood D			
Neighbourhood B	9	1.8	
School	5	1.0	
Industrial Area	10	2.0	
	24	4.8	12.0

Route 6

	minutes	miles	mph
Neighbourhood C			
Neighbourhood B	10	2.0	
School	5	1.0	
	15	3.0	12.0

Figure 8.9 Speed schedules for schedule exercise.

evenings. Certainly this sort of service goes contrary to minimum standards as was suggested in Chapter 6 in connection with the criteria for service provision. Nevertheless, it is typical of many areas and, more importantly in this context, introduces the schedules complexities of a disproportionate number of vehicles required in the peaks only. Route 2 serves a different type of area which calls for four buses per hour all day with a bifurcation near the extremity to form a fishtail to two other residential areas. Routes 3, 4, 5 and 6 comprise isolated works and school trips consisting only of morning and afternoon journeys. The speed schedules produce average speeds of 12 mph (20 km/h) to be reasonably realistic. The timetables represent the sort of specifications that might be submitted by a traffic department. The vehicle running and time schedules show how the non-standard timings of routes 3, 4, 5 and 6 have, in some cases, been interworked with the runnings of the basic services although the allocation of extra vehicles has also been necessary. Only the Monday to Friday operation has been tabled. Different traffic requirements are likely for Saturdays and Sundays but for this purpose it would be pointless to proceed laboriously through a complete set of schedules for different days of the week. On the assumption, however, that this information is also available, there is now sufficient data to compile a duty schedule and roster for a week's work.

1 Town Centre — Neighbourhood A

(TC) Town Centre	*	*	*	7.23	7.38	7.53	8.08	8.23	53	23	4.23	38	53	08	23	6.23	6.53	53	10.53	
(CW) Crossways	6.31	6.46	7.01	7.16	7.31	7.46	8.01	8.16	8.31	01	31	4.31	46	01	31	6.31	7.01	01	11.01
(A) Neighbourhood A	6.48	7.03	7.18	7.33	7.48	8.03	8.18	8.33	8.48	18	48	4.48	03	18	33	48	6.48	7.18	18	11.18

Neighbourhood A	6.55	7.25	7.40	7.55	8.10	8.25	8.40	8.55	25	55	4.25	10	25	40	55	6.40	6.55	25	10.25 11.25
Crossways	7.12	7.42	7.57	8.12	8.27	8.42	8.57	9.12	42	12	4.42	27	42	57	12	6.57	7.12	42	10.42 11.42
Town Centre	7.20	7.50	8.05	8.20	8.35	8.50	9.05	9.20	50	20	4.50	35	50	05	20	+	+	50	10.50 +

* Departs garage 2 minutes earlier
+ Arrives garage 2 minutes later
† 6.10 pm dep to Crossways and Garage only
Additional journey
Neighbourhood A to garage 5.18 pm

Journeys on Service 2
8.38 am   TC to Garage
9.08 am   TC to Garage
4.25 pm   Garage to TC
4.53 pm   Garage to TC

2 Town Centre — Neighbourhood C
2A Town Centre — Neighbourhood D

(TC) Town Centre						7.16	01	16	31	46	10.46	11.01	
(CW) Crossways						7.24	09	24	39	54	10.54	11.09	
(G) Garage	6.11	6.26	6.41	6.50	6.56	7.11	7.26	11	26	41	56	10.56	11.11
Neighbourhood B	6.25	6.40	6.55	7.04	7.10	7.25	7.40	25	40	55	10	11.10	11.25
(C) Neighbourhood C	6.35		7.05			7.35		35	05			11.35	
(D) Neighbourhood D		6.49		7.13	7.19		7.49		49	19	11.19		

Neighbourhood D	6.55	7.25	55	25	10.25	10.55	11.25	
Neighbourhood C	6.39	7.09	39	09	10.09	10.39	11.09	11.39
Neighbourhood B	6.49	7.04	7.19	7.34	49 04	19 34	10.19 10.34	11.04 11.34 11.49
Garage	7.03	7.18	7.33	7.48	03 18	33 48	10.33 10.48	11.03 11.18 11.33 11.48 12.03
Crossways	7.05	7.20	7.35	7.50	05 20	35 50	10.35 10.50	
Town Centre	7.13	7.28	7.43	7.58	13 28	43 58	10.43 10.58	

Additional journeys
Town Centre to Garage   8.38 am
                         9.08 am
Garage to Town Centre   7.25 am
                         4.25 pm
Neighbourhood D to Garage 5.32 pm

Figure 8.10 Timetables for schedule exercise.

Neighbourhood A — Industrial Area

(A)	Neighbourhood A	7.06	7.11	7.41	
(IA)	Industrial Area	7.20	7.25	7.55	
	Industrial Area	7.23		4.36	5.01
	Neighbourhood A	7.37		4.50	5.15

Neighbourhood A — School

(A)	Neighbourhood A	8.58	
(S)	School	9.05	
	School	4.15	
	Neighbourhood A	4.22	

Neighbourhood D — Industrial Area

(D)	Neighbourhood D	7.16	8.41		4.36
(B)	Neighbourhood B	7.25	8.50		4.45
(S)	School	7.30	8.55		4.50
(IA)	Industrial Area	7.40			5.00
	Industrial Area	8.05	8.14		5.05
	School	8.15	8.24	4.02	5.15
	Neighbourhood B	8.20	8.29	4.07	5.20
	Neighbourhood D	8.29	8.38	4.16	5.29

Neighbourhood C — School

(C)	Neighbourhood C	8.40	
(B)	Neighbourhood B	8.50	
(S)	School	8.55	
	School	4.10	
	Neighbourhood B	4.15	
	Neighbourhood C	4.25	

Figure 8.10 Continued.

```
Bus Running 1                           Bus Running 5                        Bus Running 9
1   6.29G   6.48A   6.55A   7.20TC      2   6.11G   6.35C   6.39C   7.13TC    2    7.11G   7.35C   7.39C   8.13TC
    7.23TC  7.48A   7.55A   8.20TC      2   7.16TC  7.49C   7.55C   8.28TC    2    8.16TC  8.49C   8.55C   9.28TC
    8.23TC  8.48A   8.55A   9.20TC      2A  8.31TC  9.05C   9.09C   9.43TC    2    9.31TC  10.05C  10.09C  10.43TC
    9.23TC  9.48A   9.55A   10.20TC     2A  9.46TC  10.19C  10.25C  10.58TC   2    10.46TC 11.19C  11.25C  11.58TC
    10.23TC 10.48A  10.55A  11.20TC     2A  11.01TC 11.35C  11.39C  12.13TC   2A   12.01TC 12.35C  12.39C  1.13TC
    11.23TC 11.48A  11.55A  12.20TC     2   12.16TC 12.49C  12.55C  1.28TC    2A   1.16TC  1.49C   1.55C   2.28TC
    12.23TC 12.48A  12.55A  1.20TC      2A  1.31TC  2.05C   2.09C   2.43TC    2A   2.31TC  3.05C   3.09C   3.43TC
    1.23TC  1.48A   1.55A   2.20TC      2A  2.46TC  3.19C   3.25C   3.58TC    2A   3.46TC  4.19C   4.25C   4.58TC
    2.23TC  2.48A   2.55A   3.20TC      2A  4.01TC  4.35C   4.39C   5.13TC    2A   5.01TC  5.35C   5.39C   6.13TC
    3.23TC  3.48A   3.55A   4.20TC      2A  5.16TC  5.49C   5.55C   5.28TC    2A   6.16TC  6.49C   6.55C   7.28TC
    4.23TC  4.48A   4.55A   5.20TC      2   6.31TC  7.05C   7.09C   7.43TC    2A   7.31TC  8.05C   8.09C   8.43TC
    5.23TC  5.48A   5.55A   6.20TC      2A  7.46TC  8.19C   8.25C   8.58TC    2    8.46TC  9.19C   9.25C   9.58TC
    6.23TC  6.48A   6.55A   7.14G       2A  9.01TC  9.35C   9.39C   10.13TC   2    10.01TC 10.35C  10.39C  11.03G
                                        2A  10.16TC 10.49C  10.55C  11.18G

Bus Running 2                           Bus Running 6                        Bus Running 10
1   6.59G   7.18A   7.25A   7.50TC      2A  6.26G   6.49C   6.55C   7.28TC    1    6.44G   7.03A   7.20IA  7.37A
    7.53TC  8.18A   8.25A   8.50TC      2   7.31TC  8.05C   8.09C   8.43TC    3    7.06A   7.20IA  7.23IA
    8.53TC  9.18A   9.25A   9.50TC      2A  8.46TC  9.19C   9.25C   9.58TC         7.41A   7.55IA
    9.53TC  10.18A  10.25A  10.50TC     2   10.01TC 10.35C  10.39C  11.13TC        8.14IA  8.38O
    10.53TC 11.18A  11.25A  11.50TC     2   11.16TC 11.49C  11.55C  12.28TC   5    8.41O
    11.53TC 12.18A  12.25A  12.50TC     2   12.31TC 1.05C   1.09C   1.43TC    5    8.58C   8.55S
    12.53TC 1.18A   1.25A   1.50TC      2A  1.46TC  2.19C   2.25C   2.58TC    DEAD 3.53G   9.07G
    1.53TC  2.18A   2.25A   2.50TC      2A  2.49TC  3.35C   3.39C   4.13TC    DEAD 4.05S   4.16O
    2.53TC  3.18A   3.25A   3.50TC      2A  4.16TC  4.49C   4.55C   5.28TC    5    4.17O   4.35IA
    3.53TC  4.18A   4.25A   4.50TC      2A  5.31TC  6.05C   6.09C   6.43TC    DEAD 4.36IA  4.50A
    4.53TC  5.18A   5.25A   5.50TC      2A  6.46TC  7.19C   7.25C   7.58TC    3    4.51A   5.00IA
    5.53TC  6.18A   6.25A   6.50TC      2A  8.01TC  8.35C   8.39C   9.13TC    DEAD 5.01IA  5.15A
    6.53TC  7.18A   7.25A   7.50TC      2A  9.16TC  9.49C   9.55O   10.28TC   1    5.18A   5.37C
    7.53TC  8.18A   8.25A   9.50TC      2   10.31TC 10.55C  11.05C  11.33G
    9.53TC  10.18A  10.25A  10.50TC
    10.53TC 11.18A  11.25A  11.44G

Bus Running 3                           Bus Running 7                        Bus Running 11
1    6.49G   7.08A   7.11A   7.25IA     2    6.41G   7.05C   7.09C   7.43TC   2A   6.48G   7.130   8.05IA  8.29O
DEAD 7.28IA  7.37A   7.40A   8.05TC     2A   7.46TC  8.19C   8.25C   8.58TC   5    7.16O   7.40IA
     8.08TC  8.33A   8.40A   9.05TC     2    9.01TC  9.35C   9.39C   10.13TC  DEAD 8.32O   8.37C
2    9.08TC  9.18G   4.25G   4.35TC     2A   10.16TC 10.49C  10.55C  11.28TC  6    8.40O   8.55S   9.04G   3.58G
1    4.38TC  5.03A   5.10A   5.35TC     2A   11.31TC 12.05C  12.09C  12.43TC  DEAD 8.55S   9.04G
     5.38TC  6.03A   6.10A   5.29G      2A   12.46TC 1.19C   1.25C   1.58TC   6    4.10S   4.25C   4.25C   4.07S
                                        2    2.01TC  2.35C   2.39C   3.13TC   DEAD 4.28C   4.33O
Bus Running 4                           2A   3.16TC  3.49C   3.55C   4.28TC   5    4.36O   5.00IA
2    7.25G   7.35TC                     2    4.31TC  5.05C   5.09C   5.43TC   5    5.05IA  5.29O
1    7.38TC  8.03A   8.10A   8.35TC     2A   5.46TC  6.19C   6.25C   6.58TC   2A   5.32O   5.55O
DEAD 8.38TC  8.38TC                     2    7.01TC  7.35C   7.39C   8.13TC
4    8.58A   9.05S                      2A   8.16TC  8.55C   9.09C   9.28TC
DEAD 9.08S   9.17G   4.03C   4.12S      2A   9.31TC  10.05C  10.09C  10.43TC
4    4.15S   4.22A   4.40A   5.05TC     2A   10.46TC 11.19C  11.25C  11.48G
1    6.08TC  6.33A   6.40A   6.59G
                                        Bus Running 8
                                        2A   6.56G   7.19C   7.25C   7.58TC
                                        2    8.01TC  8.35C   8.39C   9.13TC
                                        2A   9.16TC  9.49C   9.55C   10.28TC
```

Figure 8.11 Vehicle runnings for schedule exercise.

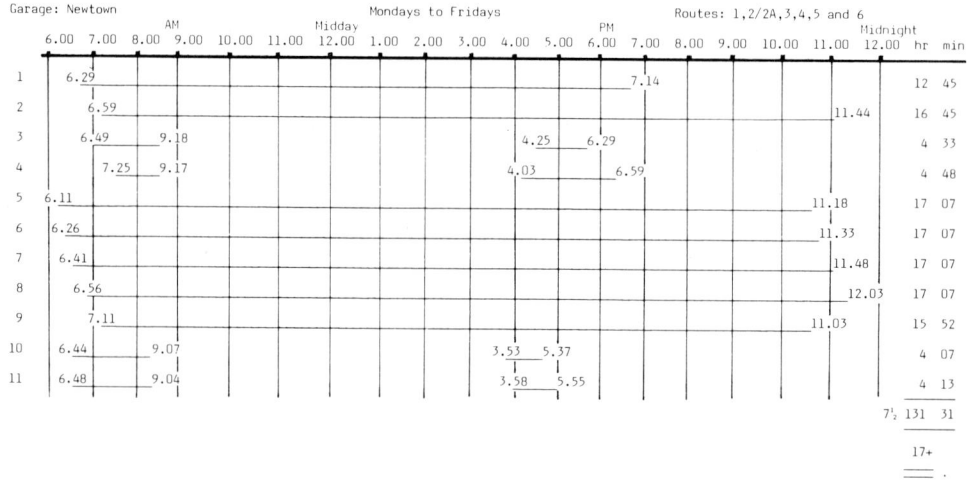

Figure 8.12 Time schedule for schedule exercise.

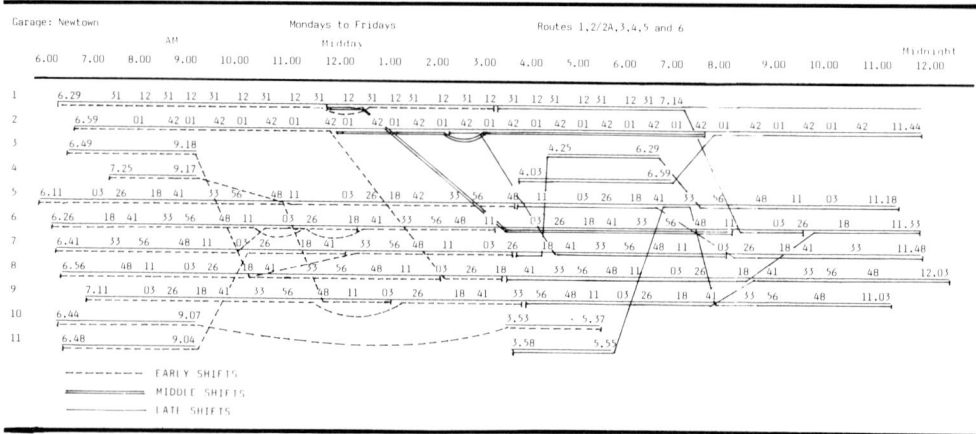

Figure 8.13 Duty allocation for schedule exercise.

Duty schedule

Reference has already been made to the acquired art of the duty schedule compiler. He spends his working life selecting pieces of the time schedule jigsaw puzzle and assembling them to produce workable schedules which:

1. Are acceptable to management in that they make maximum use of staff within the various parameters (which is the very antithesis of what the platform staff are likely to seek).
2. Conform to the statutory limitations on drivers' hours referred to in Chapter 5.
3. Comply with trade union agreements (which might be more rigorous than the statutory limitations) and are acceptable to the trade union representatives. (Conformity with an agreement has, unfortunately, proved to be no guarantee

of acceptance and apart from pay, duty schedules are perhaps one of the most common causes of disputes in the industry.)

It is emphasized that the example that follows is but one method of compilation and presentation. To keep the figures as realistic as possible for readers in Great Britain, the domestic drivers' hours regulations have been kept in mind but it must be appreciated that the purpose of the exercise is not to demonstrate the implications of such restrictions. Neither does the final production constitute a 'model schedule' or purport to give what might be in practice the optimum solution whilst meeting the requirements of (1), (2) and (3) above. Only the very simplest staff agreement has been observed. This elimination of the trimmings will, however, hopefully make the stages of compilation that much clearer and thereby enhance the value of what is no more than a textbook exercise.

In the preparation of this specimen duty schedule the imposed restraints are simplified compared with actual practice and are:

Abridged drivers' hours regulations:

Maximum continuous driving	5½ hours
Minimum required break	30 minutes
Maximum driving in a day	10 hours
Maximum on duty in a day	16 hours
Minimum daily rest	10 hours (but 8½ hours three times a week)
Minimum rest days	1 per fortnight

Important note: The above does not constitute the entire drivers' hours requirements and must NOT be interpreted as such.

Staff agreement (all one-man operated services):

Sign-on time	15 minutes
Sign-off time	15 minutes
Minimum turning plus stand time (other than dead workings)	3 minutes
Working week	40 hours over 5 days
Spreadover limitations	
9hr 1min to 10 hr	up to 10% of whole
10hr 1min to 11hr 30min max	up to 5% of whole

It is now necessary to return to the time schedule and select pieces of work which, when put together, comprise a driver's (and conductor's) duty within the required constraints. It is helpful here to mark on the running schedule each time that the bus passes the crew relief point. In this case the crew change point is at the garage for all except route 1 which, apart from the 'when working' journeys to and from the garage, is at Crossways. There is an agreed 10 minutes' walking time between Crossways and the garage. Drivers are required to sign on and off at the garage, and they are paid walking time for the meal break as well so that they can take advantage of canteen facilities. As the different parts of the bus runnings are covered, so they are underlined covering first the early and late journeys and then filling in the middle. The job is finished when the entire bus runnings are so covered. For purpose of illustration the possible crew relief times and the duty allocations have been superimposed on a second copy of the time schedule (*Figure 8.13*).

Duty No.	Sign on hr min	Route No.	Bus Running	Duty Start hr min	Finish hr min	Sign off hr min	Time Worked hr min	Total Spreadover hr min	Allowances
		Mondays to Fridays							
1	5.56	2/A	5	6.11G	11.11G*				
			9	11.48G	1.03G	1.18	6.45	7.22	
2	6.11	2/A	6	6.26G	10.11*				
			6	11.26G	12.41G	12.56	5.30	6.45	
3	6.14	1	1	6.29G	11.31CW				
		Walk		11.31CW	11.41G*				
		Walk		12.21G	12.31CW				
		1	1	12.31CW	3.12CW				
		Walk		3.12CW	3.22G	3.37	8.43	9.23	
4	6.26	2/A	7	6.41G	10.03G				
			6	10.11G	11.26G*				
			6	12.41G	3.11G	3.26	7.45	9.00	
5	6.29	3/5	10	6.44G	9.07G*				
			10	3.53G	5.37G	5.52	4.37	11.23	
6	6.33	5/6	11	6.48G	9.04G*				
		2/A	7	10.03	12.33G	12.48	5.16	6.15	
7	6.34	1	3	6.49G	9.18G*				
		2/A	8	10.18G	2.03G	2.18	6.44	7.44	
8	6.41	2/A	8	6.56G	10.18G*				
			7	12.33G	3.26G	3.41	6.45	9.00	
9	6.44	1	2	6.59G	11.42CW				
		Walk		11.42CW	11.52G*				
		2/A	8	2.03G	3.18G	3.33	6.38	8.49	
10	6.56	2/A	9	7.11G	11.48G*				
			9	1.03G	3.33G	3.48	7.37	8.52	
11	7.10	1	4	7.25G	9.17G*				
		2/A	5	11.11G	3.48G	4.03	6.59	8.53	
12	11.06	Walk		11.21G	11.31CW				
		1	1	11.31CW	12.31CW				
		Walk		12.31CW	12.41G*				
		2/A	6	3.11G	8.11G	8.26	6.50	9.20	
13	11.17	Walk		11.32G	11.42CW				
		1	2	11.42CW	2.01CW				
		Walk		2.01CW	2.11G*				
		Walk		2.51G	3.01CW				
		1	2	3.01CW	7.42CW				
		Walk		7.42CW	7.52G	8.07	8.10	8.50	
14	1.36	Walk		1.51G	2.01CW				
		1	2	2.01CW	3.01CW				
		Walk		3.01CW	3.11G*				
		2	7	4.18G	8.03G	8.18	5.35	6.42	

Figure 8.14 Duty schedule for schedule exercise.

Duty No.	Sign on hr min	Route No.	Bus Running	Duty Start hr min	Finish hr min	Sign off hr min	Time Worked hr min	Total Spreadover hr min	Allowances
15	2.47	Walk		3.02G	3.12CW				
		1	1	3.12CW	7.14G*				
		2/A	6	8.11G	9.26G	9.41	5.57	6.54	
16	3.03	2/A	8	3.18G	8.18G*				
			6	9.26G	11.33G	11.48	7.37	8.45	
17	3.11	2/A	7	3.26G	4.18G				
		1	3	4.25G	6.29G*				
		2/A	5	7.33G	11.18G	11.33	7.18	8.22	
18	3.18	2/A	9	3.33G	7.41G*				
			8	8.18G	12.03G	12.18	8.23	9.00	
19	3.33	2/A	5	3.48	6.41G*				
			7	8.03G	11.48G	12.03	7.08	8.30	
20	3.43	5/6	11	3.58G	5.55G*				
		2/A	5	6.41G	7.33G				
			9	7.41G	11.03G	11.18	6.49	7.35	
21	3.48	4/1	4	4.03G	6.59G*				
		Walk		7.32G	7.42CW				
		1	2	7.42CW	11.44G	11.59	7.38	8.11	

(Total time worked) (144.44)
(Average work content) (6.53)

Saturdays
30
31
32
33
34
35
36
37
38
39
40
41
42
43
44
45
46
47
48
49
Sundays
60
61
62
63
64
65
66
67

Figure 8.12 shows that the total daily (Monday to Friday) runnings of all 11 buses amounts to 131hr 31min. A working week of 40 hours over 5 days means 8 hours per day, but with an allowance of 15 minutes for signing on and 15 minutes for signing off (or 30 minutes per day) there is a theoretical driving day of only 7½ hours. The 7½ hours goes into the total of 131hr 31min, 17+times. On a strict time basis, therefore, 18 duties would cover the work. However, in both the morning and evening peaks, 11 buses are on the road simultaneously and unless the same drivers can cover both peaks, there must be 11 sets of duties for the morning and another set of 11 for the evening or, in other words, 22 overall.

The last bus to leave the garage in the morning is running number 4 at 7.25 and the first bus to finish in the evening is running number 10 at 5.37. With the 30 minutes signing on and off time, this gives a total spreadover of 10hr 42min, but according to the staff agreement of this imaginary outfit, no more than 5% of the duties may have spreadovers of this length. In this case this means one duty. On this basis, therefore, the 22 duties can be cut to 21 and this is what has been done, the resultant split being:

up to 9 hours	18
9hr 1min to 10hr	2 or 10%
10hr 1min to 11hr 30min	1 or 5%
	21

There is an average work content per duty of 6hr 53min. As, however, there would be a guaranteed 8 hours pay per duty, this is not particularly efficient but such are the diseconomies of the peaks. Duties could, of course, be saved by imposing more onerous conditions. They could also be saved by leaving short pieces of work to be covered locally by unscheduled voluntary overtime. If some of the low mileage peak hour buses remained unscheduled and were covered in this way there might be a considerable saving in duties and a higher average work content for the remainder. But overtime would involve a premium rate and might even incur penalty payments as well. Nevertheless, it could be cheaper to do it this way. Voluntary overtime does, however, introduce an element of unreliability and banning overtime is a favourite tactic for industrial action. For the larger and more impersonal undertakings it is a practice that is not particularly recommended. More will be said about this in Chapter 10.

Note that there are no entries in the column for allowances in the written-up duties (*Figure 8.13*). Some duties will probably carry penalty payments such as for starting before or finishing after certain times, working on Saturday afternoons and Sundays (i.e. unsocial hours) and time for a meal break in excess of 1 hour, for example, could be paid for. In short, different duties have different earning powers over and above the flat rate. Overall this duty schedule is not a particularly onerous one. There are spells of 5 hours continuous driving which might result in union representation. If this was the case then in duty 1, for example, bus 5 could be relieved at 10.48am instead of 11.11am. Duty 11 could take over bus 5 that much earlier and still have an adequate meal break. This has not been done as duty 1 already has the lower work content of the two, but it would nevertheless be possible.

Of significance in connection with duty schedule compilation, and this is a continuation of a point made in Chapter 2, is the siting of the operating garage.

With the relatively short but high-frequency services used in the illustrations, the connection between garage location and schedule efficiency does not have the same impact but there is still an affinity between the two. In order to achieve maximum work content of a duty, the agreed spells, be they the driver's hours regulations or as negotiated locally, should fit conveniently into return journey or part journey times of the services concerned. Take, for example, a route from A to C via B with a throughout running time of 1hr 25min and which passes near garages Y and Z as in the following diagram:

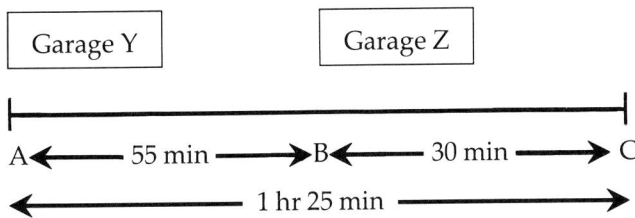

If crews were allocated to Garage Y and took charge of their vehicles at A, a round trip to C would take 2hr 50min plus stand time at C. Two round trips to C would take 5hr 40min plus two periods of stand time at C and one at A, which would exceed the maximum permitted spell of continuous work. Unless, therefore, other work was available on a shorter route from Garage Y, the crew could do no more than one return trip before coming off for a break. The second spell of duty would, in the absence of any work on another route, again be one trip to C. This would produce a duty with a total work content of 5hr 40min plus stand time. The agreed conditions of service, however, will undoubtedly call for a guaranteed daily wage equivalent to about 8 hours work, in which case, in this example (and ignoring stand time) 2hr 20min would be paid per man per day for no work at all.

Consider now the position as it would be if staff were attached instead to Garage Z. The route would not now consist only of a single 'block' of 2hr 50min but one of 1hr (30min × 2) B to C, another of 1hr 50min (55min × 2) B to A and others consisting of any combination of these two. A duty comprising B-C-A-C-B (3hr 50min) in both the first and second spells would produce a duty of 7hr 40min which might well be within the terms of the agreements, again disregarding for this purpose the additional time necessitated on layover at the termini and time taken to sign on and take over the vehicle and to sign off and pay in cash for which there must be due allowance.

In the specimen schedule exercise, if the operating garage was so sited that the crew relief point was at the town centre, then the only available spells of duty would have been 54 minutes on route 1 and 1hr 12min on route 2/2A. In this particular case blocks of this length would be reasonable enough for duty schedule compilation, but a glance again at the time schedule at which the passing times of the crew relief points have been appended (*Figure 8.13*) will show that a far greater range of permutations is available. The chances of maximizing efficiency and at the same time meeting staff agreements etc. are, therefore, that much better. As an example, the point made about the 5-hour spell in duty 1 and the adjustment with duty 11 took advantage of the passing times at the changeover point of bus 5 being only 23 minutes apart. A crew change point part way along a route gives greater flexibility but geography is nevertheless also important. In the examples the fact that the garage is not on the direct line of route 1 carries a disadvantage in that it necessitates 10-minute penalty payments in terms of walking time on each occasion that a crew is relieved.

Duty roster

Having prepared the time and duty schedules, the final task of the schedules section is to prepare a duty roster. It is this document that details, in effect, who will work what and as, in this example, the agreement calls for a 5-day week, where the rest days will be. A specimen duty roster is appended as a follow-up from the duty schedule (*Figure 8.15*).

The exercise as progressed so far has indicated a need for 21 duties on each day Monday to Friday. As said at the outset, it is not proposed to cover the same ground again for Saturdays and Sundays but for this purpose let it be assumed that there are 20 duties on Saturdays and 8 on Sundays, all with a work content of 7hr 50min. The number of duties per week, therefore, is:

Monday–Friday	21 × 5	105
Saturday		20
Sunday		8
Total		133

As each driver works a 5-day week the total number of staff required is 133 divided by five, which calls for either 26 with three duties not covered or 27 with two duties to instructions without any scheduled work. This means that in the case of a 26-week roster (i.e. 26 drivers in regular scheduled employment) three duties would have to be covered locally by spare staff (if any) or by overtime or rest day working or, if a 27-week roster, two spare duties would be available to cover absences, approved or otherwise. In the example the latter alternative has been selected.

The preparation of the duty roster is best done by first filling in on the skeleton the rest days with, in this case, 27 lines. There must be two rest days per week (per line) and as far as possible, staff might like to have them consecutively. If drivers drop down one line each week, a Friday/Saturday rest 1 week and a Sunday/Monday the next gives 4 days off together. They might also prefer an early in front of the rest days and a late after. The more popular roster is a week of earlies, then rest followed by a week of lates although it does not always work out as neatly as that. Services are now often very much thinner on Sundays which means that there must be a preponderance of Sunday rests. A similar situation cannot, of course, apply to Mondays, which means that some split rest days cannot be avoided. Care must be taken to ensure that an adequate period of rest is available should a driver work a late turn followed by an early. In the example, the actual time worked is shown as well as the duty number. Many duties, however, will have allowances and penalty payments according to local agreements and in practice it might be convenient to indicate the monetary value (if any) of each duty over and above the 8 hours flat rate.

Duty roster

Garage: Newtown
Routes: 1, 2/2A, 3, 4, 5 and 6

Rota Number	Sun	Mon	Tues	Wed	Thurs	Fri	Sat	Total work for week
1	REST	14 5.35	14 5.35	14 5.35	REST	1 6.45	30 7.50	31.20
2	60 7.50	1 6.45	1 6.45	1 6.45	1 6.45	REST	REST	34.50
3	REST	REST	21 7.38	21 7.38	21 7.38	21 7.38	49 7.50	38.22
4	REST	9 6.38	9 6.38	9 6.38	REST	10 7.37	47 7.50	35.21
5	66 7.50	19 7.08	REST	REST	9 6.38	9 6.38	39 7.50	36.04
6	REST	17 7.18	17 7.18	17 7.18	17 7.18	17 7.18	REST	36.30
7	REST	11 6.59	11 6.59	REST	11 6.59	11 6.59	37 7.50	35.46
8	REST	16 7.37	16 7.37	16 7.37	REST	INST 8.00	38 7.50	38.41
9	62 7.50	7 6.44	7 6.44	7 6.44	7 6.44	REST	REST	34.46
10	REST	REST	19 7.08	19 7.08	19 7.08	19 7.08	40 7.50	36.22
11	63 7.50	3 8.43	REST	REST	6 5.16	6 5.16	46 7.50	34.55
12	REST	18 8.23	REST	11 6.59	14 5.35	14 5.35	35 7.50	34.22
13	REST	4 7.45	4 7.45	4 7.45	4 7.45	4 7.45	REST	38.45
14	REST	REST	18 8.23	18 8.23	18 8.23	18 8.23	41 7.50	41.22
15	64 7.50	15 5.57	REST	REST	8 6.45	8 6.45	36 7.50	35.07
16	REST	REST	8 6.45	8 6.45	5 4.37	7 6.44	44 7.50	32.41
17	REST	20 6.49	12 6.50	6 5.16	REST	2 5.30	34 7.50	32.15
18	61 7.50	2 5.30	2 5.30	2 5.30	2 5.30	REST	REST	29.50
19	REST	REST	20 6.49	20 6.49	20 6.49	20 6.49	48 7.50	35.06
20	REST	6 5.16	6 5.16	REST	13 8.10	INST 8.00	43 7.50	34.32
21	REST	13 8.10	13 8.10	13 8.10	REST	13 8.10	31 7.50	40.30
22	65 7.50	10 7.37	10 7.37	10 7.37	10 7.37	REST	REST	38.18
23	REST	REST	15 5.57	15 5.57	15 5.57	15 5.57	45 7.50	31.38
24	REST	5 4.37	5 4.37	5 4.37	REST	5 4.37	32 7.50	26.18
25	67 7.50	21 7.38	REST	12 6.50	12 6.50	12 6.50	REST	35.58
26	REST	8 6.45	3 8.43	REST	16 7.37	16 7.37	42 7.50	38.32
27	REST	12 6.50	REST	3 8.43	3 8.43	3 8.43	33 7.50	40.49

Figure 8.15 Duty roster for schedule exercise.

Conclusion

This is a most complex and specialized part of bus operation. The financial welfare of the company depends very much on the skill and efficiency of the schedule compiler and it takes about 2 years to become proficient in this particular art. The foregoing is an introduction to the subject and the general approach is fairly standard but there are various ways of presenting the finished product. There are also different policies for the grouping of services for schedules purposes. Some undertakings might have separate schedules and rosters for each separate service at any one garage (but it would have to be a high-frequency service if maximum efficiency is to be achieved). Others might group the routes into two or more separate schedules and rosters whilst another alternative is maximum flexibility by containing everything within one schedule and roster. This means that drivers would have to work through and hence be familiar with them all. If there are any routes that have some special characteristic such as, perhaps a long-distance express or a night service which carries a higher rate of pay or has vehicles allocated on which drivers must be specially trained then it is likely that they would be on a separate roster, perhaps being appointed on a seniority basis.

Although there are different methods of presentation, the author feels that the layouts as shown are as good as any. It is suggested that readers who will need to know more than they know at present about schedule compilation read through this chapter again slowly and follow through the exercise by close scrutiny of the examples illustrated for each of the different stages. This is one topic where little can be absorbed from a first, quick run-through.

9 Fare collection

The need for a fare collection system

A money transaction is inevitable in the sale of goods or services, and this is as true in transport as in other trading activity. Even if passenger transport is regarded as a social service and some of its costs are met from public funds, money must be collected from the users and cash must still change hands. The problems are in no way lessened by the fact that not all of the income has to be collected through fares. It is only when a completely free system, that is free to the users at the time of travel, is introduced that the situation becomes different, and this brings with it other problems which were considered in Chapter 7. Apart from the 'free fare' issue, therefore, it must be accepted that, in the case of passenger transport, the customers must pay fares for the journeys that they take. Indeed, regardless of what is the economic function of transport, as explained in the companion book *Principles of Transport*, the reason why entrepreneurs first went into the transport business was to make a living. Even in a non-commercial situation it is still very much in the interests of managements that everybody who travels pays the correct fare and that is what this topic of fare collection is all about.

Other chapters discuss fare structures and also statistical information—both of which are to some extent linked with fare collection—and it is debatable which should be considered first. Methods and types of ticket issue can vary according to the fare structure, and ticket issue can also be a source of much statistical data. It could be argued, therefore, that the fare structure and the required statistics should first be determined and the fare collection method made to suit those requirements. This is all good theory but there are practical and financial limitations on the methods and equipment used to collect fares. Although important, statistics cannot be regarded as more than a useful by-product of ticket issue. It is also quite useless to introduce a fare structure for which no satisfactory method of implementation within the set parameters, whatever they may be, can be devised.

The important fundamental issue must not be forgotten. Operators need to ensure that as far as possible they receive all revenue to which they are entitled. To do this, not only must passengers pay the correct fare; those responsible for collecting that fare must surrender the money to their employer and must not divert it to themselves. Cash so collected is handled by various people at different levels within an organization and cross-checks are, therefore, necessary. Whilst it is right and proper for employers to expect their staff to be honest, in the opinion of the writer it is wrong to submit an employee to temptation unnecessarily. If a person is handling large sums on which he knows there is no check, any lapse is at least deserving of some understanding, if not excuse. There should, therefore, be a system of control. It is when proper audit has been instituted and the misdemeanant has then deliberately set himself out to beat the system that severity can be justified.

Basic principles

Having established that some sort of transaction is necessary in respect of each passenger journey; that many employees at different levels within the organization are responsible for collecting and handling cash and there is a clear requirement that management needs to receive all the money to which it is entitled, the methods of collection must now be examined.

For long-distance travel, be it by aircraft, boat, coach or train, a system of pre-payment is readily accepted by passengers. Such transactions are made in the seclusion of a purpose-built office away from the rough and tumble of actual travel. Tickets will be prepared and cash handled by a booking clerk who is adept at that particular type of work and who will have at his disposal all the necessary aids for ticket preparation and cash security. The actual method of issue may be manual or mechanical and may be linked to a system of seat reservation. Large organizations, notably airlines, have now computerized this work with the result that intending passengers can state their requirements at any one of a chain of booking offices and the clerk is able to confirm promptly the booking (if there is accommodation), ascertain the fare and issue the ticket. Even with advance bookings, however, coach drivers should be in possession of a book of blank tickets to be filled in by hand (with a carbon copy for audit) to cater for any person who arrives without a ticket. As was said in Chapter 7, no potential passenger should be turned away and if the fare collection procedure causes this to happen then there is something wrong with the system.

Figure 9.1 An alternative method of fare collection with a two-man crew and where an excess of standing passengers prevents the conductor circulating through the bus is for the conductor to remain seated at the rear. With a circulating area at the back passengers can board, the conductor can supervise the door and give the signal to start and then collect fares before passengers pass through into the body of the bus, as in this example of Athens Bus Corporation (EAS), Athens, Greece.

For the shorter journeys on buses and trams the issue of pre-paid tickets in the form of multi-journey tickets or display-type zonal travel passes as were referred to in Chapter 7 are becoming more popular. But as far as cash customers are concerned, the fare collection problems are very different to those of the long-distance services. In the large built-up areas, particularly during the morning and evening peaks, many thousands of people strain the vehicle resources, some travelling for perhaps quite short distances. Regardless of how they pay (if they pay in advance the availability of the 'pass' has to be checked), if speed is to be combined with efficiency, fare collection becomes a science in itself. On the assumption that some people will still wish to pay at the time of travel—and operators should ensure that they can; again it is not good business to turn away potential traffic—then the provision of an on-bus fare collection system remains a necessity. The next few paragraphs discuss fare collection by drivers (and conductors) and are followed by a review of the various pre-paid systems.

Tickets

If a scale of charges is to be properly enforced, which means that every passenger pays his proper fare for the journey taken and at the end of the day that money is credited to the transport undertaking, then a system of ticket issue becomes necessary. A ticket is, in effect, a receipt for the fare paid and an entitlement to travel for that particular journey. Tickets also constitute a record of sales. The driver or whoever is selling them can, therefore, be held to account for the cash collected. Tickets should contain at least the following information:

1. Fare paid.
2. Availability (such as stage boarded).
3. Identification (such as number of machine).
4. Serial number.

With these details the passenger has proof of payment and entitlement to travel. The ticket is available for inspection and this in turn deters overriding. As far as the ticket issuer is concerned, ticket sales are recorded on a waybill and he is hence accountable for cash so collected.

It was in the early 1880s that the long defunct London Road Car Company first issued to conductors of its horse-drawn buses rolls of pre-printed and serially numbered tickets showing fare values. A similar system was introduced by the erstwhile London General Omnibus Company some 10 years later and the fact that at the time this contributed to strike action by drivers and conductors suggests that their take-home pay in real terms might perhaps have been lessened as a result. If this was the case, then the need for some form of ticket issue becomes all the more apparent.

The Bell Punch system

At this juncture it is appropriate to consider what was at one time the most popularly accepted system of fare collection on buses and trams. It was in use from the era of the horse until the advent and general acceptance of mechanical

188

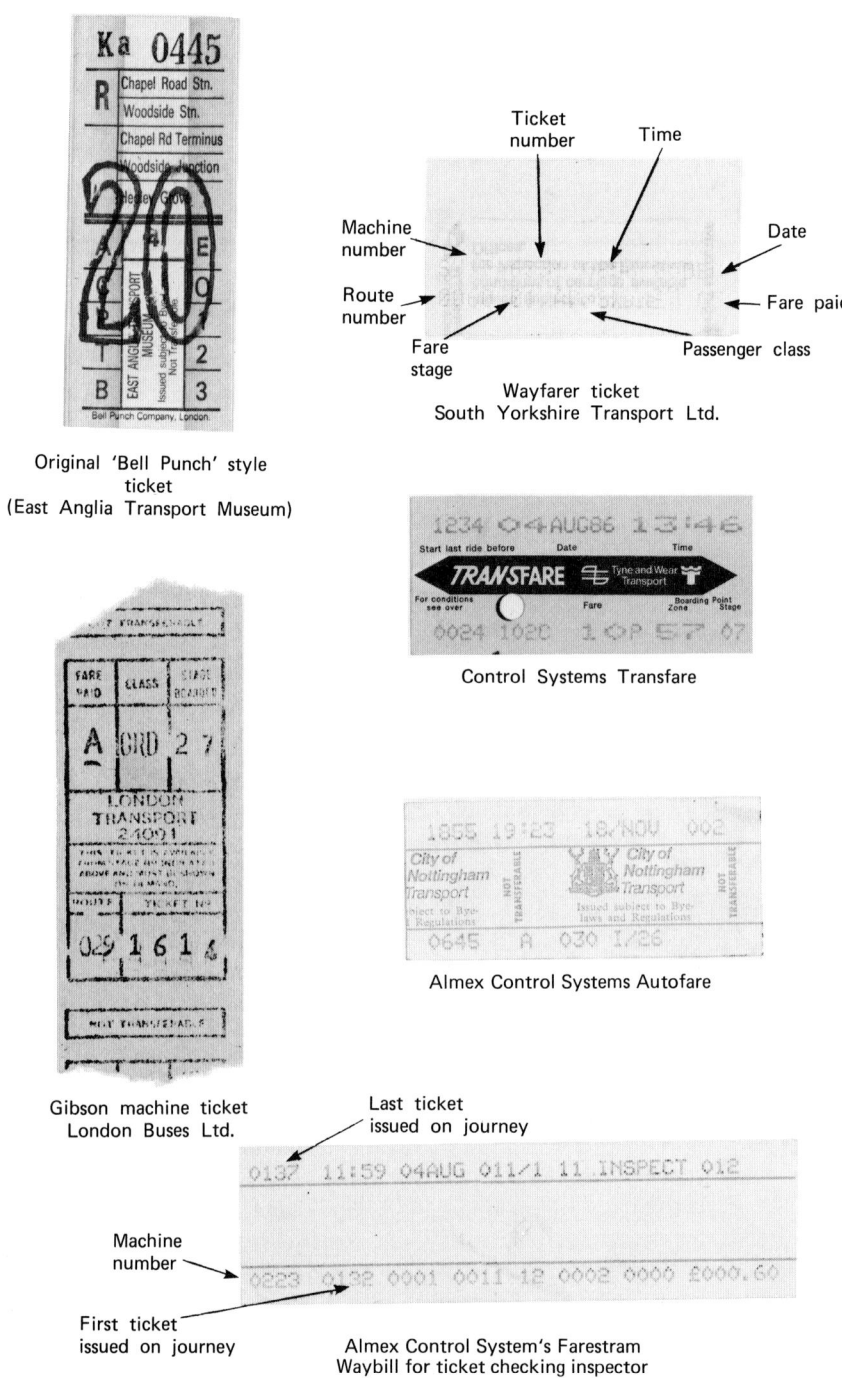

Original 'Bell Punch' style
ticket
(East Anglia Transport Museum)

Wayfarer ticket
South Yorkshire Transport Ltd.

Control Systems Transfare

Almex Control Systems Autofare

Gibson machine ticket
London Buses Ltd.

Almex Control System's Farestram
Waybill for ticket checking inspector

Figure 9.2 Types of tickets.

Strip ticket valid on buses and trams throughout Holland. Passengers cancel the appropriate number of zones which identifies the machine, gives the date and the time of boarding.

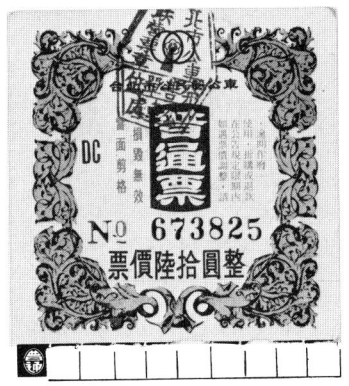

Multi journey bus ticket in Taipei, Taiwan. (Nine journeys have been used).

Prepaid ticket – RATP (Paris) Valid on buses and metro.

Serial number   Time

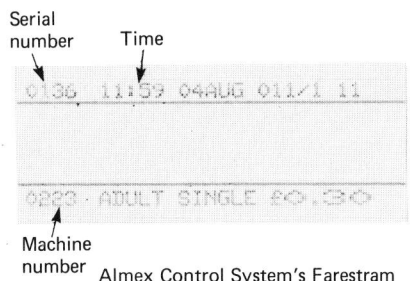

Machine number   Almex Control System's Farestram ticket

equipment and it still survives in various parts of the world even today. Its description is synonymous with what was then the title of a well-known but not the only manufacturer of tickets and equipment, namely the Bell Punch Company, although as a result of mergers, the tradename 'Bell Punch' has now become Almex Control Systems.

The original 'bell punch' system involved the issue to conductors of packs of serially numbered and pre-printed tickets, each denomination having a distinctive colour and all being carried in a rack. As the tickets were sold to passengers they were punched so as to indicate availability, e.g. at the stage boarded, the clipping being retained within the punch. A bell within the punch rang each time a ticket was clipped, which gave audible confirmation of a genuine cancellation. The punch also contained a counter which recorded each time a ticket was so punched and which, incidentally, would not function unless one, and only one, ticket was inserted. The opening numbers and quantity of all tickets issued from stock to conductors were recorded on a waybill. At the close of duty the conductor recorded for subsequent check the closing numbers and arithmetically calculated total sales and hence cash taken for paying-in. The punch register needed to agree with the recorded sales and as a further check, the coloured clippings within the punch were available for counting as each denomination was recognizable by its distinctive colour. Ending numbers could be entered on the waybill by the conductor as required throughout the duty, say at the commencement of each journey and intermediately to the extent considered necessary for purpose of supervision by ticket checking inspectors.

So far so good. The system possessed all of the attributes that have been stipulated. The necessary information was contained on the ticket in a clear and understandable way and the conductor had a complete record of sales. Statistics could be derived from the waybill and the system was suitable for any fares structure including return tickets. Very little in life is foolproof, particularly where money is involved and this is as true with fare collection and the bell punch system as with anything else. Over the years many interesting cases have passed through the courts as a result of ingenious devices to embezzle. But this was not the reason for change. The bell punch system served the industry well for a span of more than 50 years. There were other reasons which made this manual system of ticket issue no longer appropriate for present-day conditions. Nevertheless, by becoming as it did so much a part of the business, the system tends to be regarded by busmen today as a standard against which the merits or otherwise of mechanization are measured.

The disadvantages of a manual system of ticket issue may be summarized as follows:

1. The fact that conductors are issued with stocks of preprinted value tickets for which they are held to account means that waybills must be compiled and all of the conductors' figures checked. This means a lot of clerical work.
2. The conductor is involved in a large amount of arithmetic.
3. Pre-printed tickets of a quality suitable for issue manually must be a part of the expendable equipment.
4. The act of selecting and removing a ticket from the rack and punching it accurately is a cumbersome process.
5. The need for the conductor to carry a ticket rack inhibits free movement

(although the writer has knowledge of this particular piece of equipment being a useful albeit unauthorized weapon for self-defence!).

The upshot of all this is that the system is expensive in terms of clerical labour and in the production of pre-printed tickets; conductors must be held responsible for the face value of their tickets which if lost could be misappropriated; waybill compilation could be arduous for conductors who have no particular aptitude for this type of work; and operationally, the whole process is relatively slow, both in ticket issue on the vehicle and waybill compilation. It was the combination of these factors together with the ever-increasing capacity of new generations of vehicles which put a premium on speed of ticket issue. This led to thoughts of mechanization and hence the virtual demise of the old bell punch.

Mechanical ticket machines

Ideally, any system of mechanized ticket issue on the vehicle should possess all of the attributes of the old bell punch but should overcome its deficiencies (1) to (5) as described. Numerous manufacturers, several of whom were very old established but have now lost their original identities due to acquisitions and amalgamations, have undertaken a lot of development work in this field. As ticket machines came before widespread conversion to one-man operation the original thoughts were to produce equipment suitable for a conductor to carry around. Consequently it had to be not too bulky and not too heavy. With one-man operation, fare collection equipment can in one sense become a part of the vehicle and can, therefore, be more sophisticated. However, to carry the story through, brief mention will be made of machines that are suitable for conductors.

The machines that came as a direct replacement of the ticket rack and bundles of pre-printed tickets used blank rolls with the required information printed and registered on issue. Examples are Setright and TIM (now part of Almex Control Systems) and the Gibson (introduced by what was then London Transport). Many of these machines are still in operation today both in Great Britain and world-wide (in the case of OMO they are attached to the vehicle structure to the side of the driver and may be electrically operated). The fare to be paid (1) and availability (2) is obtained by rotating knobs or dials. Identification (3) and ticket serial number (4) are pre-set (the serial number automatically increases by one each time a ticket is issued). There are various designs for doing this but whatever the method, it must be a straightforward, quick and simple job to set the machine, which must be robust and reliable, and then activate it to issue a ticket many times in rapid succession in a crowded and moving vehicle. Operators must be selective in the types of machines that they purchase depending on the length of routes and fare structures. Features to be taken into account are the range of fare values, ease of settings and production of statistics. Some have registers which record cumulatively the total ticket issues and total cash value of tickets sold, which virtually eliminates the need for arithmetic when completing the waybill. The Gibson machine had a very much reduced range but had separate registers for each fare denomination although no cash totals. Hence there was more statistical information (i.e., sales of each fare value) but disadvantages in other directions. With the former type a very much simplified waybill becomes possible, as with only two sets of readings it is just the starting numbers of the ticket register and cash that are recorded at the outset of duty and again at the close. By subtracting one from the other, totals in terms of tickets and cash are ascertained and the cash figure is what the conductor is required to pay in. This is the money that he should have in his bag. The tickets themselves are printed on a blank roll of paper which has no intrinsic value. It is not until a ticket is actually issued and hence is recorded by the machine that the conductor becomes responsible for the cash taken.

If attention is again turned to the alleged disadvantages of the manual system of ticket issue, it will be seen that a portable machine which possesses the features as described in the previous paragraph and functions satisfactorily under arduous conditions effects a substantial improvement in all of these shortcomings. It will be recalled, however, that the point was made that, apart from the stated deficiencies, the Bell Punch system met the required specifications for a satisfactory fare collection system. The next question, therefore, is whether mechanization has, in meeting the bell punch deficiencies, created other shortcomings where the bell punch was satisfactory. The four essentials (1) to (4) as mentioned have certainly been met. However, the texture of a ticket issued from a machine is likely to be inferior to that issued manually from a rack; it will not be of a distinctive colour and hence not immediately obvious that the correct denomination has been issued and the availability will be indicated only by a stage number which the passenger might well not understand. This latter feature could and did arise with a bell punch ticket, as although it is perfectly feasible in this case to pre-print stage names instead of numbers on tickets, in order to facilitate interchangeability between different routes, even some bell punch tickets bore only numbers. At the time, this was often referred to colloquially as the 'deaf and dumb' ticket because it did not tell you anything. As far as short journeys are concerned, there are few tickets issued from mechanical machines that do tell you anything. What is even worse, with some types of equipment, constant fares revisions make it impossible to retain compatibility between the range of values which the machine can issue and actual fare scales. Under these circumstances there is a practice of replacing the monetary value as shown on the ticket by a code number. Notwithstanding notices on buses, with this system there can be little doubt that few passengers will be able to check that they have been issued with the correct ticket even if they wished to do so, and even fewer would be sufficiently sure of themselves to challenge the driver or conductor if they thought it was wrong. Maybe improvement does not always follow progress.

One further point concerns statistics. Remember that with separate packs of tickets, not only for each denomination but, if required, for each separate class, for example, ordinary single, return or child, there is a complete record of sales. For the machines as described point entries may be made as necessary, perhaps at the end of each journey, or even intermediately, but for most types this will disclose only total tickets sold without a split by fare values. Setrights, for example, provided a statistical counter to check the number of tickets issued for any one fare. This fare could be pre-set at will and could, therefore, produce a sample statistic in respect of that one denomination. By judicious use of this counter daily total tickets sold of each denomination over a period could be estimated and this went some way towards the production of the required figures. The results in this case are not, therefore, as good as the bell punch, but are the figures really required? Or has the industry in the past employed staff to extract information, some of which serves no real purpose and is never acted upon? This is another matter and one that was considered in Chapters 4 and 6.

One-man operation

One-man operation is not new. It is of passing interest that the West Metropolitan Tramways Company (a predecessor of London United Tramways which in turn was absorbed by London Transport), when it first introduced horse trams on the western periphery of the metropolis in the 1880s, adopted one-man operation on two sections of its lines. There was a flat fare of a penny which passengers placed in a glass box and the driver gave change if required. In the 1920s, the London United adopted one-man operation on one of its electric tram routes which lasted for several years, but by that time many small 20-seater buses were also running without conductors, generally outside the more built-up areas. What is relatively new is the extension of the system to large vehicles. In Great Britain it was not until the late 1960s that double-deck one-man operation became legally possible, facilitated by the front-entrance, rear-engined vehicles as described in Chapter 3. This development put a new dimension on fare collection as with a 78-seater vehicle speed is not only desirable, it is crucial if excessive delays at stops are to be avoided.

At this stage it is appropriate to consider one-man operation and to see why the system has spread so rapidly over the past decade. Although not strictly within the terms of this chapter, one-man operation (OMO) cannot be divorced from the subject of fare collection as the success of the former is dependent on the efficiency of the latter. The other contributory factor is vehicle design which is dealt with elsewhere. It is the development of double deck OMO which has stimulated extensive research into what has almost become a science in its own right—fare collection without a conductor.

Bus operators on the continent of Europe and elsewhere have long decried the established British practice of employing a crew of two on a bus, one to drive and the other to collect fares. For many years now, European operators have sought alternative methods of fare collection and where conductors are employed they are usually seated at the point of entry owing to the impracticability of circulating in a large crush-loading standee-type vehicle. In order to minimize time spent at stops, numerous devices have been introduced, the most important of which involves the advance purchase of tickets with self-cancelling on the vehicle, subject only to occasional spot checks by inspectors. These various methods are to be examined but before so doing—lest it be thought that British busmen are backward compared with what might be regarded as their more enterprising continental colleagues—let it be said that there are good reasons why the Europeans have been able to go where the British have feared to tread. These reasons will be discussed as the pre-paid ticket system is explained.

First, however, it is necessary for thoughts to return to the one-time conventional conductor and consider a direct transfer of the conductor's duties to the driver, utilizing the same scales of charges and a similar ticket system. It is one thing to do this on a 20-seater single-deck bus on an infrequent service in a semi-rural area. It is quite another to do it on a 78-seater double-deck bus on a high-frequency service in a heavily congested area. Under these circumstances, delays at stops whilst drivers are collecting fares could easily become intolerable, both to passengers and to other traffic and these delays would quickly result in the bunching of vehicles and hence a very ragged service. There must not, therefore, be delays.

There is no reason why a ticket machine cannot be transferred to the driver, although he does not wear it as does the conductor. It is instead fixed to the bus on the near side of the cab. At the same time this brings with it an advantage as it then becomes possible to plug it in to the vehicle's electrical system and issue tickets from the machine so adapted by the press of a button. This is easier and faster than by turning a handle which the conductor is required to do. Generally, therefore, ticket machines similar to those used by conductors can be modified for use by drivers. This method has, in fact, been widely adopted, both in the UK and overseas, particularly in areas where there has been a strong British influence. It has been applied both to single-deck and to double-deck buses with reasonable success except on the very busiest services already referred to, particularly where there is a heavy short-distance on/off movement. It is here that the driver really requires some assistance over and above that of an electrically operated ticket machine. It is here also where both operators and manufacturers have undertaken much research into the need for a fare collection system which is adequate under the circumstances described, complies with the operator's specifications (that is, it can be adapted to the chosen scale of charges) and is acceptable to and understood by passengers. The latest equipment will be reviewed later in this chapter. Before so doing, however, there are other thoughts on this subject which must be discussed.

Fare fixing as distinct from fare collection was considered in Chapter 7. As was said in that chapter, fare scales are set by either economic or political dictates according to circumstances. Ideally, the collection system should fit the fares and not the fares the collection system. In practice, however, some systems are more efficient if used in conjunction with only certain types of fares. This means that there must sometimes be discretion when deciding whether to surrender or modify a chosen method of charging in order to improve the efficiency of collection. By referring again to Chapter 7, it was seen that in Great Britain by custom and practice, a graduated fare scale is generally adopted, which means that there are many different fare stages and fares. This materially adds to the complexity of ticket issue. At the other end of the scale maximum simplicity is derived from a flat fare but the zonal system is a good compromise.

A fare collection system must satisfy all reasonable passenger demands as well as being acceptable to the 'establishment'. In the days when one-man operation was confined to the 20-seater buses and drivers had a bell punch and a rack of tickets, they were able to allow all passengers to board quickly at the busier stops and then go round the bus and collect fares either before driving away or even at the next stop if it was in a quieter place. With a larger bus this is no longer practicable and with a fixed ticket machine impossible. Payment on entry must, therefore, be enforced at all times. This not only produces problems when buses are unattended on a stand, which is another matter, it also means that passengers must queue outside the bus to pay, even after it has arrived at a stop, regardless of the weather. It is important, therefore, for more than one reason that passengers can board as expeditiously as possible.

Two-stream boarding

Vehicle design has repercussions on time spent at stops and the controversy over a separate centre exit was discussed in Chapter 3. As far as fare collection is concerned, one device to reduce waiting time is to permit two streams of people to board simultaneously. Whilst one stream is required to pay the driver in the conventional manner, the other must utilize self-service equipment. Various manufacturers have produced ideas in this field. One system is for the second stream of passengers to put money into a machine to get a ticket which records the essential details. The only action required by the driver in this instance is to change the stage number by remote control at each fare point unless, of course, management requires the last driver of the day to empty the machine and pay in the money to the cash office. This is a separate issue which is discussed in Chapter 10.

Figure 9.3 Two-stream boarding is a popular device to reduce dwell time at stops, one paying the driver and the other using help yourself equipment. This example at Rennes in France shows those in possession of tickets boarding on the left to use a cancelling machine and those paying the driver on the right. But once the driver is engaged on fare collection he cannot also check that the other stream of passengers do actually pay a fare.

As a broad principle, the two-stream system of boarding has the advantage that in theory it virtually halves the time spent at stops providing passengers split themselves equally between the two different methods of payment. In practice this seldom happens. There is usually a preference to pay the driver for one of the following reasons:

1. Passengers either imagine they do not know how to use the machine or they are nervous of it with a fear that they might lose their money in full view of spectators—the people already seated in the lower deck.
2. They do not know the fare or, therefore, how much money to put in the machine.
3. They know the fare but do not have the correct money and therefore require change, which only the driver can give.
4. They are seeking psychological reassurance that they are on the right bus.

A disadvantage of two-stream boarding to the operator is that there is a greater chance of loss of revenue through fare avoidance. At busy stops a driver will be fully occupied with the first stream through issuing tickets and giving change. He will make no attempt to challenge other passengers passing by, ostensibly to help themselves to a ticket. Unfortunately, there are occasions when some passengers misunderstand the operators' intentions, walk past not only the driver but the machine as well and help themselves instead to a free ride. For psychological reasons, this practice is encouraged if the bus has a centre exit and it is not, therefore, necessary to once again pass the driver in order to alight.

Further reference to second-stream boarding is made in connection with pre-paid tickets.

The need to give change

At this stage it is worth pondering a while on item (3) above and the vexed question of giving change. Much play has been made of the speed at which tickets can be issued. Machines are faster than the bell punch and ticket rack and some machines are faster than others because of the way the stage number and fare have to be selected. Fractions of a second are regarded as all important when choosing the machine most suitable for the job. But it is not the actual issuing of a ticket which takes the time, it is giving change that really delays the fare collection process. Many passengers offer the correct money—a few do not—and some even tender high money, in the UK perhaps a £5 note for a minimum fare. There is no legal obligation to give change. It is provided as a courtesy but this service to the few means a disservice to the many. One person demanding change for a high value note could delay some 70 other people who have boarded without bother or fuss. Operators look to give service but it is important to give it in the right places. Further reference will be made to this aspect of fare collection when the farebox is considered.

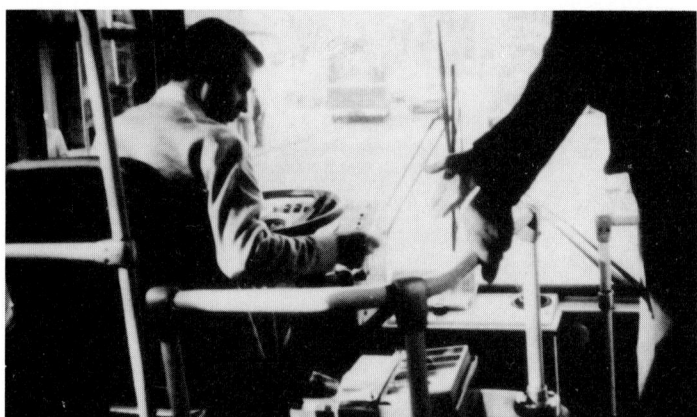

Figure 9.4 Whilst ticket issue can be a very speedy operation it is the act of giving change which is the delay factor. On this one-man operated bus in Andorra the passenger did not have the correct fare and in consequence delayed not only herself but everybody else on the bus. Changegiving is a courtesy but if it was not provided passengers would quickly learn to have the right money (they would only have to be refused once) and the service would benefit.

Pre-paid tickets

In the context of both two-stream boarding and change-giving problems, it is opportune to introduce the pre-paid ticket. Such tickets are purchased away from the vehicle and prior to travel. Sales points could be strategically sited dispensing machines or enquiry offices and agents. The all-important point is that this part of the transaction is done at leisure and not amid the hurly-burly of the bus platform. Tickets of this variety may be multi-journey, that is, valid for more than one ride (often 10 or even in multiples of any journeys up to the value of the ticket) or there could be books of tickets, each valid for one journey corresponding to its face value. If a special cancellator is provided on the vehicle, passengers boarding who have tickets then form the second stream and insert their tickets in this machine. This validates the ticket by printing the necessary details for the journey being taken and in the case of the multi-journey ticket, cancels an appropriate portion. If the latest electronic apparatus is used, there can be 'stored value' tickets. Passengers who take advantage of this system are likely to be regular riders who, therefore, should quickly become accustomed to its use. The inhibitions of using the machines as already described should not, therefore, under these circumstances, apply. The classic example of pre-paid tickets is, of course, the season ticket, sometimes referred to as a contract ticket, being a multi-journey facility sold at a specially commuted rate. The regular riders who first used them became known as commuters and the word has now found a place in our present-day transport vocabulary. Such tickets are being increasingly extended to buses, which certainly eases fare collection problems on the vehicle. The subject of season tickets, however, falls within the charging process and is therefore dealt with in Chapter 7.

Figure 9.5 The cash transaction at the time of boarding is a potential source of delay to one-man operated buses, particularly when changegiving is involved. Pre-purchased tickets speed the process and a ticket dispensing machine is seen here at the kerbside of Lauentzien Strasse in West Berlin, West Germany.

It should be noted in passing that a season ticket (or any other pass for that matter which is valid for travel) is, in effect, a display ticket and should be capable of being easily shown and its availability promptly recognized. Its size and shape should ideally be such that it can be contained within a standard season ticket wallet. A book-type document which has to be opened for inspection fails to meet these basic requirements, passengers are encouraged to show and staff to accept a valueless outside cover and the design is hence unsuitable.

Although pre-paid tickets have the operational advantage of eliminating cash transactions on the bus platform (regardless of whether a validating machine is used as they could be checked by the driver), they have their disadvantages which may be summarized as follows:

1. By using the system passengers must set aside a sum of money for what is, in effect, bulk purchase of travel. Furthermore, if the type of ticket is such that the journeys must be undertaken within a defined period, then they are committed to travel and by that means unless they are to lose their money. In any case, people have to be encouraged to put themselves out sufficiently to go to a sales point, lay out money in advance and then take care not to mislay what they have bought. To do this requires an incentive, which is likely to take the form of a cash discount. In other words, there is a cheaper fare, with the consequent repercussions on revenue.
2. The setting up of sales points does, in itself, involve additional administration and hence cost. Premises and staff must be found and sales duly accounted for and audited.
3. If dispensing machines are used, a further capital and maintenance cost is involved and there is also a security problem as is considered in Chapter 10.
4. If agents are employed, the agents might seek commission on sales, which is a further charge against revenue and cash collecting, accounting and audit is still necessary. Some agents might, however, be persuaded to sell tickets without commission as it does encourage people into their shops.

Nevertheless, the use of pre-paid 'display' tickets valid anywhere within a defined zone for periods of days, weeks or months is becoming increasingly popular.

At this juncture it is worth taking stock of British experiences and seeking reasons why, to all outward appearances, various systems seem to be working satisfactorily in Europe but run into difficulties, imaginary or real, when applied in the UK. Vehicle types are dealt with in Chapter 3 and this does have a bearing on the matter. Suffice to say here that in contrast to the areas of British influence there is, in Europe and elsewhere, a strong tendency towards single-deck vehicles with plenty of standing accommodation. The result is that there are some very high capacity vehicles, particularly where articulated buses and trams are concerned. At the same time, in some countries, unlike the patient British, the arrival of a bus means for the locals a push and scramble. A further wait to buy a ticket would not always be tolerated for very long. Operators have, therefore, taken stronger measures to enforce the sale of pre-paid tickets and in so doing they have been aided by certain circumstances which do not apply in Great Britain. The point regarding the inability of drivers to check the second stream when boarding has already been made. If boarding is permitted at entrances other than at the front then it clearly becomes quite impossible and passengers must cancel a ticket for which they have paid in advance without any question of direct supervision at the time. Under these circumstances, it is usual for European operators to employ roving inspectors to make spot checks in order to deter faredodgers. So far, nothing has happened that could not be done in Great Britain. The difference lies in the fact that in Europe inspectors impose an on-the-spot fine on those caught riding without a ticket.

Certainly it violates British PSV regulations to travel on buses with intent to avoid payment but to go to court and prove intent is a very different matter to simply accusing a person of not possessing a valid ticket and impose an automatic fine. Even so, it is questionable to what extent the on-the-spot fines in Europe do act as a real deterrent. Unless there are a lot of inspectors, and this would be expensive, the chance of being checked might be sufficiently low as to justify the risk of not paying the fare and perhaps operators might prefer not to say how much revenue they are really losing. Some passengers are seen never to attempt to pay, and on average and over a period of time money spent on fines can be less than what would have been the cost of legitimate fares. This suggests that the fines are not sufficiently high. But the steeper the rate the less is the chance of collection as the point will come when even a passenger willing to pay might not be in possession of the required sum. In any case the extraction of a fine is not exactly an enviable task. Some members of the community who frequent late-night buses pay scant regard for persons or property and when they are travelling the least of the troubles might be not paying the correct fare. In the absence of judicial support for the use of strong-arm tactics in the enforcement of proper conduct, the writer for one would have some trepidation in demanding a fine on these occasions. In some countries, more appropriate treatment of the delinquent is allowed and control is correspondingly easier.

Another feature often met outside the UK is instead of allowing a discount on the approved scale to those who purchase tickets in advance off the vehicle, to charge a fare much higher than the accepted scale to those who still wish to pay the driver. Again, this is something that is still foreign to British practice, but it does encourage the use of pre-paid tickets. It is also easier to find shops willing to sell tickets at all hours on the continent as tobacconists, for example, tend to remain open much longer there than in Great Britain.

There are reasons, therefore, why certain methods that are followed in some countries are not acceptable in others. Long-established customs and practices play a part. There is, however, one system that has many advantages, which has found general acceptance within the United States and Canada but about which operators elsewhere have been surprisingly reticent. It is the farebox.

The farebox

The principle of the farebox is popularly regarded as an import from North America. This is not, however, necessarily true as it has already been seen that some of the horse trams of the West Metropolitan Tramways Company in London carried a glass box in which passengers placed their fare. The modern farebox consists of a locked vault within a locked chamber, above which is a glass or perspex dome, within which passengers deposit the correct fare. The farebox is within view of the driver and he can see what money has been placed in the box. Even at this stage, however, the money cannot be retrieved. Once the driver is satisfied that the correct fare has been paid, he presses a button and the money drops through into the locked vault. Providing the passenger knows the fare and

Figure 9.6 In North America the farebox and locked vault system of fare collection is standard practice on urban buses. Where zone fares are in operation passengers boarding in the first zone pay on boarding and those boarding in the second zone pay on alighting. Those travelling through both zones pay on boarding and again on alighting. As those travelling only in the second zone pay nothing on boarding the driver sometimes puts his hand over the farebox to prevent a payment in error as is being done here by this driver in San Francisco, USA.

has the correct money, it is as simple as that and it is very fast—as fast as with a two-man crew. In North America, however, most people know the fare because it is normally a flat fare or at most a zone fare and no ticket is necessary. These different types of fare scales were considered in Chapter 7 but it does bring out a point already made—that although fare collection apparatus should cater for the needs of the desired fares, it sometimes helps if the fare scale is contained within what the machines can deal with. In Great Britain, there is no legal requirement to issue a ticket. However, with graduated fares, if tickets are not issued there is no check on where passengers boarded or what they paid and hence no check on overriding. It is fairly safe to assume, therefore, that any operator introducing a ticketless system with a graduated fare scale is destined to lose money. But certain manufacturers have tried to take care of this by introducing a ticket issuing arrangement in conjunction with the farebox. Instead of having one button to press to release the coins the driver has a bank of buttons. Each does the same job, it releases the coins and simultaneously issues a ticket. The price marked on the ticket, however, corresponds with whichever button is pressed. The Autofare of Almex Control Systems Limited is an example. The great advantage of this system is speed. A mixture of coins (or tokens) of any value and even paper money can be used. It is all just dropped into a receptacle, there being no slot to fumble with. Whilst it is accepted that change cannot be given (unless the driver carries a float) doubt has already been expressed on the justification of giving change. Any case of hardship can always be met by giving a passenger a voucher instead of change which could be cashed subsequently at an appointed office but with this inconvenience it is likely that passengers will do this only once. As a matter of interest it is worthy of note that the real reason for introducing the farebox in the USA was not to speed the service but for security. Armed robbery in that country is now such that for their own safety drivers cannot have money in their possession—hence the locked vault.

Speed, however, has proved to be a useful by-product and many passengers feel that this is a small price to pay for the much improved quality of service. Nevertheless, security was the real reason for the farebox and what happens in North America has a habit of spreading across the Atlantic in due course. But that is a matter for Chapter 12. A further point, however, before leaving North America is one that calls for a slight refinement to the statement that a ticketless system requires a flat fare. With a two-zone system and no tickets, passengers travelling in the first zone can pay as they enter whilst those boarding in the second zone pay as they alight. By this means those travelling through both zones (i.e. the longer riders) pay twice and still no tickets are necessary.

It was noted in Chapter 7 that if a flat fare is in operation there could be a need to offer transfer facilities. Again the best examples are in North America, and in many instances transfer facilities are available even with the farebox without ticket type of fare collection and no other sophisticated equipment. The driver has pads of dated paper transfer tickets pre-printed with lines at each quarter hour. The pad is held in place on the vehicle with a bulldog type clip, the position of which is moved every 15 minutes to accord with the time of day. When passengers alight the drivers tears off a transfer ticket on request and hands it to the passenger which is evidence that a fare has been paid and at what quarter hour the change of vehicle is being made. This piece of paper is accepted in lieu of money by the driver of the next bus who is able to check by the time that it is reasonable to regard this second trip as part of the same journey.

Having extolled the virtues of the farebox in terms of both speed and security on the bus, it does produce one complication which lies in the process of emptying. This, however, is a matter for Chapter 10.

A development of the farebox system which has found its way into the UK is the turnstile. The equipment is installed inside the bus just behind the entrance at the expense of a fair amount of seating capacity. Whilst the correct money must be dropped into a farebox, the turnstile requires not only the correct money but the right coinage as well which must be inserted in the appropriate slot to cause it to open and allow the passenger to pass through. The use of pre-paid tickets presents a problem although there could be provision for the use of tokens. This does, however, seem to be an expensive, complicated and cumbersome alternative to the farebox without any obvious advantages.

Electronic ticket machines

It is the electronic systems of fare collection that combine simplicity and speed of ticket issue with the production of full statistical data. Examples are the Wayfarer of

Microsystem Design Ltd. and the Timtronic Farestram and Transfare of Almex Control Systems Ltd. Some of the Almex Control Systems' equipment is shown in *Figures 9.7* and *9.8*.

This sophisticated apparatus is designed on the principle of a vehicle-mounted intelligence terminal with a bank of keys which may itself issue the ticket; a small memory module personalized to the driver which Timtronic calls an ACE (automatic computer entry), which Wayfarer calls a data module and which Transfare calls a STRAM (serial transportable random access memory), and with

Figure 9.7 The Transfare of Control Systems Ltd. *in situ* on a bus of Busways Travel Services Ltd. in Newcastle-upon-Tyne, UK. All transaction details are recorded by the small portable memory which the driver carries around and inserts in the machine. This system comprises two basic components, being the control module keyline (on which in the illustration the driver has placed his left hand) and the ticket issuing unit to his rear. This arrangement facilitates an orderly progression by passengers past the driver and into the bus. The two ticket dispensers are necessary in this case as in Newcastle through tickets are issued on to the local railway and rapid transit lines and passengers so transferring must be in possession of tickets which are magnetically coded. Local bus tickets are of the normal type based on standard blank paper hence two separate blank rolls are necessary. (Reproduced by kind permission of Almex Control Systems Ltd.)

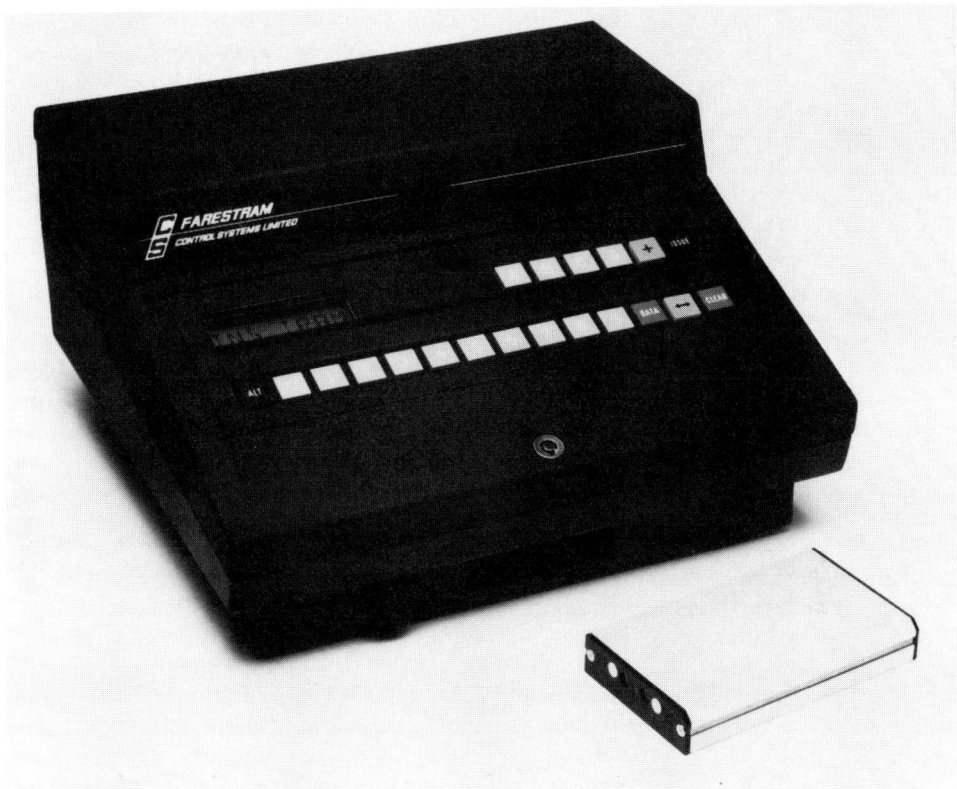

Figure 9.8 The Farestram FM2 ticket machine of Control Systems Ltd. with the memory module shown separately is illustrated here. The memory is a microprocessor based device which collects, retains and transmits data under programme control and is the part that the driver carries around with him. In this machine tickets are ejected from the slot on the left. (Reproduced by kind permission of Almex Control Systems Ltd.)

some systems a separate ticket issuing unit placed to the rear of the driver. By positioning the ticket issuer remote from the driver passengers can progress through the bus during the fare collection process which reduces boarding times.

The operational units are used in conjunction with a depot reader unit located in the traffic office at the signing-on/signing-off point and a typical sequence of events for the driver is for him to:

1. Either retain a personal memory module (it is about the size of a pocket calculator) or personalize a blank by the use of the garage-based machine.
2. Insert the memory module into the control module (i.e. the ticket machine) and key in all required details such as badge number, personal security number, route, journey number, etc., having boarded the bus.
3. Update the boarding stage as the bus progresses along the route and at terminals. (All such entries also record the time.)
4. Carry the memory module with him when leaving the bus for any reason.

5. Obtain a 'waybill' from the control module (which appears in the form of a ticket) which shows the value of tickets sold, etc., at the end of his shift.
6. Insert his memory module in the garage reader unit which downloads the day's data for subsequent analysis when he returns to garage.

The range of functions and capabilities of this type of equipment such as, for example, one or other of Almex Control Systems' Transfare or Farestram, may be summarized as follows:

1. High-speed ticket issue by using up to 40 rapid issue fare buttons pre-set to fare values.
2. Up to nine separate classes available for key entered fares with a range (in sterling) from zero to £99.99.
3. Up to three different types of display tickets such as scholars' term tickets, travel cards or senior citizens' passes may be recorded.
4. Ability to programme to suit all currencies throughout the world.
5. Multiple ticket issues automatically totalled on the drivers' display.
6. Fares memorized (as are programmed by the garage reader) and the correct fare indicated when the destination stage is keyed in.
7. Blank tickets used on which the required information is printed at the time of issue which includes for example serial number, date, route, stage boarded, machine number, class, fare paid and destination name. Printing by dot matrix in less than one second per ticket.
8. Ticket checking inspector able to obtain a 'ticket' on boarding which contains all essential control information including scheduled and actual departure times, total cash taken, details of tickets sold on current journey, etc. Summary of movements of roving inspectors as they board buses also becomes available.
9. All of the day's information stored in the memory module which is available for use by the driver for paying-in purposes and by management for statistics and audit.
10. An independent buffer memory retains information recorded by previous removals. Accumulated grand total of tickets issued and cash received held permanently (in other words, if the driver loses or misappropriates the memory, the information can still be obtained).
11. Reliance on infra-red data transfer between modules which eliminates the need for multi-pin mechanical edge connectors for this purpose.
12. Complete records kept of the drivers' and hence the vehicles' movements by time.
13. The availability of complete statistics in respect of whatever management might require.
14. The system can be used in conjunction with other equipment such as fareboxes.

A transportable electronic ticket issuing machine incorporating the revenue control system is also available. The Farespeed of Almex Control Systems Ltd. is an example. In this case the machine itself is issued to the driver rather than being a part of the bus. However, although it is advertised as light enough to be carried easily, the personal preference of the author is for the machine to be attached to the vehicle leaving the driver to carry only the memory module.

Conclusions

The fare collection process has passed through three phases:

1. Manual issue with a rack of pre-printed tickets and a punch for use by a conductor or one-man driver.
2. Mechanical issue with a machine using blank rolls of paper but worked by hand by a conductor or one-man driver. This type of machine was also modified for use with electric power when used on OMO buses.
3. Electronic ticket issue and revenue control system for use by one-man drivers.

A wealth of statistics is available from both the rack and punch system and the latest electronic equipment although the former is at the expense of a tremendous amount of time-consuming clerical work by both conductors and clerical staff. There was, however, a period in between—i.e. with the mechanical machines, when very little information could be obtained. Even with the other systems, however, holders of display tickets seriously prejudice the accuracy of any statistics. To just record them as a passenger helps but the actual journey taken is still not known unless that information also is recorded. Operators without the electronic equipment but who have a problem here might find the Almex PDR useful. This is a portable ticket machine able to store data on tape. It is issued to drivers together with a magnetic tape cassette. All passengers, including passholders, must have a ticket for the journey which they are taking (no-value or otherwise) and the tape is subsequently read by converting the recorded information to a standard code on other tape for processing and printout on a computer. Certainly all passengers must be questioned when boarding about their intended journey regardless of whether they already possess a valid ticket which can only slow boarding times and thereby negate some of the value of display tickets. If operators do not wish this procedure to be undertaken by every driver then sample techniques may be used. This can be arranged by equipping only a few drivers on each roster with PDRs and providing they rotate through each line of the roster (*see* Chapter 8) then the sample should be satisfactory.

The operator must consider what system of fare collection is most suitable for his particular circumstances. Speaking in a world-wide context then one of the first things to consider is the cost of labour. In the case of the larger undertakings in Great Britain for example, labour absorbs some 60% of total costs. Operators in Asia and Africa are likely to produce a figure substantially less than that. So much so that even one-man operation might not be attractive, let alone the expenditure of large sums of money on sophisticated equipment to save employing clerical staff which are cheap in any case. There is also the need to consider what statistics are required. It was seen from Chapter 6 that at least in the western world they are highly desirable, in fact, essential if future planning is to be realistic. And with high wages, electronic revenue control systems, costly as they are, can easily cover themselves when the value of the labour which they save is taken into account. But it is not everywhere that the driver/conductor even has to account for his takings. In third world countries in particular, owners of vehicles do sometimes lease their buses to drivers in return for a fixed daily payment. This the driver finds out of the fares which he collects and everything that he receives beyond that he keeps for himself. No very elaborate records are needed for a system of that kind.

Reverting to the west, controls can only be as good as human nature and conduct will allow. However comprehensive the records might be, everything still depends on the driver actually collecting a fare and issuing not only a ticket but, in the case of a graduated fare scale, to the amount of cash received. Remember this was an advantage of the farebox with a flat fare and a locked vault. Apart from this, the only check is a challenge by the passenger (and with the types of tickets that are issued by machines, not many of them do) or by the occasional inspector who 'jumps' the bus, and even he will not necessarily be in a position to detect the irregularity.

If the capital expenditure involved with fare collection is used only to obtain statistics, then the information obtained is expensive indeed and if it is bought then it must be put to good and proper use. For fare collection alone excessive sums do not have to be spent. A simple pair of hand clippers without any form of register is cheap and the driver can cancel a ticket as quickly as can any machine.

To take another example, in Taipei, the capital of Taiwan, Republic of China, cards with provision for 10 rides (no dates or time limits) are sold by shops and roadside stalls. The driver (or conductor) clips out one journey on boarding until the card is exhausted. Nothing could be quicker or cheaper to operate than that, except there is more than one bus undertaking operating in Taipei. There is one large one and a host of smaller ones and the bus ticket is valid on them all. The clippings from the tickets must therefore be retained in the clippers, counted at the garage and again in a clearing house in order that the different operators get their rightful dues. Back, therefore, to square one! Maybe there is a case for something more sophisticated than a simple pair of clippers. But enough has been said for operators to see that it is a case of looking at their own requirements and getting what they require to suit their particular system from the range of high-quality equipment that is now available.

10 Operational control

Introduction

All that has been said so far and what follows in Chapter 11 relates to the infrastructure, equipment, functions and professions which collectively form the ingredients of a passenger transport system. Without such hardware and expertise there could be no foundation and no direction or guidance. But the engineers, accountants, planners and staff managers, important as they may be, cannot alone actually make the thing tick. They may lay down the framework, give guidance and provide the wherewithal. There is, however, another band of people at ground floor level, the controllers and supervisors under an operating manager, who are in direct day to day control and in whose success or otherwise the efficiency of the undertaking will be judged. They work at or are attached to garages, depots or similar establishments, are responsible for implementing the procedures and directives imposed upon them by their headquarters organization and they must transmit those orders to the platform staff. If things go wrong (and they do sometimes) it is for them to take the immediate remedial measures. If the results of their endeavours are not satisfactory then the situation quickly catches the public eye. Passengers complain if the service is disrupted; staff complain if they are asked to do something a little more onerous than they expected and it is the supervisors on the road and in the garages who are on the spot to collect these reactions which in any case can only result from circumstances over which they have had little or no control. Surely, then, this is the 'heart' of the business. The supervisors and other garage staff are the links between management/ administration, platform staff and customers, and the control rooms and garage offices are the places where the pulse beats and is kept even (*Figure 10.1*).

This is the level where theory and the written directives become practical reality. Services have to be maintained, emergencies have to be dealt with, shop stewards have to be consulted, platform staff have to be solicited (agreements regarding duty changes might preclude the right to give a direct order) and quick decisions have to be made. There are occasions when many things happen at once. The conflicting demands of the passengers and the staff have to be reconciled with the rules of the job and resources are often limited. If, therefore, there is a level where experience counts, then this is it and no busman can really regard himself as having graduated until he has served for a year or two in these various traffic supervisory roles. This chapter deals with this day to day work.

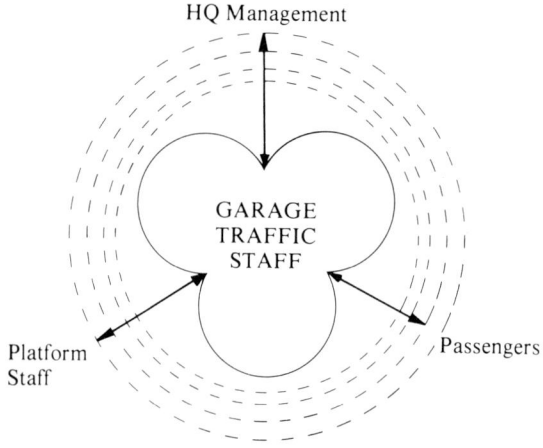

HQ Management

Platform Staff

Passengers

GARAGE
TRAFFIC
STAFF

Figure 10.1 Relationships with garage traffic staff.

Bus control and supervision

Speed schedules

The time allowances contained in the scheduled vehicle runnings (and this means both the average speed of the service and the amount of layover time at the terminal) have a marked effect on the standard of timekeeping and the ability to rectify late running. Unfortunately, what is advantageous during periods of heavy vehicular traffic has the opposite effect when the roads are clear and not enough running time in the peaks is no more detrimental to good timekeeping than is too much running time in the slack. The only difference is that in one instance buses run late and in the other they run early and the latter is something that should never be condoned. This leads into the subject of determination of average speeds which is a prerequisite for time schedule compilation as was seen in Chapter 8.

It was acknowledged in Chapter 8 that trade unions like to play a significant role in schedule preparation and speed schedules, service by service, do not escape their interest. In the schedules exercise an average speed of 12 mph (19 km/h) was set but in practice it will vary according to circumstances, and for some routes 12 mph might prove to be a little fast. However, the relevance in this context is that it is at local superintendent level that time tests will be conducted and agreed with representatives of the platform staff. To ameliorate late running in the peaks a popular device is to introduce differential running times, that is, varying average speeds according to the time of day and day of week. Certainly this helps but to express a personal opinion, the writer is against such a practice for the following reasons:

1. The degree of congestion is not necessarily consistent day by day and it is not always the same journeys that are affected. Additional running time cannot therefore be applied with any precision.
2. When congestion is really bad the few minutes extra per trip which might be given will still not be realistic and to allocate more would produce an unnecessarily unattractive timetable, bearing in mind that some of the time lost will hopefully be made up *en route* anyway.

3. It was said in Chapter 8 that regular repetitive timings are the ideal and they can be more easily remembered by passengers. With differential running times this is not possible and irregular headways must result.

The view of the author is that any allowances for late running should be built not into running time but into additional layover or recovery time at terminals. By this means buses do at least have a better chance of making the return journey according to schedule without the disadvantages outlined at (1), (2) and (3). However, the industry is not unanimous on this point.

What there can be no argument about, and this should be clear from Chapter 8, is that if additional running time has to be provided, even if it is only an extra minute, it could have a profound effect on schedules and hence costs. If existing schedules are efficient then there is likely to be no slack in which to accommodate anything extra. If more running time is to be provided then it can only mean more vehicles and more staff with poor utilization. It is part of the job of the local chief inspector, superintendent or whoever to agree running times with the platform staff and a lot depends on the success of his endeavours.

The bus control office

The control inspector is responsible for the maintenance of scheduled services. If everything is running and running on time then his work is not particularly difficult, but with a large and complex network this is seldom the case. It depends on physical factors whether, in fact, there is a separate control organization at all. In the smaller provincial towns, for example, with a rural hinterland the degree of congestion and late running and the number of untoward incidents might not be very great and certainly nothing that could not be dealt with by the output staff at the garage and the general duty inspectors on the road. On the other hand, the job of keeping the service going is, in some areas, of sufficient magnitude in its own right to justify a separate organization for the purpose.

The most sophisticated method of control is that which was touched upon in Chapter 2 in connection with urban traffic control. Remember the references that were made to closed circuit television and the possible linkage with bus managements. This, of course, is quite practicable. Bus controllers are able to have their own set of closed circuit television screens and be provided with the same traffic information as is available to the highway authority or police responsible for general vehicle movement. Coupled with this a two-way radio system enables controllers to make contact with drivers on the road and possibly with mobile inspectors as well. Other equipment is available (although not widely used) which gives a visual indication of the times that buses pass certain points and this type of control office also invariably has direct lines to the emergency services—police, ambulance and fire. This, then, is the ultimate in control equipment. It is costly to install but if its potential is properly exploited it is invaluable in maintaining the best possible services where traffic conditions are difficult. The two-way element in the use of radio is important and if the system is to be successful, drivers must co-operate and keep control properly informed of the changing road conditions. Any resistance on the part of trade unions could, therefore, render the whole concept ineffective. This, however, would be a particularly ill-conceived and short-sighted approach as a better standard of service is in the interests of everybody, including the staff, and the availability of radio with which the driver is able to summon the police quickly in the event of an emergency gives him added security.

Radio has particular significance in the case of the dial-a-bus service as referred to in Chapters 6 and 7. Indeed, this method of operation could not function without it as the whole concept of dial-a-bus is to pick up passengers where they are and take them to where they want to go; that is, subject to physical practicalities and within a defined area. To summon a bus, passengers telephone the control office from where the driver on the road is contacted.

Control work really comes into its own when buses are either missing or running late owing to heavy traffic, breakdown, accident, sickness, non-availability of staff or any of the many other causes that might prevent the bus from getting through. Corrective measures include on-the-spot instructions to staff to turn short in order to regain lost time, working through but covering their second spell of duty, working through to a different destination on another service, arranging for substitute vehicles, transferring passengers to other services and any other emergency arrangements that might have to be made. Liaison is necessary with the staff or duties clerk and the engineering staff at the garage if there are revised but important changes in staff or vehicle requirements. Bigger problems arise, of course, when these additional resources are not available, and very often they are not.

It is because of the control aspect that there tends to be a divergence of views on the merits of cross-town services in urban areas. What were seen as advantages in this type of route in Chapter 6 are likely to be viewed in a different way by the local operators whose job it is to maintain service. If buses come into town and layover prior to return to the place from whence they came then there is a chance to minimize and localize the effects of traffic delays but if they are on a through cross-town service there is no such possibility, and any dislocation experienced on one side of the town is likely to be projected through to the other. To give a recovery allowance in the centre on a through service would be irritating to passengers and would defeat the object of providing such a facility as well as having to find more stands in what is likely to be a very congested area.

Coach control

Just as the traffic characteristics of the long-distance services are different to those of local buses, certain aspects of control work are also rather specialized for coach controllers. The work is highly seasonal and a somewhat meagre basic timetable needs to be augmented at busy periods by substantial duplication according to demand at the time. Although many of the basic services are now of the 'non-stop' variety using motorways, on services where this is not the case (i.e., with intermediate stops) non-stop duplicates are often provided when the demand is heavy. One object is to attract full-length-ride passengers who get journey times that are competitive with the private car but there is also the operating advantage of being able to bypass the more congested areas by the use of special routes, and to segregate through riders from those not making the full journey. In the peak weeks it is usually easy to segregate terminal-to-terminal passengers so that a relief vehicle can run by the fastest practicable route, allowing for the need for occasional halts for refreshment. It is important that such routes be defined properly and there are distinct advantages in preparing a drivers' instruction leaflet for each service where all relative instructions are not only put in easy-to-follow form, but are also accompanied by maps showing routes through or round towns, picking-up points, garages for use in emergency, and so on. Drivers will often have to be found from several depots, as well as be supplied (with vehicles) by other operators and so the better the briefing the less likelihood there is of trouble of any kind. Relief vehicles can be staffed then by anyone, but the actual service vehicle should always be handled by those wholly familiar with the route and its operating practices. That coach must adhere to advertised intermediate timings.

Past experience offers a guide to what the total demand may be on any one day, so that when desired a number of duplicates can be arranged at 2 or 3 days' notice. But it may still be economically sound to have a 'floater' or two available, so that last-minute 'overflow' traffic on any route can be carried. When hiring is practised the operator concerned may make a limited number of definite bookings of coaches some weeks ahead; the others may be arranged only a couple of days before the date of movement. There is not necessarily any difficulty in obtaining vehicles in this way as the commitments on contract work is often less at weekends.

In contrast to bus control work which is usually at maximum pressure during the Monday to Friday peaks and particularly during inclement weather, the coach controller has his seasonal fluctuations with the masses presenting themselves for travel—hence unscheduled vehicles and staff need to be found—at weekends in the summer.

Inspectors' duties

Bus operation is centred around the schedules as described in Chapter 8. Examples of bus runnings identified by running numbers were appended as also was a specimen duty schedule. The crew will be in possession of a copy of the actual duty being worked and a copy of the bus running will remain on the vehicle for the entire day, being collected from the garage office by the first driver and handed in by the last driver. The scheduled working of the bus is, therefore, known by the crew and any inspector who may care to board and inspect its running plate. Inspectors will be in possession of timetables but if a road inspector is stationed at a roadside control point which is passed by a large number of buses, perhaps on different services, a 'straightdown' is desirable. This is, in effect, a list of departures in chronological order showing route number, running number and destination. Many inspectors compile this information for themselves from the main schedule but it is a laborious task, and with the advent of computers it is possible to produce this information easily by this means. What is also of material assistance to road inspectors is the display of the running number outside the vehicle. In this way each bus can be readily identified without the need to board but surprisingly few undertakings adopt this practice.

Then there is the unscheduled bus and coach work, always of course within the limits of available resources. This is work that is arranged locally, usually on inspector's instructions, according to demand, probably in the form of duplication and covered by either spare staff, overtime or rest-day working. Once on the road, however, these vehicles are subject to the same control as are the regular scheduled services. In fact they must have more attention as to avoid waste they need to be curtailed or withdrawn as soon as they are no longer required.

The uniformed road inspector is a general supervisor with many different responsibilities. He is the eyes and the ears of the undertaking and he performs a key public relations role. His observations are important and it is through his reports that management might first hear of changing demands, surplus accommodation, inadequacies and any new circumstances that might affect future traffic patterns. There may be different grades of inspector undertaking different types of work, the two basic groups being those who are basically static at a roadside control point and the roving inspector on ticket checking duties and dealing with anything else that presents itself at the time. Duties might be arranged to do part and part, perhaps a little bit of control work at the busier times, but what is important is that ticket checking contains an element of surprise. For this reason there should be no pre-determined schedule of buses to be checked. It should be left to the inspector's discretion and his daily checking sheet will contain a record of the work done. It is customary for checking sheets to show in respect of all vehicles checked the route, running and vehicle numbers, place and time boarded and alighted, number of passengers on the bus and any irregularities found for subsequent processing by a chief inspector or some other appropriately senior official through the disciplinary procedure. If the offence is a serious one, the driver or conductor concerned might wish to be accompanied at a hearing by a union official, and it is likely that the inspector would need to be available to give evidence if required. Under these circumstances, a decision, which might range from a warning to suspension or discharge, is likely to be subject to the right of appeal to more senior management. The arrangements might be that the official conducting the first interview has limited powers and if he considers that the gravity of the charge warrants more than he is empowered to award, he would himself refer the matter to higher authority.

Road inspectors are often equipped with a portable two-way radio in a similar way to police constables. This is a valuable aid for road control purposes and some

Figure 10.2 For many years London Buses and its predecessors have displayed the running numbers on both sides of the vehicles. This practice is very helpful to supervisors on the road who can immediately identify any particular bus without needing to board and inspect the driver's running plate. It is surprising that more operators have not adopted this practice. In the example shown the letter represents the garage concerned (N is the code for Norwood) and the number is the scheduled running on which the bus is working on that particular day. For control purposes, therefore, no reference need be made to the permanent vehicle number which is painted on the bus and appears to the right of the picture.

undertakings adopt this practice as a cheaper alternative to equipping all of the vehicles. Although in urban areas most inspectors are on foot, it is impossible to cover a wide rural area in this way, particularly if the services are infrequent. For coverage of territory of this type there is advantage in making inspectors more mobile by the allocation of a small van or car. Unless, however, they travel in pairs, an inspector must find his own way back to his vehicle which he left to board and check a bus. The system of employing a squad or travelling inspectors to check buses over a wide area is not unknown. It has the added advantage that these inspectors are more likely to be strangers to bus crews. Some local officials are inclined to mix with platform staff on rather familiar terms and this arrangement, rather like the village policeman, does not create the best atmosphere in which to enforce discipline.

One other grade of supervisor employed by some undertakings to considerable advantage is the plain clothes inspector. The system is only practicable in a large organization as, if they are to be effective, they must remain completely unknown to the staff. They can be afforded no privileges. They must take their turn in the queue to board and they must pay their fare. But this, of course, is an essential part of the exercise as they are then in a good position to check the re-issue of dead tickets, tickets issued under value and all other operating irregularities. Plain clothes inspectors cannot of course undertake road control work.

Accident procedure

An accident to a bus in service generally takes the form of a collision with another vehicle or pedestrian or a fall within the bus itself. It does not necessarily involve serious personal injury or, indeed, any injury at all but there is usually a delay factor and often a subsequent claim for damages. It is important, therefore, that management is in possession of the full facts and that is why every incident has to be reported in considerable detail. It is, of course, the bus crew that is immediately on the spot and the first steps following an accident must be taken by them. An official may be present by coincidence although if the vehicle is fitted with radio one can be quickly summoned, as can the emergency services. Should a lengthy delay be expected, the onus is on the driver or conductor to transfer passengers to another bus, assuming that one is available and to contact the bus controller for further instructions.

In view of the subsequent importance of the availability of complete and accurate information, staff should not only be properly versed in the procedure to be followed but also provided with a printed form, the completion of which will ensure that no detail has been omitted. This form will contain provision for at least a description of what happened with a diagram if appropriate, particulars of injuries and/or damage to property, insurance details of other vehicles, names and addresses of people concerned and witnesses as well as date, time, place, etc. Whilst the police and the fire and ambulance services will look after their own particular responsibilities, it is incumbent upon the operator not only to restore normal service as quickly as possible but also, if necessary, to remove any of its vehicles if they are disabled. Many of the larger undertakings have their own vehicle recovery service, but it is legal for the vehicle concerned to be towed away by another PSV.

Staff coverage

This is about the allocation of drivers and conductors to buses. It is a task that has to be done at the local operating garages and may be undertaken by depot inspectors or by a special duties clerk. Once again it is necessary to refer back to Chapter 8 which dealt with schedule compilation and which produced a specimen duty schedule and duty roster. If the system suggested is followed then the duties clerk at the garage will have played no part in the preparation of the schedules. He will have received the duties and the roster as a finished job and all he has to do is to fit names to it. So far so good and if he has got sufficient names to set against the roster and having so allocated the staff they do not go sick or absent or on holiday, then the job is done. But that is not always the case.

The specimen roster contained in Chapter 8 had 27 lines. Therefore, at least 27 drivers (or drivers plus conductors) are required. It is a question of fitting names to the lines and then to drop them down one line each week in order that they rotate through all of the early and late shifts with their different rest days. It was noted at the time that this is something with which the staff show a particular interest. They expect to be consulted when the schedules are prepared and they look for similar treatment with day-to-day allocation at garage level. This means, however, that there are many different systems in operation. An interesting point is that in some countries, the USA being one and Israel another, it is common practice for staff not to rotate through the schedule but to select in order of seniority their line on the roster and keep to it for the life of the schedule. This means that they work precisely the same journeys each week, be they early or late, and take the same rest days. Operationally, there is merit in this as the driver becomes more personal. To the staff, the more senior they are, the wider is their choice. They might, for example, prefer a line with fairly light duties. On the other hand, they might like long spreadovers which have low work content but high penalty payments. The more common British practice, however, is for staff to drop down one line each week. In cases where conductors are still employed and management does not wish pairs of staff to remain together as a permanent crew, one arrangement is for drivers to drop down one line and conductors move up one line each week. It is all a matter of local arrangements. If this type of system is adopted, a duty list must be prepared week by week which fits names to lines on the roster and changes accordingly. It might, however, involve more than 27 drivers (to quote the example). Even if there is no lateness and absence without leave, there is always holidays and sickness to be covered, which necessitates spare staff. It might be reasonable, therefore, to add, say another three drivers to make 30 in all, the bottom three lines being to instructions, that is, to work as allocated locally by the garage duty clerk.

The real problem with staff coverage arises when not only is there insufficient staff to carry spares but insufficient to cover even the basic scheduled requirements, or, in other words, there are blanks on the duty list. This means that scheduled duties have to be covered by overtime and rest-day working as well as taking care of any unscheduled requirements. It is here, of course, that the drivers' hours regulations really aggravate the issue and their sheer complexity does nothing to assist the duties clerk in his arduous task of covering all of the bits and pieces of duties that remain unstaffed. If they cannot be covered, then buses must come out of service. Some journeys are missed more easily than are others. One bus might have a driver but no conductor, another has a conductor but no driver. Rapid adjustments have to be made, assuming always that the staff are willing and prepared to co-operate. This is the responsibility of the official in charge of output who will also issue ticket machines, running plates and any other necessary items of equipment. At the end of the day a complete record must be made of what everybody has worked if the right money is subsequently to appear in their respective pay packets.

Under the system described, if the payrolls officer had a copy of the duty roster and weekly duty list, he would know what every man was entitled to be paid assuming that he worked his schedule job. It might be convenient, therefore, and this practice is adopted by some undertakings, for the garage officials to advise the payrolls department only of any variations to rostered duties and positive advice would have to be given only in respect of spare staff who are not rostered for any specific work. The alternative is for garage officials to supply information in respect of the entire workforce for pay purposes. In a small undertaking they might even prepare the payroll themselves but the work is more suitable for a specialized department. However, the garage staff might be required to make up the packets and pay out.

One further point on staff coverage is the economics of maintaining a full complement of staff even if it is possible to do so. The cost of a driver (or conductor) is rather more than his weekly pay as the following items must be borne in respect of each employee to the extent applicable:

1. Employer's contribution to national insurance.
2. Employer's contribution to superannuation.
3. Allowance for paid holidays.
4. Allowance for paid sickness.
5. Allowance for any staff amenities.
6. Uniform.
7. Cost of staff administration.

It is a question of balancing this cost against the premium payments for a limited amount of overtime and rest day working to cover vacancies. It could be that a small shortage could be financially beneficial and could also be preferred by the staff as it gives them the chance of extra work and hence extra pay which would not otherwise be available. A policy, however, which relies to a small extent on voluntary overtime does make the system more vulnerable in the event of industrial action.

Receipt and safe custody of cash

Security

Remember from Chapter 9 that the use of buses involves payment, usually at the time of travel. Many hundreds of thousands of separate financial transactions, therefore, take place daily. Each one involves the collection of a small amount of cash for which a receipt (in the form of a ticket) is normally given. Straight away, therefore, there is a big security question. In this context, however, security is not interpreted as drivers and conductors receiving and accounting for the proper fares. That aspect was dealt with in Chapter 9 and in the earlier part of this chapter which covered the duties of inspectors. At this stage it is assumed that the correct fares have been paid, proper tickets have been issued and the money is in the possession of the platform staff. Adequate facilities must, therefore, be available for one-man drivers and conductors to dispose of that cash with safeguards for both the undertaking and themselves. Having got thus far, those responsible for collecting the money on behalf of management must also have facilities and safeguards and bulk cash must in turn be disposed of into the banking system. That is what security is all about.

Paying-in

Cash offices need to be placed at strategic points where it is convenient for platform staff to finish duty. These paying-in points are often but not necessarily a part of the garage traffic office. In order to avoid the need for staff to carry unnecessarily large amounts of money around with them it is reasonable to allow them to pay in money part way through their duty if they happen to be in the vicinity of a paying-in point as well as at the end. In any case, there must be a pay-in at the end of the duty and it follows that the process could take place at almost any time of the day or night. What is quite clear is that much of the paying-in will take place outside normal office hours, which is traditionally a middle shift. The question arises, therefore, whether depot inspectors, garage cash clerks or whatever they might be designated be on duty throughout the traffic day or should their numbers be fewer and confined to normal office hours; or should, indeed, they accept cash direct from drivers and conductors at all? If the latter alternatives are adopted it is certainly cheaper in terms of salaries of garage officials but some method is necessary for staff to pay in without an official in attendance. This can be overcome by putting the cash and completed waybill into a special bag and depositing it into a drop safe or night safe as it is sometimes called. The contents of these bags are then counted the following day. Whilst, however, this overcomes the shift problems of the cash clerks, the disadvantage of this system is that the driver or conductor is not present when the money is checked and he is not therefore available for challenge should there be a shortage. This can lead to disputes which can only partially be resolved by the bags being opened and the contents counted in the presence of a second official as a witness or, what might be preferable to staff, one of their own representatives. The system is not ideal and machine manufacturers have developed systems which enable staff to deposit their money and have it counted with the amount being indicated to them. If they are satisfied they can then release it for deposit in a secure place and at the same time receive an appropriate receipt. Suitable records are also made for the garage staff to check subsequently the amount paid in by each person against the respective waybills.

Fareboxes

All that has been said so far relates to cash collected in exchange for the issue of serially numbered tickets for which there is a record. There is a cross-check and each stage is subject to audit. This is not the case, however, with the farebox type of fare collection system as was described in Chapter 9. Here it will be recalled money is deposited by passengers into a box which can only be released (by the driver) into a locked vault. Where flat fares or zone fares are applied as in the

United States, no ticket is necessary. For graduated fares, a ticket must be issued if there is to be any check on overriding and the Autofare system of Almex Control Systems Limited, for example, does combine the issue of a ticket with a farebox. However, there is no adequate direct cross-check as such and in any case the cash contents at the end of the day will have been received by several different drivers. In short, buses arrive at the garage on run-in with full boxes but with no record (or certainly no adequate record for which staff could be held to account) of how much has been put in. This presents no problem to the driver. The most he will do is take the locked vault to the cash office. He might not even do that, but the fact remains that by some means the locked vaults must be conveyed from the bus to the cash counting centre. Once inside they will be opened and the contents counted, probably by emptying into the receptable of a coin-counting and sorting machine. The weakness lies in the fact that in the absence of records, the staff of the cash office are not subject to check and temptation is put in their way.

Some of the larger undertakings in the United States go to great lengths to reduce this risk and consequent theft and thereby protect their interests. Examples are a bank of machines at a centralized counting house attended by several cash counting officials who are required to change from their outdoor clothes on the premises into special pocketless overalls and pass through a metal detector with the window of the chief cashier's office (fitted with one-way glass) overlooking the counting area and all under the watchful eye of armed guards. Still, of course, there is no positive check against theft, only every possible discouragement. Perhaps the most ambitious method adopted in the United States is the emptying of farebox vaults by vacuum whilst *in situ* on the bus. With this system a large pipe links the base of the farebox with the receiving end of a coin counting and sorting machine and the contents are counted with the minimum of human contact. Nevertheless, there is still a point where unscrupulous hands might find their way into the hopper of the counting machine. The ideal, of course, is for this to be impossible until the coins have passed through the apparatus and are registered, after which it does not matter if they are accessible as there is a cross-check and the cash counting staff can be held responsible for the money recorded.

To this extent, therefore, there is a degree of weakness in the system which brings in locked boxes of money without any record of what the contents should be. On the other hand, this method of fare collection has been developed largely for security reasons, but on the road and not in the garage. In many parts of the United States and particularly in certain neighbourhoods of the larger towns on the eastern side, it is quite unsafe for staff (or passengers) to carry money. They cannot even have provision for a float for the purpose of giving change as drivers have been killed through armed robbery. The solution is a locked vault which is accessible (by orthodox means) only by authorized garage staff. The security aspect of the farebox method of fare collection is, therefore, very real. It also has considerable advantages in service in terms of speed and this is something which was considered in Chapter 9. If the farebox method is to be introduced, and there is much to commend it, particularly as it can be linked to a system of ticket issue, it is likely to be advantageous to count all of the cash in a centralized counting house. An exception would be if the vacuum method of emptying was used as this is done in the garage. Otherwise, it might be economic to convey the vaults in vans between the garages and a single counting house. Whilst transport involves cost, there then needs to be only one set of sophisticated equipment and security arrangements.

Coin counting

Regardless of the method of fare collection, large quantities of coins have to be counted in the cash office. Just as ticket issue was at one time done manually by the conductor, so the cash clerk physically counted the coins, aided only by scales which acted as a cross-check on the filled bags of silver.

Coin counting machines are now available for this purpose, an excellent example of which is the 'Condor' produced by International Coin Counters (ICC Machines Limited) (*Figure 10.3*). This machine can accept, sort and bag as required mixed coinage (and/or tokens) of up to seven different denominations at a speed of upwards of 600 coins per minute. Before acceptance and recording, its electronic 'Triple Checking' system ensures validation by monitoring diameter, thickness and metallic presence and any spurious material is ejected. This is a significant feature as not only is it important for obvious reasons that foreign matter does not enter the bags of cash to be banked, neither must it jam the machine. The ejection facility which is built in to this latest design could therefore be adapted to overcome to a large extent the problem referred to of counting unrecorded cash from fareboxes.

This type of coin counter can if required be linked with the aid of a computer to a complete currency control system to provide a fast and efficient means of recording and storing details of cash (including bank notes and tokens which can be keyed in) allowing the user to print, display and transfer to other devices, holding details of the data in a range of formats as appropriate. Cash clerks merely use the keyboard to enter necessary details such as date and the driver's number and duty number. The machine then verifies and counts and with notes, tokens or whatever as advised, transfers the information to the computer for an analysis of the takings. If this system is utilized and applied alongside an electronic ticket issuing system as was described in Chapter 9 then figures can be reconciled, any driver's debits and credits ascertained and complete statistical information to the extent required becomes available.

Retention and disposal of cash

Once an undertaking has accepted the cash from its platform staff it must be safely stored until such time as it can be banked, either on the following day or as soon as possible thereafter. This calls for the provision of an adequate safe or strong-room in garage offices or wherever the money is paid in and proper defined procedures which determine responsibilities of the staff concerned. Disposal of cash to the bank is often entrusted to an outside contractor who specializes in this type of work. It could, of course, be undertaken internally, possibly by the use of a spare bus and driver subject to the availability of suitable escorts. What tends to be to some extent unique is that money collected for bus rides usually contains a high percentage of coins. With the farebox system this is even more so as passengers will be tendering the exact fare. Even quite a small undertaking can produce several tons of coinage each day and this is not necessarily popular with banks. Suitable arrangements must, therefore, be negotiated and the question of bank charges will arise. The alternative method of selling prepaid tickets and tokens does ease the banking problem imposed by bulk coinage.

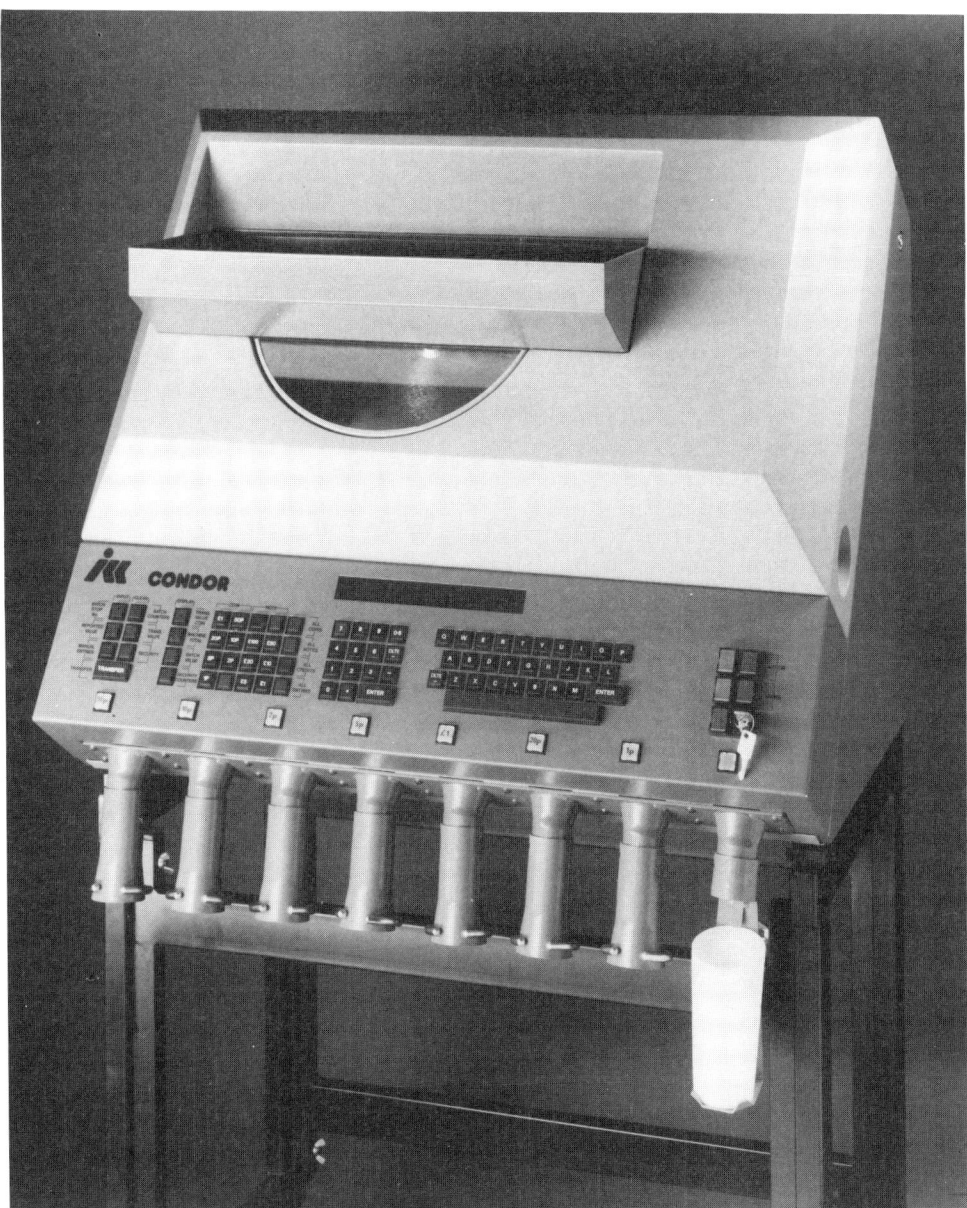

Figure 10.3 The Condor machine of International Coin Counters which can handle up to seven different coin denominations and/or tokens. The seven outlets can be seen to which bags are attached, the supply automatically stopping when a bag has the correct amount and needs to be changed. The outlet on the extreme right is where rejected material is deposited. Money is tipped into the hopper above. It sorts, counts, batches and registers and, depending on the model, can include a printer with full receipt and second print-out capabilities, a dot matrix printer, an advanced program which itemizes and totals non-cash items such as notes and cheques with or without a printer giving fully itemized print-outs. (Reproduced by kind permission of ICC Machines Ltd.)

Prepaid tickets and tokens

The issue of prepaid tickets (which includes season and 'anywhere' type tickets) is primarily a commercial consideration and as such has been mentioned in Chapter 7. But the subject does also impinge on security. If a passenger is in possession of a prepaid ticket, be it valid for one ride or is a multi-journey type, the driver may cancel part of it, the passenger could insert it in a machine to do the same thing or, if it is an unrestricted pass, the driver would merely inspect it. The important point in this context is that no money changes hands and the amount of cash for which the driver or conductor is responsible is reduced accordingly. If tokens are used, then the platform staff receive them in lieu of the national currency but their intrinsic value is not quite the same. They are paid in in the same way as other coins, they can be used in fareboxes and (assuming that they are made of metal) be sorted and counted through the normal machines. They do not, however, have to be banked but merely returned to the selling points for reissue. To this extent, therefore, the use of prepaid tickets or tokens considerably lessens the security risks. In reducing one problem, however, it creates another. Sales points become necessary, the economics of which have been considered in Chapter 7. But they must be conveniently sited for easy purchase and if a sales counter is not practicable an alternative is to install a vending machine. But herein lies a security risk as the machine has to be replenished and emptied of cash in a public place. This is not ideal. The machine is also liable to be a target for vandalism and at the extreme the contents ransacked. This naturally leads into another aspect of security; protection from vandalism.

Vandalism

So commonplace has the habit of wilful and wanton destruction of other people's property become that the Vandals, who in the fourth and fifth centuries ravaged the area around the western Mediterranean, have become immortalized with their name now accepted by general consent as a household term used to describe the malicious practices undertaken by some members of the community today. Public property in public places is a common target for their activities. Public transport is no exception and the majority suffers at the hands of a minority. What has been rampant in the United States for a number of years has now spread eastwards across the Atlantic and is making its mark on the British public transport system. Buses and the crews who man them are targets for attack, particularly in the late evening. Payment of fares is refused, behaviour is obscene, vehicles are damaged, often delayed and sometimes even destroyed. Staff are injured and instances of industrial action in the form of refusal to operate last journeys are growing. It is not the job of bus managements to cure this social malaise, they can only live with it; but in so doing it does to some extent influence the way in which they run their services and probably it will do more so as time passes. The subject is for further discussion in Chapter 12. As it is, vehicles, and particularly the seats, have to be designed with this in mind; publicity often cannot be maintained at bus stops; and costly aids to deter and detect are being introduced, particularly radio but also television cameras with recording video tape. Those in charge of public transport have always had to plan for the travel requirements of their passengers; they now also have to plan how to minimize the effects of wilful destruction inflicted by a few of those passengers. It is now a part of the operating scene.

Lost property

The necessity to handle lost property is one of the minor irritants of all passenger transport undertakings. Whilst operators would wish to give every consideration to their customers, the careless act of leaving belongings on a bus does have a strong nuisance value and not only to the person who suffers the loss. Lost property has to be taken into custody by drivers, cleaners or whoever might have the job of searching the vehicles. It has to be conveyed to a supervisor, duly registered and forwarded to a lost property centre. If it is not claimed it has to be disposed of. Enquiries have to be dealt with. All of this involves administration, and this means expense. It puts additional work on to staff who must adhere to a strict procedure. Valuable items involve greater responsibility and temptation. If staff fail to observe the lost property regulations there is trouble and although there can be no excuse, it does seem a little unfortunate when a breach of this kind which involves disciplinary action would never have happened in the first place but for somebody else's negligence. As far as buses and coaches (public service vehicles) in Great Britain are concerned, the procedure to be followed is covered by law.

11 Finance

Introduction

As is the case with mechanical engineering, finance and accounting is an essential part of the job of running buses. But it is a profession in its own right; and—important as it is to the science of transport—finance is a separate and, in this sense, ancillary discipline. For this reason there is no pretence here to try to teach this very specialized subject. The purpose of this chapter is to examine the financial issues rather than the accounting methods. It is a subject which has assumed greater significance over recent years with some of the revenue now coming in as a form of subsidy or in compensation for the provision of some special facility rather than direct from the passenger. There is a need to see how revenue is obtained (being partly from fares but also partly from public funds) and the machinery which has been established to deal with this matter. Governments must, of course, be involved in such issues. In so far as financial support from public funds is concerned, in what follows the arrangements as adopted in Great Britain are quoted as an example and as in previous chapters, references to statutory controls relate to British law. To some extent the system of financial support as described is unique to the United Kingdom.

Revenue

Although very pertinent to this chapter, revenue is also considered in various other places in this book as the subject impinges on several facets of operation. Suffice to say here that whatever services are provided costs will be incurred and those costs must be recovered, either from fares or from some other source. Revenue obtained through fares, either on or off the vehicles, must be collected and the various methods of doing this were considered in Chapter 9. Having received the money, proper arrangements must be made for its security and banking, and this was covered in Chapter 10. To maximize revenue, facilities must be as attractive as possible and this was a matter for Chapter 7. Any shortfall must be made up in the form of a subsidy, something again considered in Chapter 7.

If revenue is insufficient to cover direct working expenses—that is, not enough to pay the drivers' wages and buy fuel—then the undertaking would cease trading very quickly. If these costs could be met but there was insufficient to cover overheads then again business could not continue and it would eventually go into liquidation. If all costs including interest on loans could be covered but there was nothing left to remunerate shareholders then those concerned would still be encouraged to dispose of their assets and reinvest in a more lucrative industry. This is how private enterprise must work and there is a clear incentive to combine economy with service and give the maximum in return for the least if patronage is to be encouraged and a living is to be made. The principle is not altered by public ownership. For example, the Scottish Transport Group (*vide* Section 41 of the Transport Act, 1968) and London Regional Transport (*vide* Section 15 of the London Regional Transport Act, 1984) are required to pay their way. This means that revenue from the farebox together with any revenue support which might be forthcoming must cover costs.

To follow on from what was said in Chapter 7, local transport, even if not viable, can be a social necessity. If this is the case then a political decision to give revenue support from public funds is likely, and in the UK county councils have power to do this.

Subsidies

The need for subsidies

It has been seen that the financial difficulties of the bus have come largely because traffic has been eroded by the private car. It was suggested in Chapter 1 that in Great Britain it was around the late 1950s when the industry began to gasp for

Figure 11.1 In some of the less affluent countries, lack of cash and foreign exchange means a shortage of vehicles and equipment. Vehicles therefore become overloaded and poorly maintained as is this bus of the Calcutta State Transport Corporation seen emerging from Howrah Bridge in Calcutta, India.

breath and that was at a stage when the level of private car ownership was around 80 vehicles for every 1000 people. In 1985 that figure had grown to 291 cars for every 1000 people (*see Table 1.1*) and in some areas, particularly North America, it is much more than that. In the USA the figure quoted by *Transport Statistics* (HMSO) is 540, West Germany 412 and even the lowest figure for western Europe (Greece) is 116. However, in the developing countries of Africa and Asia levels are very substantially below that and certainly way under the '80 threshold'. In many cases they are in single figures. On this reasoning, therefore (subject to any other special circumstances) in these areas the stage has not yet been reached where it is impossible to run urban bus services as a commercial enterprise. The main financial problem here is likely to be not insufficient demand but a lack of foreign exchange to buy vehicles (or perhaps chassis for locally built bodies). If this is the case then the only financial help that might be justified is in the form of capital grants for this purpose. Otherwise, insolvency is more likely to be through political interference or a lack of prudent management rather than a lack of passengers.

British legislation

Grants

The final section of Chapter 1 drew attention to the need to support public transport financially and noted that the 1968 Transport Act brought with it, among other things, provision for subsidies under certain circumstances for local services. Much of what was contained in the 1968 Act has now been changed by the Transport Act, 1985. However, certain remnants remain which are as follows:

Section 13—As amended by Schedule 3 of the 1985 Act, enables passenger transport authorities to make grants to passenger transport executives in passenger transport areas.

Section 33—Which amended Section 92 of the Finance Act, 1965 and which itself has been amended by Section 110 of the 1985 Act, provides for grants to cover the duty charged on fuel used by buses on local services other than excursions and tours.

Section 34—As amended by Schedule 7 of the 1985 Act, enables the Council of the Isles of Scilly to make grants or loans towards the cost of rural bus services. (Very minor.)

Section 56—As amended by Schedule 7 of the 1985 Act provides for infrastructure grants at the discretion of the Secretary of State for the provision, improvement or development of facilities for public passenger transport. But note that the 1985 Act also requires the authorities responsible for expenditure on public transport— passenger transport authorities and executives, non-metropolitan county and district councils in England and Wales and regional and islands councils in Scotland—not to do anything that might inhibit competition. In this case this is effected by Section 57 which inserts a Section 9A to the 1968 Act (for PTAs and PTEs) and by Section 63 (for local authorities). Any such grant applications would, therefore, have to take this aspect into account.

The 1985 Act gives special albeit limited help for rural bus services. Section 108 makes provision for grants at the discretion of the Secretary of State for rural services in Wales and Scotland and he may also under certain circumstances make transitional grants for rural services anywhere outside London *vide* Section 109 over a defined period (4 years).

Section 106 of the 1985 Act permits the responsible authorities (as just described) to make grants towards the provision of special facilities for the disabled and Section 107 enables London Regional Transport to make grants to voluntary organizations in providing transport for the disabled.

Without wishing to become too involved in the peculiarities of one area in one country, for the sake of completeness in this review of British law as it relates to bus finances, it must be mentioned that as was the case with quantity licensing, financial arrangements are different for local bus services operating in the Greater London area. Other than for grants in respect of transport for the disabled as has just been mentioned, it is the London Regional Transport Act, 1984 which gives statutory sanction in this instance. Section 12 of this Act empowers the Secretary of State (who in turn may make levies on local rating authorities) to make grants to London Regional Transport in aid of capital investment or operating costs in respect of the services of its own subsidiaries or others with whom it has a working agreement. It is also the Secretary of State who may determine financial objectives and policies to be followed by LRT. As far as covering unprofitable routes is concerned, LRT is in a similar position to that of the PTEs and county councils outside Greater London to the extent that Section 6 of the 1984 Act requires it to invite tenders. It is the system of tendering which is now to be described.

Tendering

The main source of financial support for buses in Great Britain is based on the principle of tendering for specific routes, being those that are deemed to be socially desirable but which are not provided voluntarily by operators on a commercial basis.

Remember from Chapter 5 that quantity control of services has been abolished. The subsidization of networks has similarly gone and there is also a swing towards private ownership with services provided on a commercial basis and routes determined by the forces of free enterprise. But even the smaller operators with their lower overheads will not cover all of the services that were hitherto provided within subsidized networks. Accordingly Section 89 of the 1985 Act provides for the responsible authorities as stated in the previous sub-section to determine which routes should be so covered and then to invite tenders for the provision of the required facilities. Acceptance by the authority concerned must be based on the tender that offers the most effective and economic application of the funds at its disposal for the payment of service subsidies. As with the provision of facilities, so also with tendering, operators must work in a competitive environment, and here it is Section 92 that prevents the authorities from doing anything that might inhibit competition between persons wishing to provide bus services. This Section also makes provision for limiting by regulation the amount that may be paid out in service subsidies. Note also that the Rates Act, 1984 enables the Secretary of State to limit the rates made and precepts issued by local authorities.

Contracts may be let on a fixed price or minimum subsidy basis with the operator keeping the farebox revenue and taking the risk or on a revenue guaranteed basis.

Concessionary fares

Finally for mention in this examination of ways in which British operators can obtain money from sources other than from passengers are the arrangements in respect of travel concessions.

Section 93 *et seq.* of the 1985 Act enables the responsible authorities as already defined to introduce travel concessions on local bus services for eligible persons—senior citizens, those of 16 years of age or under (18 or under if in full-time education), the blind, those whose disability makes it difficult for them to walk and others who may be defined. Arrangements are made for operators to be compensated for loss of revenue in such a way that they should not be any better off or any worse off as a result of these concessions. Operators will therefore need to ensure that they do not suffer loss through such schemes. They will look for a make-up of revenue that they have lost (i.e., the difference between what they would have had if normal fares had been charged and what they actually received) plus additional costs incurred as a result of any extra traffic generated. There is, however, always the point that if such extra traffic could be contained within the existing facilities and that seats are therefore filled which would otherwise have remained empty there would be a net benefit. This is something that the authority might not overlook. In accordance with Section 94, the administrative arrangements are determined by regulations. Although the appropriate Statutory Instrument—*No. 77 Travel Concessions Schemes Regulations, 1986*—protects operators from being forced to divulge confidential information relating to such things as costs, profits and individual route results, the writer notes with some concern that the authorities have a right to survey on buses passengers travelling at concessionary fares (which means with people other than those who are employees of the bus company). Certainly the authorities will need information and they could require operators to use suitable electronic equipment for this purpose. Again costs must be watched and it is appropriate here to remind readers of Section 56 of the 1968 Act (infrastructure grants) which has already been mentioned.

Whilst operators have a right to participate in such schemes there is also provision for them to be required to do so on a compulsory basis in order that the authorities can maintain proper coverage within their respective areas. Concessions may also be provided on services other than local bus services—e.g. non-local bus services, taxis, social cars and trams—but in these cases operators have no participation rights and compulsory participation notices cannot be served.

In Greater London it is Section 50 *et seq.* of the London Regional Transport Act, 1984 which contains the statutory authority and arrangements for travel concessions in that area.

Statutory plans

In Great Britain the passenger transport executives and London Regional Transport are required to prepare plans setting out the policies that they intend to follow. Although these plans relate to various matters, finance is an important element and for this reason they are mentioned in this chapter.

Section 3 of the Transport Act, 1983 requires passenger transport executives to prepare annually and submit to the appropriate passenger transport authorities plans containing their proposals for the ensuing 3 years with respect to the general level of services to be provided and fares to be charged. The proposals are required to be such as to enable their financial duty as contained in Section 2 of the 1983 Act, i.e. to ensure that revenues are adequate to cover charges properly chargeable to revenue account, to be met. Also to be recognized is the duty imposed on the executives *vide* Section 9A(3) of the Transport Act, 1968, i.e. to secure the provision of such services as they consider appropriate for meeting the public transport requirements of the areas in accordance with policies formulated by the authorities. Remember that it is the duty of the authorities (*vide* Section 9A(1) of the 1968 Act) to formulate policies regarding the services which they consider it appropriate for the executives to secure—those that are necessary to cater for any requirements that would not otherwise be met. The plans are prepared on the assumption that the authorities will make revenue grants as appropriate and will include details of costs, levels of demand and benefits. In preparing these plans, executives are required to take into account any advice given by the Secretary of State.

Upon receipt of such plans the authorities will consider and either approve the proposals or request modifications and they also will take advice from the Secretary of State, particularly regarding the maximum amount of revenue grants. In accordance with Section 5 of the 1983 Act, this is the only way in which revenue grants may be made by authorities to executives.

As far as London Regional Transport is concerned, it is Section 7 of the London Regional Transport Act, 1984 which calls for three-yearly statements setting out, *inter alia*, the policies that it is intended to follow with a view to the discharge of its duty imposed by Section 2(1) of the 1984 Act, i.e. to secure the provision of public passenger transport services for Greater London. The financial prospects of LRT are dealt with in this plan after having had regard to any financial objectives as determined by the Secretary of State in accordance with Section 16 of the 1984 Act.

Other methods of financial support

The previous section has described albeit briefly British legislation in so far as it relates to the financial aspects of bus operation. It will have been seen that there are now no network subsidies as such but in the spirit of de-regulation and free enterprise machinery is available to support at public expense socially necessary services which cannot be provided commercially. But even this is done through a process of competitive tendering. Elsewhere in the world there are many examples of network subsidies but the sources of the necessary funds vary. The basics of this particular topic were covered in Chapter 7 where the political influence that comes with subsidies was discussed at some length.

To follow on from what was said in Chapter 7, in principle the sources of public assistance for bus services may come from central or local governments or both or at their instigation and may take various forms such as:

1. Grants (capital and revenue support).
2. Loans with favourable repayment rates.
3. Tax relief or exemption.
4. Funds raised from specific local taxes. For example:
   (a) Payroll tax on employers
   (b) Sale of petrol or any non-essential commodity such as cigarettes, chewing gum, etc.
5. Revenue from local road or bridge tolls, etc.

The method of determining the extent of such assistance and the repercussions on services and fares were considered in Chapter 7. In this context, however, operators should be aware that there are three aspects of their businesses which are liable to become subject to political deliberation. Consider the following diagram:

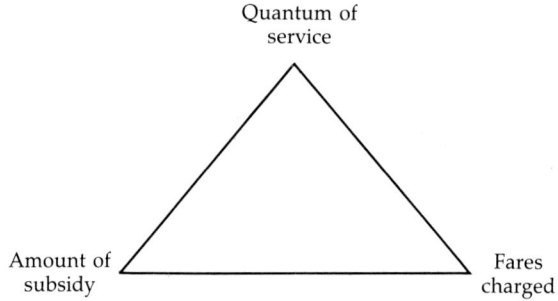

All of the three factors as illustrated are matters for political consideration. Elected representatives will be held to account by their constituents on all of them. Not only will there be interest in the total amount of public money that is being spent on buses but also what is being achieved in return in the form of the service provided in terms of routes and frequencies and the fares that are charged. Accordingly, politicians will doubtless like to determine all three issues which, if not done with exceptional consideration, could put operators in impossible situations. In reality only two of these features can be fixed by an outside third party. Subject to maximum efficiency on the part of the operator, the quantum of service provided determines the cost of operation and the fare levels determine the revenue. If, therefore, the costs and the revenue are fixed by an independent authority then the deficit, being the excess of costs over revenue, will automatically be settled and that is the amount of subsidy which will be required. Similarly, if costs and subsidy are fixed then fares must find their own level and if subsidy and fares are set (which together determines the total income) then total costs and hence the quantum of service becomes fixed. It is when all three are determined by some arbitrary method by politicians with reasons other than bus operating technicalities foremost in their minds that financial disaster must come with, at the end of the day, bus companies needing to be bailed out with money which has not been properly budgeted for in the national or municipal treasury.

It is important that operators are aware of these circumstances and do not run their businesses in a way that their total costs can be legitimately challenged. Subject to this, there can be no proper justification for political control of all three of the factors described. It is nevertheless acknowledged that managements of undertakings which are in public ownership, closely related to a branch of government and whose ultimate masters are politicians are liable to experience particular difficulties when dealing with these financial issues.

Route costing

So far this chapter has centred mainly on the statutory background for financing the deficits incurred by buses in Great Britain. It has done little more than list rules as decreed by parliament and it relates to British law. What is now to follow has no reference to legal niceties but instead covers a certain product of the finance function which is a most useful tool for those responsible for route and timetable planning. It is the profit or loss statement of each individual route.

The purpose of a costing system

There are limitations to what the financial accounting system of a business can provide to enable a firm to be run effectively. Financial accounting falls short on two counts; it gives a historical picture and deals only with the costs of the business in total. This is insufficient for forward planning. It is, of course, true that for fare fixing purposes, total revenue must exceed total costs if the business is to survive but even then, as has just been seen, economic circumstances are such that some of the revenue might have to come in the form of a subsidy. Route costing is not concerned with the preparation of data necessary for price fixing. Total costs and average costs per mile are obtainable through normal financial accounting and fares can be set on this basis. Unless, however, a bus or coach undertaking operates only one route, management will need to know the financial viability of each individual service just as a manufacturer needs to know the profitability of each separate product. If it does not, then any changing fortunes of a particular service cannot be identified and the consequent lack of or application of the wrong remedial action would result in an inevitable deterioration of the financial situation.

Classification of costs

The subject of route costing has been examined by the Chartered Institute of Public Finance and Accountancy (CIPFA). The resultant recommendations provide a uniformed basis for information to be presented and are as summarized below.

For costing generally, expenses can be classified under four main headings:

1. Cost of materials used directly in the manufacture of goods or provision of a service.
2. Cost of labour directly associated with (1).
3. Other expenses associated with goods or service.
4. Expenses which cannot be directly identified with or attributed to the goods or service.

The first two are variable and are known as direct costs. The third can be regarded as semi-variable whilst the fourth category is usually known as overheads. All four make up total costs. Translated into bus operating terms, the more important of the various expenses may be classified as under. The list of items is by no means exhaustive:

1./2. Variable:
    (a) Drivers' and conductor's wages and expenses.
    (b) Fuel.
    (c) Tyres.
    (d) Servicing of vehicles.
3.   Semi-variable:
    (a) Vehicle depreciation including spares.
    (b) Vehicle maintenance.
    (c) Vehicle licences.

(d) Fare collection equipment.

(e) Supervisory and traffic staff salaries and expenses.

(f) Publicity.

4.   Fixed:

(a) General administration including salaries and costs of management and administrative staff.

(b) Rent and rates.

(c) Legal costs.

(d) Maintenance of buildings and plant.

The categorizations are suggested as the most appropriate but they must not be regarded as inviolable. The classifications can alter according to circumstances and the time periods. Variable costs relate directly to the service provided and if the particular buses did not run then these expenses should be saved. This is certainly true of fuel and tyres and if vehicles are serviced on a mileage basis, the same reasoning would apply. It is also a fair assumption that if the service did not run, drivers and conductors would not have to be paid. However, staff are generally employed on a guaranteed weekly wage basis, and if savings are to be made, any reductions would need to be sufficient to actually save duties and not just to produce shorter spells of work. Turning to the semi-variable costs, if the complete service was withdrawn, the vehicles would be saved, unless, of course, they worked on other routes as well. Nevertheless, assuming that buses did become redundant, they might not be disposed of immediately although they certainly would not have to be replaced when they became time expired. Similarly, publicity costs might be reduced in due course. Whilst overall publicity would still go on, roadside timetable display would no longer be required. Conversely, additional vehicles and publicity are likely to be required when new services are introduced. Inspectors and traffic staff employed in the direct operation of the buses, such as staff controllers and schedule compilers, will vary in numbers according to the quantum of service provided and any substantial changes will have fairly short-term effects. On the other hand, the management team and general administration, the costs of offices, other buildings such as garages and the associated equipment and all other such expenses known collectively as the overheads, would still go on regardless of service changes. Even then, however, there would come a time when, if the trends were significant, the overhead expenses would be affected. The size of the administration would, in the long term, require adjustment, new garages might be required or some might be closed as the case may be.

One small point here on the subject of the relationship of costs with mileage operated is worth noting in passing. In terms of timetable compilation, supervision, publicity and public relations, an infrequent service could cost more than a frequent one and it would certainly not cost less. With wide headways, each journey has a specific purpose and inconvenience and even hardship might arise if the full service failed to operate. A few journeys of this type might occupy as much time of the people mentioned as would a frequent all day route. But on the other (and major) items, costs would, of course, be less.

Costing method

So much for the classification of costs. They now have to be apportioned route by route. As far as the direct expenses are concerned, fuel and tyres present no problems as their costs are based on mileage and the mileage is known. Drivers' and conductors' wages and vehicle servicing, which is also mostly wages, is rather different as they are based on time. Certainly the number of hours worked on a given route could be calculated and multiplied up by the rate per hour but this takes no account of a basic guaranteed weekly wage, penalty payments and other costs such as allowances for superannuation and national insurance contributions, sick pay, holidays, uniform, etc. The position becomes yet more complicated if, as is so often the case, platform staff work on more than one service in the course of a duty and the same difficulty arises with all of the semi-variable and fixed costs. They all have to be apportioned route by route on either a time or mileage basis.

Receipts have to be dealt with similarly and here again complications can arise. Whilst cash received by conductors on the bus was at one time relatively straightforward, it has now become more difficult to get this information for reasons which were explained in Chapter 9 except that the advent of electronic equipment will once again produce adequate statistics. Even so, some theoretical allocations to services have to be made in respect of revenue received in the form of, say, a general subsidy to either maintain a group of routes, to hold down the level of fares or for travel concessions for elderly people, season tickets valid on more than one service, etc.

Once these allocations have been made, the total costs can be set against the total revenue for each service and its financial state determined on a daily, weekly, four weekly or annual basis. To bring each service to a common denominator, all of the figures may be divided by the mileage operated to produce costs, receipts and profit or loss per mile, route by route.

Interpretation

Contained in Chapter 8 is a schedules exercise based on six imaginary services. To quote some equally imaginary but proportionately realistic figures, an individual route result statement based on the mythical Newtown garage might look something like as is shown in *Table 11.1*. The figures bear a little examination, and to do this it is helpful to glance again at Chapter 8 to see what sort of services are involved. The timetables and vehicle runnings are set out in *Figures 8.10* and *8.11*. Service 2/A is the mainstay of the network and earns enough surplus not only to cover itself but also to compensate for the combined losses of the remainder. This is

Table 11.1 Specimen route results of the services depicted in the schedules exercise in Chapter 8

Four weeks ended..................19......

Route number	Costs				Receipts	Net surplus (+) or deficit (−)
	Variable	Semi-variable	Fixed	Total		
	Mondays to Fridays					
1	4625	2158	694	7477	7028	−449
2/A	11 242	4309	1312	16 863	18 258	+1395
3	178	169	44	391	221	−170
4	34	122	29	185	52	−133
5	355	343	101	799	470	−329
6	72	139	34	245	104	−141
Total	16 506	7240	2214	25 960	26 133	+173

an example of cross-subsidization (which is difficult under British de-regulation with a loss of the network principle). However, never mind that, notwithstanding the highly profitable service 2/A, the system as a whole shows a very meagre profit and prudent management would wish to do something about it if possible.

Looking again at the schedules exercise in Chapter 8, service 2/A has a regular 15-minute service throughout the day. In other words, it has a consistently good traffic without the need for heavy peaking. Service 1 covers a different type of area where there is a high car ownership. Only a bus every 30 minutes can be justified here except that in the peaks four buses in the hour are required but in the evenings it drops to a 60-minute frequency. This means that vehicle utilization will not be as good and the buses that work the extra mileage in the peaks will be considerably under-utilized. They are, in fact, running numbers 3 and 4 and a look at their scheduled work confirms the point. What this means, therefore, is that the same vehicle costs will be spread over much less mileage (and less revenue). This makes the service results unfavourable in comparison with service 2/A and in purely financial terms, the route loses money and something must be done. However, ignoring the disturbance to traffic aspect, it could be assumed for this purpose that withdrawal would save the variable and the semi-variable or, in other words, the avoidable costs. This means that in the period quoted above a figure of 4625 plus 2158 or 6783 would be saved but the receipts which amount to 7028 would be lost. (The unit of currency is disregarded.) Assuming therefore, that the overheads would remain, this course of action would make the undertaking worse off to the extent of 245. This suggests that if fixed costs cannot be reduced then any contribution towards them, which is the excess of receipts over the avoidable costs is better than nothing. To make a worthwhile saving would be to reduce the peak commitment but another glance at bus running 4 shows that this vehicle also works journeys on service 4. If those journeys had to be maintained then any reduction of the service 1 work would result only in crews and vehicles lying idle for longer periods than they already are with minimal savings (tyres and fuel). The other low-mileage buses, being runnings 10 and 11 cover services 3, 5 and 6 which are confined to works and school journeys and because of this they show up badly and they would have a very high cost and deficit per mile. If the peak hour extras on service 1 had a different route number and were costed separately they would produce a similarly adverse result but the basic service would be improved and maybe become even profitable, although the total would, of course, be the same. The results of these individual route statements are, therefore, influenced by the numbering system. If services 5 and 6 were re-numbered 2B and 2C respectively and costed within a single route 2 group, the result would show a profit, albeit a lower one. Two loss making services would have been deleted from the books. But this is only playing with figures and that is one reason why it is so important to interpret the results correctly.

These are the things that management must consider when the monetary alarm bells ring and something has to be done. In going through the finances of the imaginary system the problems encountered when attempting to take remedial action have been highlighted but no recommendations have been proposed. But these figures are produced by the finance officer. It is for the traffic manager to do something about it, and this goes back to Chapter 6.

It was said when discussing costing methods that if the different cost figures produced were divided by the mileage of the route concerned to indicate all such costs on a mileage basis, true comparisons could be made as there would then be a common base. By this means, a situation might be revealed that need not necessarily be detected from the figures as they stand. For example, high crew costs per mile indicate an inefficient duty schedule, high vehicle costs per mile indicate slack in the vehicle runnings, high peaking, etc.

There is one other feature in cost statements which must be recognized. Some services run daily, others on weekdays only and there are those that run on Mondays to Fridays or perhaps even just on Sundays. Whenever they run, the maximum vehicle requirement for urban services is likely to be in the Monday to Friday peaks; and the vehicles, fare collection equipment and all of the overheads will be geared to accommodate the maximum level of service which prevails at this time. There is a different type of traffic with different demands and hence different levels of service required on Mondays to Fridays compared with Saturdays and Sundays. Furthermore, premium payments are likely to be made to staff on Sundays and perhaps also on Saturdays. In planning timetable changes, management will need to see separate results for these days and over recent years Sunday traffic has been particularly vulnerable to abstraction by the private car. If separate figures are to be prepared then it is for note that as vehicles etc. must be available for the Monday to Friday peak maximum requirements, they will be there in any case on Saturdays and Sundays regardless of whether they are used. If the Monday to Friday service is to bear the full vehicle costs then the theory is valid. If, however, those (fewer) vehicles which continue to run daily bear only five sevenths of their total costs on Mondays to Fridays, then M-F costs will cheapen but a proportion must be borne on Saturdays and Sundays. This leads in to marginal costing.

Marginal costing

The marginal cost of running an extra journey or a new service—which is the actual additional cost that would be incurred in putting it on or, conversely, what would be saved by taking it off—has already been touched upon. There is a big difference between properly allocated costs and marginal costs but it is sometimes appropriate to bear in mind the marginal cost aspect. Consider what the extra cost would be of putting on one more bus or one more service or even one more journey. In the latter case the marginal cost might only be fuel and tyres if there is enough slack in the schedules. Think also about what could be saved in real terms if a service or a journey was withdrawn. Again, in the case of the latter, it might well be only fuel and tyres and it might need only one or perhaps two passengers on the bus to cover that. Both the arguments and the use of marginal costing must, however, be approached with caution. In the short run it may be justified (e.g. partly utilized vehicle) but in the long run all costs must be covered, and to ignore fixed costs completely will court disaster sooner or later.

Referring once again to the schedules exercise in Chapter 8, services 4 and 6 are special school services and they incur deficits. A possibility here is to ask the local education authority to meet the cost of these journeys. If the services were withdrawn the buses concerned would still be required for work on service 1 (running number 4) and service 5 (running number 11) and it is unlikely, therefore, that any actual costs would be saved except fuel and tyres. The marginal costs of these services are, therefore, very small and are likely to be more than covered by revenue. The question then is what should be charged for the service. The writer considers that there is every reason to support the view of the Chartered Institute of Public Finance and Accountancy that whilst accepting that there should always be an element of flexibility to allow for special circumstances, as a general policy; figures should reflect a full allocation of costs. The main reason given is that all costs must be recovered by some means and it is only possible for any one service to make less than its proper contribution to overheads if other services contribute more. Route costing is a long-term planning tool and it is important, therefore, that all costs are properly accounted for and any variation from this practice should be done only as an exception based on carefully considered commercial policy. Even so, remember what was said in Chapter 7 about costing a Sunday private hire when a bus is available which would not otherwise be used. Consider the merits or otherwise of losing the job because of a quotation which is not competitive whilst a lower charge would still have produced money in excess of direct costs and which would not otherwise have been earned.

Modal costs

Introduction

Reference was made in Chapter 2 to the different modes which collectively produce a system of inland passenger transport. Remember they ranged from the diesel bus to the fast main-line railway train. The two extremities cater for different movements but although this book is about buses, there are other modes that cater for the same traffic, in fact everything from trolleybuses to rapid transit and perhaps even suburban railways. Each of these modes has different characteristics and their capacities were considered in Chapter 6. Their costs are also different. It is impracticable to quote actual figures, particularly in the case of fixed track systems, as there are substantial variations due to local circumstances and in any case information of this kind becomes quickly dated. Nevertheless, for comparison purposes, at least within the modes which have relevance to this text, some sort of a guide is desirable. Although it is the policy of the author to deal only with general theory, in this instance and by way of illustration the figures and/or conclusions of three specific undertakings with more than one mode will now be discussed as the information is illuminating.

Modal comparisons

Blackpool Transport Services Ltd.

Blackpool Transport Services Ltd. (UK) operates buses and trams and the information contained in *Table 11.2* is derived from information contained in the accounts of Blackpool Corporation Transport Department (the operator at the time) for the year 1984/85. In order to produce a common denominator for comparison purposes, mileage costs have been translated into factors of 100 based on the bus figure. It will be seen that the total mileage costs of the trams are according to this information more than 100% above the buses and even in theory must be at least 70% above. If this sounds a little bit like playing with figures it only gives emphasis to the fact that costing information must not just be accepted at its face value without examination and interpretation of the circumstances. A discussion on *Table 11.2* and particularly the 'theoretical' column 3 is therefore necessary.

Table 11.2 Comparative mileage costs of diesel buses and electric trams of Blackpool Transport Services Ltd. with the total bus figure based on 100. Note: These figures do NOT represent pence per mile. Source: *Annual Accounts 1984/85* of Blackpool Corporation Transport Department.

Item	Diesel bus per mile	Electric tram per mile	Theoretical* electric tram per mile
Traffic operations:			
Staff costs	55.2	74.0	55.2
Traffic revenue control	7.7	7.7	7.7
Traffic equipment of routes	0.9	1.9	0.9
Other expenses	0.2	0.2	0.2
	64.0	83.8	64.0
Servicing vehicles and routes:			
Heating, lighting and cleaning depots	0.6	1.7	0.6
Cleaning and servicing vehicles	3.7	5.5	3.9
Cleaning, salting and sanding track	—	1.1	1.1
	4.3	8.3	5.6
Fuel and power	7.4	6.8	6.8
Tyres	0.8	—	—
Leasing	0.3	0.3	0.3
Repairs and maintenance:			
Permanent way	—	29.9	28.8
Electrical equipment of line	—	17.7	17.7
Vehicles	13.6	40.1	40.1
Buildings and fixtures	0.4	1.4	0.4
	14.0	89.11	87.0
Vehicle licences	0.3	—	—
Rent and rates	0.9	3.5	0.9
Management and general expenses	8.0	9.5	8.0
Total expenditure	100.0	201.3	172.6

*See text.

Looking first at column 2, the major item within traffic operations is staff costs, the bulk of which is drivers' and conductors' wages. In this case it may be more one-man operation on the buses than on the trams. If this is so then the comparison is not strictly valid as it is not a modal characteristic. Similarly there is probably no modal reason why the cost of heating, lighting and cleaning of depots or management and general expenses is heavier specifically on the trams. It could well be for quite a different reason. Repairs and maintenance of the permanent way includes an item for illuminations which, whilst correct as far as the accounts are concerned, is a little unfair on the trams if counted for comparison purposes.

This has really now become as much a lesson in interpretation as in modal costs but it would seem reasonable to make some theoretical adjustments to the tram figures before they are used to compare with the buses. This has been done in column 3. Here, the items contained in traffic operations, leasing, rent and rates and management and general expenses have been kept constant with the buses. The actual figure for leasing has also been retained but was the same in any case although this is not necessarily attributable to the mode. It could be influenced for example by the local programme of vehicle acquisitions as for the same figure more buses might have been obtained than trams in the particular period. Similarly, the actual figure for the repair and maintenance of the trams has been retained as it would be different to the buses but if the buses were new and the trams were part of an ageing fleet then again the comparison would not be a fair one. At this stage it is not necessary to delve into all of these possibilities—only to bear them in mind.

Looking now at column 3, the total costs per mile of the trams are, on this reasoning, some 73% higher than the buses because of the cost of the specialized way plus the higher vehicle maintenance charges where, as has been seen, the comparison might be suspect. But remember from Chapter 6 that a tramway has a higher capacity potential than does the bus, particularly if it is on a segregated way. The estimated capacity of 15 000 passengers per hour as suggested in Chapter 6 would involve two Blackpool trams coupled together on a 1-minute headway. This would be the absolute maximum and probably seldom achieved but if they ran singly they could still offer space for 7500 per hour. Even then, in practice, traffic would not be as consistent as this but it could still be up to say 50% greater than the bus. This suggests that trams could become cost effective at a point where traffic is consistently heavy as although mileage costs are higher, less mileage needs to be run to cater for an equivalent number of people. This now leads into the next example.

Toronto Transit Commission

Although an example (the only example) of comparative costs of buses and trams within a British undertaking has been examined, no mention has been made so far of trolleybuses. Toronto Transit Commission (Canada) operates buses (with a few of a smaller than standard size), trams and trolleybuses (as well as a metro which is outside this discussion) and in 1983 that undertaking undertook an evaluation of broad policy options to determine the future composition of its surface fleet. ('Surface' means the vehicles which use the roads as opposed to the underground railway system). Under consideration was whether to expand, maintain or reduce its trams, trolleybuses and smaller buses and also whether to introduce articulated vehicles, remembering that they can appear in any of these three forms. As what follows has been extracted from the TTC report, and the Canadian terminology has been retained, it might be helpful for readers outside North America if the descriptions are clarified. More familiar terms might be as follows:

Canadian term	*Approximate British equivalent within the sense of the Report*
30ft diesel bus	Single-deck bus (not standee)
40ft diesel bus	Double-deck bus (in terms of capacity)
60ft diesel bus	Articulated bus
40ft trolley coach	Double-deck trolleybus (in terms of capacity)
60ft trolley coach	Articulated trolleybus
Streetcar or LRV (Light Rail Vehicle)	Tram or more modern tram
ALRV	Articulated tram

The cost performance of the various transit modes were analysed using a generalized cost methodology applied to a variety of route circumstances and service options. In the three modes being considered, namely streetcars, trolley coaches and diesel buses, the major inherent differences were of course infrastructure requirements and motive power. New technology such as alternative fuel for buses or hybrid trolley coaches were not considered at the time but high-capacity articulated versions of these modes together with the smaller 30ft diesel buses were. The analysis was further restricted to consider the peak period demand of under 3600 passenger places per hour which TTC regards as the maximum which it is practicable to budget for on a surface route in mixed traffic operations, being the equivalent of one standard 40ft bus every minute (60 per hour).

It is not proposed to detail here the costing methodology but to the operator the results are interesting and are depicted in *Figure 11.2*. The standard vehicle in Toronto (as throughout North America) is the 40ft diesel and it is on this type which all of the others have been judged. Hence on the chart it is the 40ft diesel which represents 100 and the alternatives are shown as a ratio of that base. As is to be expected, the costs of the electric modes are considerably higher at low levels of passenger demand due largely to the greater fixed costs (notably track and/or overhead wire) but as the peak demand increases the relative costs of the electric modes improve since the greater scale of operations helps to defray these fixed

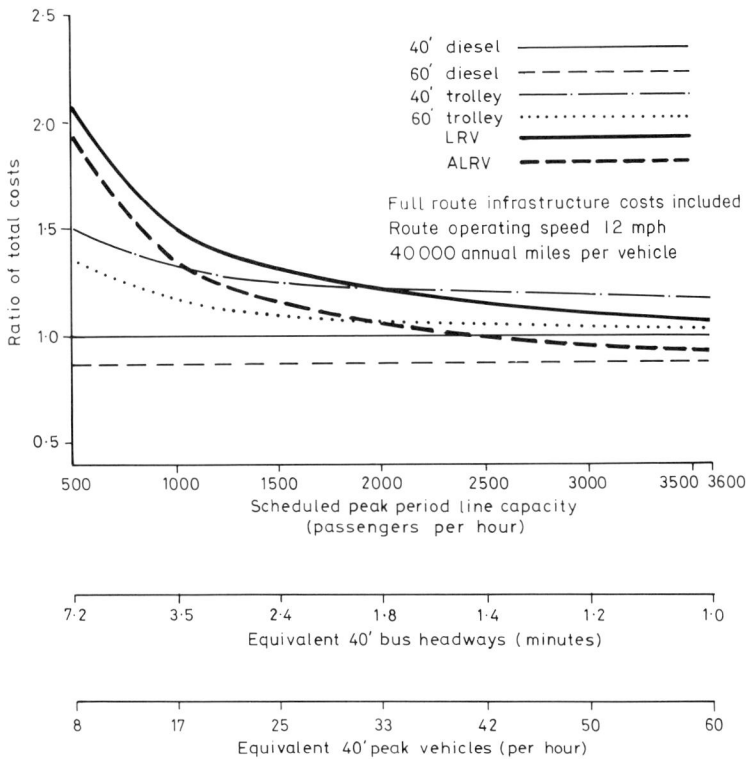

Figure 11.2 Ratios of total average annual costs of various modes relative to 40′ diesel (Reproduced by kind permission of Toronto Transit Commission).

infrastructure costs. The study found that the average annual total costs of streetcars only became comparable with 40ft diesels at about 3600 passenger places per hour whilst 40ft trolleys did not break even within this range. Articulated versions offered substantial savings over the regular vehicles if substituted on a two for three basis as the equivalent line capacity could be provided with a one-third reduction in vehicles and, more importantly, driver labour costs which more than offset the greater capital costs of the high-capacity vehicles.

As a matter of interest, TTC, as a result of this study, does still see the standard 40ft bus as the largest component of its surface fleet. It is cost-competitive relative to the other modes over a range of circumstances and offers the greatest flexibility in terms of tailoring services to meet demand. Whilst articulated vehicles should make an important contribution on high demand routes the wider headways involved would be acceptable only on the very frequent services. TTC also recognizes certain operational disadvantages associated with articulated vehicles, including fare collection, but this is only going back to what was said in Chapter 3. A future is seen for the streetcar network but only where the peak demand is likely to exceed 3000 passengers per hour with a relatively high level of off-peak traffic as well. Even then, it is felt that this level of service would likely require transit priority right-of-way with signals or grade separated track. No evidence was found to justify retention of the trolley coaches or the 30ft diesels other than on certain very low demand routes where use of the smaller bus is perceived to be less intrusive.

City of Johannesburg Transport Department

The City of Johannesburg Transport Department (South Africa) is a 'conventional British style' undertaking which converted its trams to trolleybuses (British built AECs, Sunbeams and BUTs) and some remained operational until 1985, much later than in Great Britain. Their extended period of life was accompanied in the latter years by a trolleybus demonstration project to decide the future of the system. Accordingly seven prototype vehicles were purchased to evaluate their economic suitability for the Johannesburg Metropolitan Area. Five were double-deck and two were single-deck articulated vehicles. All had emergency drive equipment.

At this juncture it is interesting to note that the Johannesburg undertaking is on record as recognizing a passenger preference for double-decks. To quote from one of its reports:

'Buses having low seating and high standing capacity are unpopular. It has been observed that when vehicles with standing room only stop for intending passengers the latter hold back in the hope that seats will be available on the following bus. Double decks can be designed in such a manner that 100 passengers out of 110 can be seated. This aspect together with the easy access to the seats has made double-deck buses more popular among passengers in Johannesburg.'

The capacity aspect is of course yet another input to the bus versus trolleybus consideration. As in Great Britain but unlike Canada, Johannesburg passengers seek a greater standard of comfort and the bus operator accepts that this is a factor in the considerations. Although the average British double-deck bus seats around 80, *Figure 3.21* depicts a three-axle bus of China Motor Bus with 108 seats. In

Johannesburg nearly 60% of the double-deck fleet has 98 seats with 12 standing. It is claimed that this capacity cannot be matched by trolleybuses.

Some of the more interesting and apposite conclusions from this study are summarized as follows:

1. When comparing energy consumption based on the ESCOM and SASOL coal conversion processes, the trolleybus is twice as energy efficient as the diesel bus.
2. In terms of speed and acceleration performance on gradients the trolleybus is slightly better than the diesel bus.
3. The additional mass of the electric traction equipment means that the passenger capacity has to be reduced from 110 to 90 when compared with an equivalent diesel bus but for mobility in depots and on routes when power failures occur it is essential to have an emergency drive system.
4. The value of a typical trolleybus system with emergency drive engines shows a 72-vehicle trolleybus system to be 68% more expensive than an equivalent diesel bus system.
5. Passenger capacity, the maintenance and repair of the overhead system and the purchase price of new trolleybuses are the most cost-sensitive items.

The conclusions of Johannesburg were that for the foreseeable future the operation of trolleybuses is not economically viable although in the national interest the advantage of having a system based on an alternative energy source was noted. However, the fleet is now 100% diesel bus.

Conclusions

Three different systems in three different countries in three different continents have been discussed with totally different approaches. Nevertheless the message comes through that although the diesel bus is the most economical form of road passenger transport, the possibility of a tramway system is worth looking at if the traffic is upwards of 3000 people per hour. As passengers in North America are not accustomed to the same degree of comfort on short trips as are their British or South African counterparts, their standard bus is a 40ft single-deck crush loader rather than a double-deck but regardless of this, the average capacity is comparable between the UK and Canada. However, it does mean that the crush-loading conditions of an articulated bus, necessary if its capacity potential is to be fully exploited, will be accepted more readily in North America than in the case of the countries in the other two examples. Except in special circumstances TTC sees little future for its smaller buses which supports the author's views on midi- and minibuses expressed in Chapter 6. Like South Africa, neither does it see justification for the retention of its trolleybuses. This view could run contrary to feelings in the UK and referred to in Chapter 12. However, the Toronto study was undertaken in 1983 and both British trials and some European continental systems are now exploring new trolleybus technology which Toronto at the time and to some extent South Africa did not, and this could be an added influence. In any case the relative costs of diesel and electricity could be different in Canada and South Africa compared with Europe. What has been said here should not be construed by the reader as an indictment against trolleybuses generally.

Enough has been said to give operators a general idea of when and where to start looking should a conversion to electric power come up for consideration. In conclusion acknowledgements are due to the managements of Blackpool Corporation Transport Department, Toronto Transit Commission and the City of Johannesburg Transport Department for supplying information in respect of their own systems for discussion in these pages.

12 The future

A projection from the past

This book began with a brief review of the past. That was a straightforward exercise because the facts were known. The salient features were discussed in the hope that the reader might thereby get a clearer reason why things are done in the way that they are today. The thought was expressed in the very first paragraph that by studying this process of evolution a trend might be established which could help to predict what might happen in the future. If this chapter was being written in the late 1950s, with the benefit of hindsight, it could have been predicted that buses would get larger, their engines would move from the front to the back whilst the entrances would move from the back to the front. A lot more one-man operation would appear, including double decks. There would, therefore, be greater productivity. Now, apart from any possibility of more use of articulated vehicles, it is difficult to see how buses can get bigger, particularly with one-man operation. Route patterns would not be changing in the immediate future (the origins of some services can still be traced back to the horse tram era). Many timetables were to be reduced in frequency, and numerous services, particularly in rural areas, were to disappear altogether. But there were to be substantial reorganizations, changes of direction and changes of control. A reorganization of local government in Great Britain in the early 1970s was to be accompanied by a certain devolution of power with much tighter financial and hence policy control of local bus services in the hands of county councils.

Notes such as this if written in, say, 1957 would have given some idea of at least a few of the things which were to happen in the ensuing 30 years. A lot has been accomplished and there have been many changes. On the other hand, to the man in the street it could be said that so far there might not be very much noticeable effect except for rising fares which have made their mark on bus travel. In some cases to ride on a bus has become prohibitively expensive and the counter-attractions of motoring and television have tended to reduce interest in public transport except for essential journeys. This factor is important: public habits and preferences have changed and with it travel patterns and the use of buses. Many people are now able to seek the convenience of their own private cars with the result that the use made of public transport for local journeys, particularly for pleasure purposes, has fallen dramatically whilst the congestion and parking problems created by private cars are becoming intolerable.

But the British bus industry is now passing through a phase of immense change. With privatization, de-regulation (and hence unfettered competition) and financial support reduced to selected specific routes that would not otherwise be provided, the future becomes even more obscure and the industry itself is unable to forecast what might happen even in the immediate future. The Bus and Coach Council is on record as saying that:

'Decreased financial support means fewer buses and higher fares. The consequences of a reduction in bus services are congestion with more cars on the road, more pollution, longer waiting times and in some cases no bus service at all, all of which have a direct effect on the way of life.'

However, the Government in its White Paper *Buses* says:

'It is too easy for local authorities and operators to claim that the only alternative to high subsidies is massive fare increases and drastic service cuts. The other way is to improve efficiency and reduce costs. The licensing and subsidy arrangements (as hitherto existed) without the spur of competition protect the operators rather than their customers.'

And so, as this book appears, the industry has entered the unknown. In view of the uncertainties operators are being understandably slow in placing orders for new vehicles and equipment which in turn has repercussions on manufacturers. But just as the long-distance coaches have survived and flourished since their de-regulation in 1980 (as has road haulage since 1968), the writer predicts that the busmen's ingenuity will also suitably weather the local services through what in the end might prove to be a passing storm.

As can be seen from the foregoing, there are claims that the industry will suffer and there are counter-claims that it will be stimulated, but, be that as it may, if the trends of the past are projected forward like lines on a graph the result becomes illogical. Buses would no longer be required regardless of any loss of financial support as within the foreseeable future the last passenger would have completed his journey and thereafter they would instead all be in their cars. These, in turn, would not be able to move, at least in urban areas, because there would be too many of them in the available road space. There would, therefore, be no need for wage claims to price the buses out of business or for staff militancy to lower the quality of the service as the demand would have disappeared. But more than that—in the immediate past oil was readily available at a reasonable price. The predicted energy situation could alter things. Something more than a simple progression is therefore necessary if there is to be an intelligent assessment of what is to come. Technology and politics—which cannot be included on a straight projection of trends—have a commanding influence on the future.

Future demand

The demand for public transport is not necessarily falling. Airline traffic is buoyant as is that of the short sea ferries. Inter-city railway trains have good loadings, and long-distance scheduled coach services as well as excursions and tours are not without their clientele. It is the medium- and shorter distance services, particularly in rural areas, that have suffered. For these journeys most people prefer to use their own private cars, which suggests that patronage of public transport is at risk in cases where private transport is a feasible alternative. But for some people, private transport will never be an option, being precluded by age or physical condition. Regardless of the popularity of the private car, therefore, a hardcore will inevitably remain in need of the public services and will suffer hardship if they are not provided. This, of course, assumes that there will still be the same demand to move around. Optional travel must surely remain. People will still wish to visit their relatives and friends and to change their environment in their hours of leisure but the private car is a strong competitor for journeys of that kind. Whether there will always be the same need for journeys to work and for shopping is not quite as predictable. Depending on developments in other spheres of activity, the pattern of life could change dramatically just as television has emaciated the cinema queues of 30 years ago. It is conceivable, therefore, that there might not be the same need or even desire for mobility as there is today.

Environmental and social issues

Environmental and social aspects have already been examined. The separation of vehicles and pedestrians was discussed in Chapter 6 and it can be anticipated that in the years to come lonely footpaths landscaped with bushes even in residential areas will be no places for people to walk alone any more than they are in parts of the USA today. Perhaps, therefore, revised concepts for town planning will come with further repercussions on bus routeings and the policy of segregation abandoned as a social failure in the same way that high-rise flats are regarded today. The impact of the private car—with its insatiable demand for more roads, wider roads and faster roads along with its noise and pollution of the air—is a particularly sensitive issue. There is no shortage of opinion and advice on this matter from the environmentalists but, nevertheless, they, like other people, enjoy the convenience that the car provides. What this can only mean is that private transport is a bad thing for everybody except them. Be that as it may, it is abundantly clear that people will continue to want cars and, as was said in Chapter 2, no government is going to suffer the unpopularity which restraints would undoubtedly bring without some compelling reason, able to be seen and generally understood. It is likely, therefore, that local buses will continue to run into the red if indeed they run at all. Nevertheless, as at least a limited demand is likely to remain then, other things being equal (but they might not be), urban and rural transport could become still more of a social service. It seems inevitable, therefore, that such provision will remain a political issue and, in the UK, a controversial one at that. Financial support means public expenditure for which there are competing demands. There must be a limit to the amount of money that can be made available through rates and taxes.

The allocation of public money raises the question of priorities which is not something that transport managements will have to decide or a subject that is appropriate for further discussion here. But government decisions, whatever they might be, will have a profound effect on managements who must continue to keep the sectional interests of their own particular industry to the fore when such matters are considered. The UK is behind the rest of Europe in giving public support to public transport. In some other European countries the degree of subsidy for local transport tends to be much greater and is more of an accepted way of life unaccompanied by reactions from the press and elsewhere.

When machinery for bus subsidies through county councils came to Great Britain in the early 1970s, those in command had been reared in true commercial style at a time when buses were run on a shoestring but nevertheless giving a good service at no cost to the community other than reasonable fares. Custom and practice dies hard and it was not easy to change so fundamentally. Now, the subsequent generation of bus managers has grown up within the social concept and they must now accustom themselves to the rigours of the commercial world from which they have hitherto been given shelter. The Bus and Coach Council, in a title to a publication issued in 1984, an extract of which has already been quoted, asserts that 'Buses mean Business'. The challenge is there. The writer has just expressed the thought that once acclimatized they will succeed. Perhaps it would be equally appropriate to say that buses will stay in business.

Still on the social plane is the malaise referred to in Chapters 5 and 10—violence and the destruction of property, which is now rampant. There is a grave danger that this will escalate in the future, and this increase will have its effect on the pattern of demand for public transport in the years to come. In some areas people will be in yet more fear of walking the streets; they certainly will not use segregated pedestrian ways except at times when there is safety in numbers, nor will they stand at lonely bus stops. Potential riders, could, therefore, be confined to those whom the bus crews will not be prepared to carry. Seats in buses will have to be the uncomfortable fibre-glass variety, drivers will not be able to have possession of money, which means only fareboxes or pre-paid tickets and protection from passengers at least in the form of a screen and acceptance by passengers of an unattended upper deck will be unlikely. The writer has expressed a preference for double-deck buses wherever practicable but it could become unsafe to ride on top.

It is inevitable that those who man the buses are in the front line against attack from the rougher members of the community. Bus conductors suffer abuse and violence when they seek their rightful dues. Their situation is not an enviable one and they are incensed when they do not get the support of other passengers when they are attacked. Industrial action results and late-night journeys fail to operate.

Maybe passengers do not always go to the assistance of bus crews because they in turn are displeased with the service (or lack of it) which has on occasions been meted out to them. Bus crews have been known to run early and leave people stranded, fail to stop when hailed, refuse passengers when seats are available, show misleading information on destination blinds, sit and smoke at the terminus and thereby pollute the atmosphere in the bus, depart late and when spoken to leave civility wanting. They will complain, rightly or wrongly, that their standard of remuneration leaves something to be desired. It is accepted that driving a one-man bus is a responsible job but have they maintained the reliability, prestige and self-esteem generated by their grandfathers 60 years ago? If appearances and, in the case of some, standards are anything to go by, they have not, which is sometimes in contrast with their colleagues overseas. However, it is not fair to censure only bus crews for changes in values in society. This is only leading on from what was said in Chapter 4, but outside Great Britain there is a much greater appreciation and acceptance of the fact that if employees are to prosper then their employing organizations must also prosper. No more real money can be got out of a machine than is put into it and the way ahead depends very much on whether organized labour accepts this fact of life. If it does not, then the service will suffer and job satisfaction will continue to deteriorate with falling standards further discouraging traffic.

This was part of the British scene when a Transport Bill was being debated which eventually became the 1985 Transport Act. The new element of competition which it has introduced will perhaps enable (or maybe compel?) managements to manage and hence improve standards. If this is the outcome then the changes can be justified but the price might be high. Loss of the established networks built up over many years with the resultant vacuum filled by fleets of midi-buses, unregulated and uncoordinated, if that is what is to come, is not something that can be accepted lightly. Viewed with dismay might be a more appropriate comment, but perhaps a newer breed of midi-bus driver will regain the public goodwill which has been wilfully destroyed by some of his counterparts on the conventional buses.

Of those who read these lines, some may be bus crews. Some of them will be seeking betterment. Some will reach supervisory and control status and others will become the managers of tomorrow. They will no doubt understand the points being made and are not likely to be contributing to this industrial disease. Not everybody is. It is hoped that they will play their part in the difficult task of restoring pride in the service. This is surely one of the things that will have a profound effect on the years that lie ahead and whether those who provide bus services indeed have any future at all.

From the gloom and despondency that has been dispensed so far, readers might be excused should they begin to doubt the wisdom of their choice of calling. But not to despair. Hopefully, the years to come will prove that the confidence hitherto expressed will be justified and that the previous paragraph is a timely warning rather than an accurate prediction. It has already been said that some people will always need buses but in meeting that need there is one other factor that is very topical to this chapter and that could change everybody's way of life. It is the energy situation.

The energy situation

There is much talk of a forthcoming energy crisis. The generally accepted view is that oil is formed from plant and animal material which was buried in sediments millions of years ago (i.e. it is a fossil fuel). As such it is claimed that there is really no doubt that the world's supply of oil will one day be exhausted—the only uncertainty is when.

There is an alternative less publicized and so far unproved theory by D. Osborne in his article *The Origin of Petroleum*: that oil is not of biological origin but that hydrocarbons (oil and gas) leak upwards from materials that were buried within the earth during its formation with a consequent migration of gases from great depths. Should this idea have substance then there could be a lot more oil than the geologists have imagined. However, this is mentioned only to emphasize the imponderables when looking into the future and particularly where the availability of oil is concerned. At present there is still plenty left and oil products remain freely available. The full benefits of Britain's own oil production is being realized and new sources may yet be discovered.

Commercial production has been geared to accessibility and fields regarded as uneconomic have not yet been exploited. Scarcity increases value which brings justification for working areas hitherto regarded as unviable. Under these circumstances, supplies could continue but at inflated prices. Unless the alternative theory is realistic, what might be a fair assumption for long-term planning purposes is that oil will cease to be available for energy needs perhaps sometime in the first half of the next century. Clearly that date will be conditioned by the development of new technology to enable extraction from hitherto inaccessible places and the rate at which available stocks are used. This in turn depends upon the development of alternatives.

Much has already been written and doubtless much more remains to be said on substitutes for oil as a source of power. It is not appropriate here to include a technical treatise of the problems and prospects but once again the fundamentals might give an indication of things to come.

The obvious alternative to the diesel engine is of course electricity. This is a basic and easy assumption but one that raises a host of questions. The simple course for electric power lies in fixed-track systems, the concept of which is far from new. Even without new technology, therefore, change there could be. But some power stations burn oil to generate electricity. However, coal can be and is similarly used and stocks are available, although nuclear power is now an alternative. What is important in this context, however, is not how electricity is produced in power stations but how it will be used for public and private transport.

Still with regard to the fundamentals, derv and petrol are commodities that can be carried around conveniently on the vehicle and the fuel tanks can be easily replenished. Not so with electricity which has to be fed from power stations via suitable conductors through to the motor on the vehicle; unless, of course, it could be stored on the vehicle to permit free running independent of any power cables leading in from the outside supply source. But herein lies the problem. Again, battery vehicles are not new but their application is limited. They have been in use for local milk delivery purposes for a number of years and for this role their performance is satisfactory. But heavy-duty bus work is much more demanding. Good acceleration, a fast sustained speed and a range of about 150 miles (240 km) at least before re-charge are parts of the specification, all with a high-capacity vehicle. The volume and weight of a bank of conventional batteries necessary for this performance would leave very little accommodation for passengers and new technology is, therefore, indicated. Development of new techniques in the battery field is another story but to put it briefly, all that can be said at present is that no suitable battery has so far been developed.

This, of course, has far reaching repercussions on private as well as public transport. Given that oil will be available for a time yet, the production of an acceptable battery vehicle complete with rapid re-charging facilities remains a possibility. Depending on circumstances, however, the developing process might be overtaken by a restriction on oil supplies coupled with substantial increases in cost. For an optional use, the demand for the private car has remained remarkably inelastic. So far there seems to be no financial limit beyond which the private motorist will not go to keep his car on the road although there surely must come a time when at least some of the motoring population will no longer be prepared to bear the continuous imposition of heavy surcharges, be they in the form of taxation, fuel, insurance or parking.

If this situation comes, therefore, at least a limited swing from private to public transport could be anticipated. Public transport undertakings might well wish to consider a move away from oil, and fixed track systems readily lend themselves to electric traction. But remember from Chapter 1 that the street tramway was abandoned partly because it was confined to its tracks and was considered to be unsatisfactory in heavy traffic. Rather than forsake electric traction the trolleybus came, even though it was far less flexible than the conventional bus and one reason why the mode was abandoned was that costs became high in comparison with diesel. Even though electrically powered systems are capital intensive, this trend could now be reversed with history once again repeating itself. If and when oil becomes really scarce it is conceivable that governments might step in with measures to conserve such stocks as are available. This could, for example, take the form of infrastructure grants or tax incentives for those undertakings prepared to develop electrically powered systems. If all this came to pass there would be a very real possibility that trams and trolleybuses might once again become a major part of the transport scene.

New technology

For consideration now is what sort of systems are most likely to be developed. Conventional trams and trolleybuses would certainly meet the energy crisis as would monorails and light rapid transit. Monorails would no doubt find support from the armchair planners, some of whom seem to see a mystical built-in formula which makes this particular mode the obvious answer to all urban transport problems. Unfortunately, monorails are not blessed with this virtue as witness the number of systems now in commercial service. The classic example is at Wuppertal in West Germany where the physical layout happens to suit this type of transport. In this instance there is an elongated area of commercial, industrial and residential development astride a river valley with the course of the river forming a natural path for a monorail line. In terms of both capital cost and capacity it comes somewhere between a tramway and a rapid transit system and the characteristics of the monorail happen to be suitable, both physically and operationally for the Wupper Valley. But a situation such as this is not encountered frequently, and it produces a visual intrusion.

The trolleybus has much to commend it as although technically a fixed track vehicle powered by electricity, it does not require steel rail. It is free running on a normal road surface which means that the system is less capital intensive than the trams and the vehicles are more manoeuvrable. Even past generations of trolleybuses carried a supplementary power unit in the form of batteries which enabled them to move short distances, albeit very slowly, free of any outside power supply. It is reasonable thinking then that the next stage will be a vehicle which travels under the wires along heavily used common sections of routes and then moves on its own stored power into the suburbs and back, where it would again re-charge under the wires. That might take care of the more lightly trafficked outer ends. If towards the centre, the volume of traffic was such that there was more of a case for segregated light rapid transit systems, it is not beyond imagination that the trolleybus might be adapted even for this purpose. The specially constructed way, instead of consisting of steel track would instead be so designed to give linear constraint to a rubber-tyred vehicle in the fashion of the West Midlands experiment as described in Chapter 2. If a system of this kind was developed to a state of acceptable operating performance it could combine the best of three worlds, being light rapid transit with its segregated right of way and hence high speed and capacity, the trolleybus with its need for electric power rather than oil and the conventional bus with its flexibility and minimal infrastructure requirements. Then, of course, there are the battery buses which might possess all of the attributes of diesel traction but they are still the subject of research.

At this stage of development, the following represents a summarized review of the possible options in so far as road (i.e. non-rail) vehicles are concerned.

Trolleybus

A proven system but inflexible with operational problems due to the need for overhead wires. Capital intensive and, at present levels, prices compare unfavourably with diesel buses although as far as the fuel element is concerned, this could change. Maintenance costs are cheaper than those of a diesel bus and given certain circumstances they could over the years become cost effective.

Hybrid battery/trolleybus

The hybrid would operate from overhead wires along part of the route whilst at the same time charging on board batteries which would become the source of power for the remainder of the journey. The vehicle would therefore need to accept twice the amount of current compared with the conventional trolleybus to allow for both running and charging batteries and the resultant rapid charging would shorten battery life. Costs are therefore likely to be high.

Figure 12.1 Looking into the future, one possibility is the reappearance of trolleybuses in Great Britain. What might be the first of a new generation of trolleybuses is this vehicle of South Yorkshire Transport Ltd. based on a standard Dennis Dominator chassis with Alexander bodywork but converted to take electric power. The vehicle is seen here undergoing trials on a special test track at Doncaster racecourse in South Yorkshire, UK. (Reproduced by kind permission of South Yorkshire PTE.)

Other types of hybrid

Other combinations include a diesel/trolley and a diesel/battery electric. The diesel/trolley is a vehicle with duplicated motive power; in other words a trolleybus which also has a diesel engine and can therefore run 'under the wires' or as a normal diesel bus. Such an arrangement would certainly reduce oil consumption but the initial costs are likely to be high. The diesel/battery electric would carry a small diesel engine which would run at a constant speed to drive a generator.

The trolleybus as such was discussed in Chapter 3 and remember from Chapter 1 that this is the class of vehicle that is being developed by South Yorkshire Transport Ltd.

Lead–acid battery bus

Satisfactory for specialized work such as milk delivery but the range is insufficient for bus operation. It could be extended with interchangeable batteries but this would be expensive in terms of batteries, infrastructure and staff.

Advanced battery bus

There is ongoing research into batteries capable of giving an extended range of say 160 miles (257 km) or more. This would be attractive but is not yet a reality; at present the sodium sulphur battery seems to be the most promising. If it is ever perfected its characteristics would be superior to the previous alternatives mentioned and in performance and use, comparable with that of a diesel bus as well as offering an alternative to oil.

Conclusions

From the foregoing it seems likely that the advanced battery has the greatest promise if only it was a reality; but for the present it is not. If a breakthrough came then the concept might well be superior to the trolleybus or even the hybrid. The unknown is whether the sodium sulphur battery or an equivalent will come before oil disappears. If it does then capital expenditure for trolleybus equipment would seem to be unnecessary. If it does not, then a reappearance of the conventional trolleybus (or tram) or the development of some form of hybrid becomes a distinct possibility.

Looking into the future involves a deal of speculation although it is clear that those who are new to the business will see many changes. They will see a change of behaviours and the way of life and in the types of vehicle which will be available to them to carry the traffic as it will then present itself. The managements of tomorrow will no doubt have with them many of the problems that are with us today but they might have some others as well and in this the author wishes them well.

Bibliography

The following is a list of reading for operators wishing to study in greater depth the subjects dealt with in this work. All of the titles referred to in the text are included here.

Published work

BAILEY, J.M. and LAYZELL, A.D. (1983) *Specialised Transport Services for Elderly and Disabled People*. Oxford Studies in Transport: Gower Publishing: London.
BEESLEY, M.E. (1973) *Urban Transport: Studies in Economic Policy*. Butterworths, London.
FAULKS, R.W. (1982) *Principles of Transport*, 3rd edn. Ian Allan: Shepperton.
GOODWIN, P.B. *et al.* (1983) *Subsidised Public Transport and the Demand for Travel—The South Yorkshire Example*. Oxford Studies in Transport: Gower Publishing: London.
HAY, A. (1986) *The Impact of Subsidised Low-fare Public Transport on Travel Behaviour*. Sheffield University Environment and Planning C: Government and Policy Journal, vol. 4, pp. 233–46.
HIBBS, J. (1985) *Regulation—An International Study of Bus and Coach Licensing*. Transport Publishing Projects, Cardiff.
HUTCHINSON, B.G. (1974) *Principles of Urban Transport Systems Planning*. McGraw-Hill, New York.
KITCHIN, L.D. (1985) (Duckworth, J., ed.) *Road Transport Law*. Butterworths, London.
OSBORNE, D. (1986) The origin of petroleum. *The Atlantic Monthly*, **February**, pp 39–94.

Publications of HM Government (UK) through HMSO to which references have been made in the text

Acts of Parliament

1847   Town Police Clauses Act
1865   Road Locomotive Act
1869   Metropolitan Public Carriage Act
1870   Tramways Act
1909   Development and Road Improvement Funds Act
1930   Road Traffic Act
1954   Transport Charges etc. (Miscellaneous Provisions) Act
1955   Miscellaneous Financial Provisions Act
1960   Road Traffic Act
1965   Finance Act
1967   Transport Act (Northern Ireland) Act
1968   Transport Act
1969   Post Office Act
1970   Equal Pay Act
1971   Vehicles (Excise) Act
1972   Local Government Act
1972   European Communities Act
1972   Road Traffic Act
1974   Health and Safety at Work etc. Act
1975   Sex Discrimination Act
1976   Race Relations Act
1978   Transport Act
1978   Employment Protection (Consolidation) Act
1980   Transport Act
1980   Employment Act
1980   Highways Act
1981   Public Passenger Vehicles Act
1982   Employment Act
1982   Civic Government (Scotland) Act
1983   Transport Act
1984   London Regional Transport Act
1985   Companies Act
1985   Transport Act

Statutory Instruments

1981   No. 257 The Public Service Vehicles (Conditions of Fitness, Equipment, Use and Certification) Regulations
1986   No. 77 Travel Concessions Schemes Regulations
1986   No. 1078 The Road Vehicles (Construction and Use) Regulations

Other publications of HMSO

1966   Cmnd 3057 Transport Policy

1967   Cmnd 3481 Public Transport and Traffic
1984   Cmnd 9300 Buses
Department of Environment Circular 82/73 'Bus Operation in Residential and Industrial Areas'
Sir John Buchanan 'Traffic in Towns' 1963
Highway Code
Transport Statistics Great Britain

Publications of other organizations including those to which reference has been made in the text

Transport and Road Research Laboratory publication

LR 521-1973 *Bus Boarding and Alighting Times.*

Bus and Coach Council publications

Urban Planning and Design for Road Public Transport. Revised 1986.
The Future of the Bus. 1982.
Buses mean Business. Lewis, C. 1984.
The Route towards Tomorrows Buses. 1986.
Costing your Coach for Profit. 1986.
Working for the Professionals. 1986.
A Year Working for the Professionals. 1986.

The Chartered Institute of Public Finance and Accountancy publications

Passenger Transport Operations. 1974.
Management Information for Road Passenger Transport Operators. 1976.
Passenger Transport Operations. Supplement: Peak/Off Peak Costing and Revenue Allocation. 1979.

British Road Federation publication

Basic Road Statistics. 1986.

Glossary

The following describes selected words which are in common use but peculiar to the bus and coach or associated industries. Certain of the terms have been covered in the text but where appropriate have been repeated here for easy reference.

Articulated bus   As applied to passenger vehicles, an extra-long vehicle (maximum length in UK 59 feet) with two separate parts connected by a joining mechanism which allows the unit to bend on curves whilst providing a continuous interior. The two parts will not operate singly and cannot be separated except under garage conditions with special equipment. In road haulage (and very occasionally road passenger) an articulated vehicle (an 'artic') implies a separate tractive unit which can be easily separated from its trailer.

Autorickshaw   Small three-wheeled vehicle developed from the Vespa scooter from Piaggio of Italy and used as a taxi in various parts of south-east Asia, etc. Occasionally referred to as a 'trishaw' or 'motor scooter'.

Axle weight   That part of the total vehicle weight which is borne by each axle which, in the case of buses, generally means 2 axles but occasionally 3. It is the sum of the weights transmitted to the road surface by all the wheels of that axle and it is important that these weights are compatible with the strength of the roads on which the vehicles operate. In Great Britain, maximum weights are stipulated in the Road Vehicles (Construction and Use) Regulations, 1986 (S.I. 1986 No. 1078). As a matter of interest, weights are calculated based on a vehicle fully equipped for service with a supply of fuel, oil and water plus 65 kgs (10 stone 3 lbs) per passenger.

Bus priorities   A traffic management (see below) measure whereby the bus is given an advantage over other traffic.

Capacity (modal)   The total number of people that can be moved past a fixed point in one direction per unit of time (usually 1 hour).
   (vehicle)   Total number of passenger seats or total load (seats plus standing) to give total number of 'places'. See Chapter 6.

Char-a-banc   Derived from the French 'carriage with benches'. At one time common parlance in Great Britain applied to what are now termed 'motor coaches'. Generally used in connection with open or hooded single-deck vehicles with solid tyres and rows of transverse seats without a gangway but with separate doors at both ends of each row. This was known as the 'toastrack' type of seating which gave maximum capacity with no space for standing or to manoeuvre within the vehicle.

Commuter A regular traveller, the term being derived from their commuted payment (or season ticket). See Chapter 9.

Demand responsive bus Paratransit (see below) with routes and times completely or partially determined at the time of travel by passengers. Taxis and 'dial-a-ride' services are examples. See Chapter 7.

Display ticket A prepaid ticket such as a season ticket or 'travel card' which eliminates payment at the time of travel and hence a need only to show the driver (or conductor). See Chapters 7 and 9.

Feeder service A local service designed to take passengers to and from another service for the main trunk haul, be it of the same or a different mode.

Grade separated A service with its vehicles physically disconnected from any other form of traffic or movement including that within its own mode. It is this type of service which has been dubbed 'rapid transit'. See Chapter 2.

Hybrid Generally referred to in connection with the new generation of trolleybuses being developed for propulsion by more than one source of power. See Chapter 12.

Infrastructure Subordinate parts of an undertaking such as its permanent installations. Described by the European Commission as a 'system of communication and services as backing for operation'. See Chapter 2.

Interchange A recognized place whereby passengers may transfer from one service to another of the same or a different mode. Often involves a purpose-built structure.

Jitney Service provided by paratransit (see below) such as minibuses, cars or vans along fixed routes, sometimes with minor deviations. Often seen in developing countries and is more suitable where either labour is cheap, a class category of travel is evident, regular conventional bus services are costly to operate or are inadequate or where lower standards are acceptable. See Chapter 6.

Kiss and ride Where an individual is driven by car to the boarding point for the main trunk haul by public transport. It could be to the advantage of the operator to encourage this concept, in which case facilities for setting-down and also meeting (and therefore waiting) are desirable.

Light rail transit A term now frequently applied to the more modern form of tramway, sections of which are partially segregated from other traffic. The writer is of the opinion that the term 'tramway' or 'tram' (see below) is perfectly adequate and that this new jargon is an unnecessary complication.

Light railway A conventional railway on which certain standards and legal requirements have been relaxed in return for specified operating restrictions.

Light rapid transit *See* **Rapid transit.**

Load factor Ratio of passengers carried to seats or places offered.

Metro A local urban railway network with an identity distinct from the national main line system (including its suburban lines). Also a popular name for rapid transit (see below). Sometimes referred to as 'subway' or 'the underground' (even when it is on the surface or elevated). If its tunnel has been burrowed it might be called 'the tube' and if only some lines were constructed in this way then the whole system tends to be designated erroneously as such.

Paratransit Small passenger vehicles ranging from 2 up to about 20 seats which operate informally on a fare-paying basis, often supplementary to regular bus services. They may provide either a personal door-to-door facility (e.g. a taxi or a shared taxi) or could take passengers in a similar manner to a bus. The World Bank records that this type of transit has different nomenclature in different places and quotes as examples the terms 'matatus' in Nairobi, 'jeepneys' in Manila, 'dolmus' in Istanbul and 'publicos' in Puerto Rico.

Park and ride   Where an individual drives himself in his own private conveyance to the boarding point for the main trunk haul by public transport. This movement is generally associated with the railway, which means the provision of car parks at railway stations, but it does not have to be. In the case of buses the concept is more often associated with the main haul by car to a car park on the periphery with a special bus from the car park to town (perhaps for shopping purposes).

Payload   The number of fare-paying passengers that can be accommodated on a vehicle.

Pre-metro   A system of light rapid transit (see above) designed for easy conversion to heavy rapid transit.

Private hire   A vehicle and driver hired en bloc either to another operator or a private individual to work at their discretion but under the control of the owner. Generally applied to a private party on a special occasion. For regular private hires, particularly to statutory bodies, the term 'contract' or 'charter' is often used. See Chapter 7.

Quality licensing   A system of licensing by an independent third party which regulates the standard (or quality) of the service. See Chapter 5.

Quantity licensing   A system of licensing by an independent third party which regulates the amount of provision (or quantity) of the service. See Chapter 5.

Rapid transit   A totally grade-separated (see above) system both from other modes and other services within the same mode. Usually heavy rail (i.e. standard railway size and characteristics) unless prefixed to the contrary, e.g.

    Light rapid transit (LRT)

    Bus rapid transit

See Chapter 2.

Shuttle service   In common parlance, a service on which vehicles go to and from over a short route. A special connotation is derived from EEC Regulation 117/66 wherein a shuttle service is designated as one of the categories of international services. It is there defined as an international service which, by means of repeated outward and return trips, continuously conveys previously formed groups of passengers from a single place of departure to a single foreign destination and subsequently back, collecting the first group for return on a later journey, and so on. The first reverse journey and the last outward journey of the season will therefore be empty.

Standee bus   A vehicle with minimum seating to allow maximum space for standing. Sometimes referred to as a 'crush loader'. See Chapter 3.

Swept circle   The area which is traced by any part of the body of the vehicle and not just the track of the wheels. This has a particular significance with front entrance vehicles (i.e. the entrance ahead of the front wheel) and hence a longer overhang at the front. See Chapter 3.

Tare weight   Weight of vehicle without fuel and unladen.

Toastrack   *See* **Char-a-banc.**

Tonga   An animal-hauled form of paratransit (see above) at one time prevalent in the Indian sub-continent but now tending to be superseded by mechanical power. Functioning as a taxi, a light two-wheeled vehicle drawn by a horse (or in Sri Lanka by a bullock).

Traffic engineering   Roadworks to improve the flow of traffic. See Chapter 2.

Traffic management Revised traffic arrangements to improve the general vehicular flow. See Chapter 2.

Tram Defined in the Public Passenger Vehicles Act, 1981 as any carriage used on the road by virtue of an order made under the Light Railways Act, 1896, a road being defined as any highway and any other road to which the public has access including bridges over which a road passes. Note that pedestrians do not have authorized access to the tracks of a segregated light rapid transit system, but it is likely to be possible to walk (and often drive) across the tracks of a partially segregated tramway or light rail transit line.

Index